12/22

Marked for Life

Marked for Life

One Man's Fight for Justice from the Inside

Isaac Wright Jr.

with Jon Sternfeld

St. Martin's Press
New York

First published in the United States by St. Martin's Press, an imprint of St. Martin's Publishing Group

www.stmartins.com

Insert photos courtesy of Issac Wright Jr.

Design by Jonathan Bennett

The Library of Congress Cataloging-in-Publication Data is available upon request.

ISBN 978-1-250-27748-0 (hardcover)
ISBN 978-1-250-27749-7 (ebook)

Our books may be purchased in bulk for promotional, educational, or business use. Please contact your local bookseller or the Macmillan Corporate and Premium Sales Department at 1-800-221-7945, extension 5442, or by email at MacmillanSpecialMarkets@macmillan.com.

First Edition: 2022

10 9 8 7 6 5 4 3 2 1

THIS BOOK IS DEDICATED to those who were intimately responsible for molding me into the man I was, the man I became, and the man that continues to evolve into a better man than yesterday . . . The only Protector, Provider, and Mentor in my life, Isaac Wright Sr., my father. The only Nurturer in my life, Sandra B. Wright, my mother. The only Team in my life: Quentin W. Wright, Walter D. Wright, Paportia R. Wright, Sandra J. Wright-Laribo, and Steven J. Wright, my siblings. The only reason for living, Tikealla S. Wright, my daughter. The only Teacher in my life, LIFE. And the only Guardian in my life, GOD . . .

Although this is a work of nonfiction, the names of certain individuals have been changed to protect their privacy, and dialogue has been reconstructed based on the best of Mr. Wright's recollection and on press accounts.

Contents

Acknowledgments

I WOULD LIKE TO ACKNOWLEDGE the extraordinary debt I owe to Curtis "50 Cent" Jackson. His legendary vision and foresight immediately understood the importance of my story to society. His efforts and ingenuity turned my story into the inspiration of one of the most profound social justice television shows to date, ABC's *For Life*, and made the necessity of this book a no-brainer. Thank you, Fif, for being you.

This acknowledgment must also be extended to my friends, Andy Mascot who introduced me to "50 Cent," as well as Doug Robinson and the late Allison Greenspan, executives who were instrumental in cultivating 50's vision into the *For Life* series—the prelude to the anticipation of this incredible book.

I would also like to acknowledge the people who made writing this book an enjoyable experience among the onerous responsibilities of career and life: Tikealla S. Wright for picking up the slack when the distractions of writing this book caused me to fumble in other areas of my responsibility; Frida Baicea for keeping me healthy and fit when endless hours of focus and work turned into days isolated in a room, refusing to take a break, even to eat.

Finally, I would like to acknowledge the three I refer to as the Trinity: Steve Fisher, my agent; St. Martin's Press, my publisher; and Jon Sternfeld, the heavy lifter in writing this book. Steve was the brilliant architect that brought all the pieces together. St. Martin's Press saw the vision and put the full force of its expertise and resources behind ensuring the best book we could produce. Jon, my "twin pen," was instrumental in bringing home an incredible product.

I must acknowledge Richard "Poo" Dailey and Steve Workman, lifelong friends who never said no and never let me down when the obligations of this book required me to ask them to stand in for me regarding tasks that I could not allow to take me away from writing.

A shout-out acknowledgement must go out to the people I emphatically depended on when I ran for mayor of New York City in 2021: Melody Jimenez (my campaign manager), Michael Roman (my field director/acting campaign manager), Michael Pringle (my field organizer), Sheena Li Guzman (my team leader) and Sandra J. Wright-Laribo (my communications director and personal assistant). And, a special acknowledgment to Roger "English" Francis, Eli Cohen, Andy "Hov" Moscat, and Kenneth "Jordan" Espiritusanto for all of your invaluable help and support.

Thank you all for your kindness and support.

Continue to follow my story and obtain updates on my journey, social justice initiatives and appearances, by following me on:

> Facebook: Isaac Wright Jr
> Instagram: @isaacwrightjr
> Twitter: @IsaacWrightJr

Prologue

> When nothing seems to help, I go and look at a
> stonecutter hammering away at his rock perhaps
> a hundred times without as much as a crack
> showing in it. Yet at the hundred and first blow it
> will split in two, and I know it was not that blow
> that did it, but all that had gone before.
>
> —JACOB RIIS, *THE STONECUTTER'S CREDO*

SOMERSET COUNTY COURTHOUSE, SOMERVILLE, NEW JERSEY
SEPTEMBER 4, 1996

HE WAS SQUIRMING UP ON the stand, avoiding my eyes like they were shotgun barrels. Detective James Dugan possessed the look and bearing of a military man: dirty-blond crew cut, straight-backed posture, tight-lipped expression. But the eyes. The eyes told a different story.

I didn't know what he thought when he got out of bed that morning, what was on his mind when he dressed in his crisp blue uniform or when he kissed his wife goodbye. Maybe he thought he was in the clear, that a convicted felon acting as his own lawyer couldn't do much damage. Maybe his lies about me weighed on him or maybe he buried it all deep enough that the guilt couldn't come up and bite him.

But as the momentum on my cross-examination built,

as I found my rhythm, he sensed where this was going. In prison you learn to read people's eyes quickly and decisively. It's basic survival to know friend or foe, anger or fear, impulse or plan.

Dugan's eyes gave away the game.

I woke up that morning only a couple of miles from where he did, not in the relaxed comfort of my home, but in a cramped and damp cell. Not next to my wife and across the hall from my child, but alone inside hard stone walls.

Everything you were and ever will be is squashed in prison. That's what they don't tell you, what the public doesn't understand, and what the movies don't show. Prison doesn't just take away your present, swallowing up your days, hours, and minutes. It also takes away your *past* too—drowns out your memories until they're wisps of ideas, unrecognizable, like something from a dream or a story someone once told you.

And it takes away your future, until all you can see in front of you is a blank space, so dark and empty that you can't even imagine what would fill it.

I had one clear advantage over the detectives and prosecutor who set me up, the witnesses who lied about me to save themselves, and the judge who perverted justice to seal my fate: I had thought about nothing else for over 2,600 days.

My case was my lifeblood—it pumped my heart, circulated the blood in my body, and ran through my veins. Everyone else had lives to live, schedules and plans and all the things that come with being free. But in prison, those things fall away; you have nothing to do but make it through the day. Over and over and over again. It's always right now and it's always forever.

So around the clock, from when I opened my eyes in the morning to when I put my head down at night, I thought about them: Prosecutor Bissell, Chief Detective Thornburg, Judge Imbriani, Detectives Dugan, Racz, and Buckman. Seven-plus years after my arrest, I knew them better than they knew themselves.

They called it a post-conviction relief hearing—a PCR— but it actually was more of a reckoning. These men had excised everything out of my life with near-surgical precision. And it was finally time for my answer.

In court, Dugan sat before me, boxed in, seeming so small. He was just a man; they were all just men. They had the power of the state behind them, the trust of the public, the obedience of the police force, the weight of history and institutional memory, but they didn't have my ingenuity or my will. They couldn't possibly. I was outmanned but they were outmatched.

It came to this because of a piece of paper.

I had found a seemingly harmless one-page memo in the prosecutor's files that undid their whole case against me. But using it required the element of surprise, which meant I could only use it once. *Put all your eggs in one basket,* I read somewhere, *and* watch *that basket.* That was Dugan: my eggs, my basket.

Dugan was different from the other players, not cocky

and craven like Thornburg, or ambitious and slimy like Bissell. I wouldn't say he was soft, because I knew better. Let's say dimensional. Dugan carried an air of humanity about him, which was why I had chosen him.

My goal was to get Dugan to confess about a lie, a lie that laid the foundation for all the other lies. At my trial, the cops had planned and rehearsed their fabricated version of what I did—*of who I was*—though they all denied doing it. The piece of paper proved otherwise. I picked Dugan because I sensed something different about him, a discomfort with deceit. My plan was to exploit that, burrow into his soft core and see what it could withstand.

It was simple in that it was straightforward and elegant. It was complicated in that it was nuts. Getting a police officer to confess to wrongdoing under oath is among the most difficult things a lawyer can do. It's basically impossible, the holy grail of judicial defense work. If cops regularly admitted to their deception, their dishonesty, their outright corruption, the jails would be nearly empty. Not to say all prisoners are innocent, just that few cops and lawyers are either.

But I was about to get Detective Dugan to unravel the whole entire thing. And I wasn't even a lawyer then, just an innocent man—armed with only a high school diploma—crazy enough to represent myself, a forgotten soul the public lost no sleep over. I had pinned Dugan so that he was stuck. And because God is graceful but also clever, Dugan had one way out: the truth. The detective's survival was entwined with mine because I had tied them together. I knew that in moments of desperation people did what they had to in order to survive.

I first learned it from the twins.

When I was seven years old, my family lived in Bremerhaven, Germany, where my father was stationed with the U.S. military. Once used by the Germans during World War II to make rocket weapons, the base was a U.S. staging area in 1968 for the Cold War. On a July 4 afternoon, my family—five brothers and sisters, mother and father—was picnicking by the river with other families from the base. Among the other kids were twin boys, a few years older than me, long athletic kids who were incredible swimmers.

I was shy as a young child, more comfortable in the background, so I was hanging by the grill with my mom. As I was chowing down on a hot dog in the sweet smoke, a soft breeze blew on me. My eyes wandered to the river and locked in on one of the twins out there. It was hard to tell, but it looked like he was playing around, hands flailing above the waterline.

"Mom," I said, pulling at the bottom of her summer dress. "Look."

"Not now, Junior," she said, chatting with one of the other wives.

"No, Mom." I kept pulling on her. "Look! Look at the water!" Exasperated, she followed my pointing. She saw it too—except she understood what she was seeing.

In one motion, she dropped her plate and ran toward the banks screaming, her words taken by the wind. All the other adults turned and followed her like water rushing to fill a gap. It was an unsettling sight, so many grown-ups in full panic like that. I was scared, so I moved slowly toward the crowd, the shore, the noise. On the banks, the other twin was grappling with his father, trying to wrestle out of his arms. They were locked in this dance until the boy finally wriggled free, took a running start, and dove in, a fluid splash as he broke the surface. He was going out there to save his drowning brother.

From shore, we watched as he swam out into the fierce current and reached his twin. There was an exhalation of relief, but then a heavy pause as we watched and waited. And waited. They weren't getting any closer and didn't appear to be swimming back. As the minutes passed, the boys stayed the same distance away, heads barely above water. I squinted in the sunshine and tried to make out their faces. Their mouths were moving, but their words were too far away, taken by the wind.

Then they went under.

The next day, a half of a mile downstream, local police found both of the twins' bodies. The drowning boy's hand was still clutched to his brother's wrist, solid like a sculpture. Like God had turned flesh into stone.

I played back what I saw and pieced it together. Once he reached him, the twin who dove in had been pleading with his drowning brother, begging that he let him go. He wasn't prepared for the fight his brother was giving him, and in the back and forth, he got weakened. Then he got dragged under too.

It ate at me for a long time, the senselessness of it: *Why didn't the drowning boy let his brother go? Why hold on to him to the point that they both died?* As I grew older, and went through the trials and tribulations God had devised for me, that image would remain. And that's how it sat with me, as a stubborn fact of human nature: if you get someone in enough trouble, he'll grab ahold of anything to save himself.

Part One

Chapter One

AS THE CAR PASSED US, I knew something was up. The gray sedan was nondescript, the kind of car that wanted to be ignored. It drove by slowly, deliberately. I caught the driver's stare, menacing like a flashed pistol.

"The *hell's* wrong with that guy?" I said, under my breath, more to myself than to my wife. "He's grilling me like he wants to kill me."

My wife, Sunshine, and I were sitting in my prized possession, a customized AMG Hammer. It was a specially modified Mercedes-Benz, with a candy-apple-red exterior and black interior. The car had a custom sound system with gooseneck controls, like a swivel game controller. Its trunk was bored out of a complete white fiberglass encasement for two fifteen-inch woofers, midrange speakers, and tweeters in the basin instead of a spare tire. The body was widened so far out that the side vents had to be extended from the doors into the quarter panel. The tires were low-profile Hoosier Racing Tires, and the frame was lowered a few inches from the ground. There were running lights below the headlights that in the dark made it look like a UFO creeping up on you at night.

It was the kind of car that got you noticed.

We were parked curbside on a two-way boulevard in Passaic, New Jersey, fifteen miles outside Manhattan, about an hour north of the quiet suburb where we lived. We were waiting for Carlos, who had asked me to meet him here, near his house. In nearby Paterson, Carlos owned a successful custom furniture and cabinet business. That spring he and I had decided to team up. I'd put in the money for inventory and run the business side and he'd produce custom pieces for me in a fifty-fifty partnership. He did everything in-house and his guys churned out quality work, though they didn't speak a word of English. Any time I stopped by the shop, including earlier that day, we'd have these gesture-heavy conversations around questions like *Where is Carlos? When will he be back?*

Carlos had some new furniture designs to show me, designs I'd been asking to see for almost a month. That morning on the phone he told me to meet him at the shop, but when I showed up, he wasn't there. When I finally got him on the phone again, he said he had to "make a run" near his house and I should come up to his neighborhood in Passaic. I knew that "make a run" meant a drug sale, but I paid it no mind. I wasn't involved with that side of Carlos's life and I didn't care.

I had lived in neighborhoods in Harlem in the early 1980s where you couldn't see the sidewalk beneath the river of empty crack vials crumbling under your feet. When I moved out to the Far Rockaway projects, I was still surrounded by hopelessness and desperation. Everyone was committing crimes of survival. The stickup kid, the hit man, the prostitute, the numbers runner, the burglar, the scam artist were all my neighbors, some of whom came to be my friends. As I moved up in life, I didn't see myself as any better than them. They remained my friends and it wasn't my way to worry about what every person in my orbit did. If it wasn't *my* business, it wasn't my business. That had been my attitude when I lived in New York City, and as Sunshine and I met new people and built a life in New Jersey, I carried it with me.

After almost thirty minutes waiting in the car, Sunshine started getting antsy. My wife was a music performing artist—I was her manager and producer—and she was due at a recording session in the city. I kept putting off her pleas for us to go, telling her to give it five more minutes. As we sat there, waiting for another five minutes to pass, she pointed out a parked car up ahead, its lights on in broad daylight. I didn't think much of it until I looked it over a second time. *Brake lights.* They weren't just on, they were flashing in random intervals—from a car that appeared to be empty.

"What the—" I said, putting my car in drive and rolling up the street. When I pulled alongside the car, I saw a figure crouching down under the steering wheel, his knee inadvertently pressing on the brake.

The sight shook me. *Is this guy waiting on me?* My mind ran back through the day, going over clues my subconscious must have registered: the same unfamiliar car appearing in my rearview, the same stranger's face at a different location, a pair of eyes staring at me too long. Sunshine and I were an hour from home, in a place we didn't know, directed there by someone I knew to be a drug dealer. Now we were surrounded by surveillance.

I stayed out of trouble, but this was not the first time I had encountered police. I was used to being profiled, stopped and searched illegally, harassed and aggravated by cops. But this was different: the police had located me in a place I didn't even know I'd be at. They were hiding—far removed from the bold, arrogant show of force I was accustomed to. I assumed the cops were waiting on Carlos, even though they were on *me*. But how'd they even know where I'd be? *I* didn't even know where I'd be.

Then it hit me.

"Oh, shit," I said. "They got something in this car."

"What?" Sunshine asked. "What do you mean?"

"This car," I said, lowering my voice. "There is something in this car." I tried to remain calm, but my throat was pinched, the oxygen tight. That car was my pride and joy, and somehow, at some point, the cops had gotten to it. It felt invasive. I thought back to the dealership. After I left the car to get serviced about a month back, they had called and asked me to come pick it up right away. They even offered to waive fees under a "goodwill policy" if I came and got it immediately. It didn't seem strange at the time, but now I was thinking: Why would the dealership care if I picked up my car right away?

Sunshine was still worried, firing questions. "Something like what?" she asked. "How do you know? Can we just get out of here, please?"

"It's fine. Don't worry about it," I said, trying to calm her down. I didn't let her know about the alarms going off in my head. "We got to wait. A few more minutes."

"Wait? Why?" she asked, her voice tinged with panic. "Let's just get out of here."

Sunshine's instinct was to bolt, and I understood it, but I didn't react on impulse. I knew that's what brought trouble. If I did anything rash, it could get me in serious shit. I had no idea what the police were doing there. They could've been after Carlos and waiting on him to show up. If I took off without telling Carlos, it could look like I had set him up, or at least had left him a sitting duck. Then he and I would have a problem that would require one of us to respond. That was what the streets demanded. This was my world, and the riches and spoils of the music business had done nothing to protect me from it. In fact, part of the music business, specifically hip-hop, was inextricably bound to the street.

At the time, all my worry was focused on Carlos and his people. I didn't think I had anything to fear from the police. I thought that by staying, I could warn Carlos, protect him from whatever trouble the cops might drop on him. Over the past thirty years, I've replayed that afternoon many times in my head, but I usually come back to a simple conclusion: I didn't respond like a criminal because I wasn't one.

When Carlos's red SUV appeared in my rearview, I opened my door and got out. "Wait here," I told Sunshine, then walked up the street toward him. A tall, dark-skinned Dominican in his thirties, Carlos sat in the car with a relaxed air about him.

"What's up, Isaac?" he said, nodding.

"Look, man," I said, "there's cops everywhere. I know you asked to meet me here 'cause you had to make a run, but—" I looked back toward Sunshine. "You need to be careful. Let's just meet up later."

"OK, sure. Sure," he said, making a cursory glance up the street. "Thanks, man," he said, as though it was a hiccup, no big thing. I started to walk away.

"Isaac," he said, and I turned around. "You want these cabinet plans, right?" Carlos reached under his seat. I looked back up toward Sunshine and my car idling not fifty feet away. Before I knew what was happening, Carlos tossed a tightly wrapped pack of what was clearly drugs at my chest. *Cocaine.*

I froze. As it thudded to the pavement at my feet, almost in slow motion, the sound of squealing cars rushed up the street.

That summer of 1989 I was twenty-eight years old, working as an independent music producer. I had risen through the entertainment ranks, first as a dancer and then moving on to management, establishing a footing in the hip-hop world and representing a stable of up-and-coming artists. My wife was an original member of the female trio the Cover Girls, who had gone platinum, and she had recently embarked on a solo career that I was helping to manage, along with running a record label. Our success exposed us to a freewheeling social scene, and illicit types are just part of the territory. I'd see them at the club and break bread with them; a few I might actually call friends. We didn't do business together—unless they had a foot in music—but we were in each other's circuits.

Just like when I lived in some of the worst New York City

neighborhoods, I knew about their business, but I didn't inquire or get involved. It was of no consequence to me. When I moved to New Jersey, I was a young man at the height of his powers enjoying what I'd made of myself and for myself. In hindsight, I should've been more cautious about who I associated with, and if I had a chance to do it all over again, maybe I would. But those years are gone now.

Sunshine and I married young and, after seven years in New York City, had moved out to the New Jersey suburbs to settle down and raise our six-year-old daughter. Life had been gravy for a few years and we were living well. I had an ultra-stretch limousine to chauffeur the artists I signed, in addition to the AMG Hammer, among a stable of other cars. Sunshine had a rack of furs, more jewelry than she could wear, and the finest designer clothes. The other big indulgence of mine were custom-made cowboy boots with encrusted diamonds. No Black man in the hood could pull off cowboy boots except Isaac Wright Jr. They were like my signature and I had enough street credibility that no one questioned my style. I had earned my success and though I wasn't overly flashy about it, I wasn't shy either. It hadn't been that long ago when I had nothing.

I remembered when I first got to New York City eight years earlier, a kid from the South, on a mission, intelligent but inexperienced, rough around the edges.

The hard iron bench at Columbus Circle where I spent my first night, on my back with my legs up, hoping no one would mess with me.

The seventy dollars in my pocket, which I stretched within an inch of its life.

The homeless shuffle between the Port Authority Bus Terminal and Penn Station, which moved like a wave across town every night, dodging cops on the night beat.

Biking packages through traffic to earn enough money for a room at a Times Square motel above the porn theaters.

My first place on Edgecombe Avenue in Harlem—among a row of abandoned buildings that had a crack den on the top floor, a place overrun by dreads who used it to dump bodies.

Moving to the Far Rockaway projects where I had to duck bullets just to enter and exit the building.

The first time I spotted a small crowd semicircled around a young dude dancing on the sidewalk in Midtown, a hat full of bills at his feet, and thinking: *Shit, I can do that.*

In the early eighties, hip-hop was about to blow up and breakdancing was like the canary in the coal mine. The music, dance, fashion, and culture of hip-hop rose up from the house parties and pavement of the Bronx, through the dance clubs of Manhattan, into the suburban living rooms of Middle America. I was a hustler at heart, not in the illicit sense but in the self-motivated sense. My skill was finding an opening and pushing myself through. So that's what I did. Rounding up two of my buddies from back home in South Carolina, Donald and Willie, I formed a dance crew: the Uptown Express. We performed on the street, at parties, in clubs, the crowds multiplying with each gig. Things moved pretty fast and I rode the wave, knowing it could just as easily vanish.

One day we were winning *Star Search*—the *American Idol* of its day—and then, boom: we were touring around the country, selling Burger King on TV, opening for top-selling artists like Run-DMC and Kurtis Blow, getting a taste of the world. I parlayed that into a music management career, and in what felt like a blink, I was light-years away from that Columbus Circle bench. After a life of looking from the outside in, I was the white-hot center.

I loved every damn minute of it. The speed with which it would all come crashing down on that July day is unfathomable. Even now, I still can't believe it.

"Get on the ground!"

"On the ground, motherfucker!"

"Freeze. Don't move!"

"The ground!"

"Stay right there!"

The cops' commands came from different directions and contradicted each other. I obviously couldn't get on the ground while not moving. So I slowly lifted my hands, knowing that even a flinch might trigger a fusillade of bullets.

The plainclothes cops pushed in aggressively; red-faced and jacked, reacting to their own adrenaline. As they came upon me, one held my arms down while another snapped metal cuffs onto my wrists, biting the skin like an animal's teeth.

Before I could even get a word out, two of the cops were dragging me from the curb to the middle of the street. A beefier guy bent down at my feet, yanking my boots off. Then another pressed me to my knees from behind, while arms and legs started to swing freely at my body. Punches and kicks flew at my torso and back while I tried to jerk away. Someone behind me was pressing my head down, chin to chest. "Not in the face!" one of them yelled out. "Watch the face! He's gotta take mug shots!"

Though it was hard to tell, I think there were five or six all slamming away at my kneeling and helpless body—in the middle of the street, in broad daylight. Their hard boots felt like metal shovels smacking my legs and ribs. I pulled in hard for oxygen. Then the taste of warm blood on my teeth, the crunching of my bones against the pavement, the nausea coagulating in my stomach.

I lost sense of time, but at some point, Sunshine appeared at my side, her long body hazy in the afternoon light. She had been dragged from the car to watch, her screams drowned out by the commotion. "Stop it! What are you doing?" I could hear her yell. "Why are you beating him?"

Then scattered taunts: "He ain't so big now, huh? Look at the ni**er now."

The next thing I remember is two cops picking me up by my crotch and neck, like a duffel bag, and throwing me in the back of an unmarked SUV. I remember the crushing in my ribs, the tight pain in my lungs, the blood pooling at my socked feet. Inside the car, I pressed my forehead onto the cool window. The taste of blood was warm and metallic on my tongue and an eerie silence lingered in the car as we pulled away.

At the wheel was a white cop in his midthirties with black hair and a thick mustache, running lights and riding bumpers. This was Detective Racz, though I didn't know it at the time. The one in the passenger seat was younger, clean-shaven with blond hair, a Marine seriousness about him. I stayed silent, vowing not to speak until I knew what the hell was going on.

After about ten minutes of silence, there was static on the CB radio and a voice: "Bingo," someone said through the speaker, followed by some muffled words.

Racz put in his earpiece and had a short talk at low volume. "Yep. OK. Yep, got it," he said. Then he caught my eye in the rearview. I looked away.

"Hey," he said.

I didn't speak.

"Hey!"

I looked up and met his eyes again through the mirror.

"Looks like we found a bunch of coke at your man's house," he said. I knew he meant Carlos.

The cuffs dug into my skin and I squirmed in the back seat, trying to find a position that didn't pinch. The other cop up front kept half turning, checking me out of the corner of his eye.

Who the fuck did they think I was?

Through the streaked window, I watched an industrial stretch of the New Jersey Turnpike pass into vast trees of green. I was thinking about who to call when we got to the station, where Sunshine was, who would help out with my daughter until this was all sorted out. At some point, I realized we had been driving for maybe forty-five minutes, way further than the nearest police station.

"Hey," I said, interrupting the cops' back and forth. "Where we going?"

Chapter Two

I WAS MARCHED INTO JAIL in my socks.

Franklin Township Police Department was a white-brick-and-stucco building surrounded by pristine landscaping and more trees than you'd normally see around a jail. The further west you go in New Jersey, the more rural it gets, the further back in time you travel. It doesn't take too long for the state to go green on you.

We parked out front, curbside, which struck me as strange. Cops don't bring the newly arrested through the front door like the delivery kid bringing lunch. There are police bays where patrol cars park and a service entrance of some kind in the back. That much I knew. The two cops escorted me down the bright white sidewalk to the front door like they were visitors. That's because they were: these weren't Franklin Township police officers. They were detectives out of the county prosecutor's office, though I didn't know that yet.

The arrest process is efficient in pulling your humanity right out of you. Forget what they teach schoolchildren; innocent until proven guilty is a fable. Forget that the cops read aloud your rights; that's just to distract you from the fact that you're being stripped of them. Promise something and give the opposite. Take away the very thing they're pretending to give you. That's the American way.

The public lets law enforcement do this because of a perverse kind of circular logic. Most people think the same thing: *If the cops brought you in, you must've done something.* Unbridled support for law enforcement and unyielding belief in its honor, even when it has been clearly compromised, is a protective mechanism. It allows the public to go on with its day. Admit it: at some point in your life, you've thought that way. You may still.

But everyone on the inside, from the convicted to the arrested to the police, prosecutors, district attorneys, and judges, know that there are serious integrity and veracity issues with law enforcement. They know that the general public is clueless about how the system really works. The people's naïveté and ignorance give cops a green light to do as they please. They have the public trust, which they wield like a weapon. You have the public suspicion. If you're a Black man under thirty with money in your pocket, you already carry enough public suspicion to drown you.

When you get into custody, you're dragged like a package through processing: signatures, fingerprints, searches, confiscation of your possessions. You sit here, wait behind there, stand here to have your photos taken. Your whole existence is reduced to codes and notes and paperwork. People talk at you, not to you. They ask your name, even though they know it, even though you won't need it where you're going.

That morning I woke up as Isaac Wright Jr. By sundown, I'd be a case file number.

I didn't answer a thing or make eye contact with a soul. I shut down, which was a survival response more than anything else. Whenever I meet someone, I let them reveal themselves first; when I arrive someplace new, I get a lay of the land before making a move. In that police station, among the barking cops, ringing phones, slammed file cabinets, and overall cacophony, I closed up, sank deeper inside myself. All the sounds came through muffled and distorted, like behind thick glass. Cuffed to a chair in the station, I searched for solid ground by going over the facts that I knew.

First, the simplest one: I was not a criminal. This seemed disqualifying, but clearly it was not. That left two options: a mistake or a setup. Considering the obvious planning involved in my arrest, the surveillance, the likelihood of a bug in my car, and the number of police involved, an error seemed unlikely. But at that point, I was still hopeful. Maybe it's a mistake. A gigantic, elaborate mistake.

Second, I knew Carlos was dirty, going back to before I'd even moved to New Jersey. Outside of our furniture business, I kept my distance from whatever it was he had going on. I tried to think of any conversation between us that could have been misconstrued as drug-related and I came up empty. Yet I was arrested meeting up with him in a place that he had directed me to. Then he seemed unfazed when I told him that cops were surrounding us. Finally, he threw a package of cocaine at me right before the cops closed in.

But if they were taking me in so I'd give up Carlos, why'd

they arrest me in front of him? Why'd they beat the hell out of me if they wanted my cooperation? Plus, where the hell was he?

Third, I was arrested in Passaic County in the far north reaches of New Jersey, an unfamiliar area almost an hour from my home. Then, I was transported forty-five minutes south to Franklin Township, in Somerset County. I played basketball here from time to time, but I had no legal connection to the place. I racked my brain but the only thing I could think of that tied me to that county was Gator's car.

That past winter, my friend E., whom everyone called Gator, had his car taken by the cops, supposedly because it needed to be run for fingerprints on some robbery case. (It came up empty.) As the cosigner on the car—I'd helped Gator out with some financial issues—I had to go to the Somerset County prosecutor's office and sign to get it released. While there, I met with an assistant prosecutor who gave me some paperwork, which I put my name to, and that was it. The prosecutor, a broad square of a man named De-Marco, asked far more questions about me than you'd expect for that kind of thing.

The only other connection to Franklin Township had to do with Ron, Gator's childhood friend. He'd been arrested here back in March. But I barely spoke to the guy; he was reserved around me and I neither liked nor trusted him. All I knew was that Ron had been brought in by Franklin Township cops on a drug charge and was now out on bail.

So I sat there in the police station, playing with all these disconnected facts in my head. I moved them around, like pieces on a chessboard, but I couldn't for the life of me make sense of the game.

After being processed, I was led down a narrow hall by a burly officer who opened the door to a holding cell. He made an *After you* kind of gesture, a final indignity. Glancing down at my socked feet, he smirked before closing the heavy door behind me.

The small cell was surrounded by faded red brick on three sides. Rusted white bars ran from the ground to the ceiling, and across the thin hallway was yellow glazed cinder block. It was dark in there with fading light spilling in from one high barred window. There were other cells down the corridor, but I could feel it in the dead air: they were empty.

I sat on the metal bench, inhaling slowly. Each breath crushed my rib cage, like getting kicked all over again. My knees and shins stung, the scrapes rubbed up against the denim, and every movement was like being cut by little razor blades. The blood on my toes had dried, sticking my socks to my feet. My head was pounding like a shovel knocking against my skull. I closed my eyes and tried to leave my body.

I don't know how much time had passed when I heard a call of "Wright!" The guard came back, opened my cell and cuffed me, and took me back up the hall. Being restrained like that changes your body posture, your way of walking; it tips your balance and tightens your shoulders. My senses became amplified: the feel of my socked feet on the dirty linoleum, the sound of typewriters clacking and copy machines whirring, the smell from the burnt coffee—it all hit me intensely.

I was escorted into a starkly blank room. Dark plastic chairs surrounded a wooden table on which lay a phone, its cord running to a jack behind the door. One of the walls had a giant one-way mirror with an infrared dot showing through, obviously a video camera. I knew cops, likely the detectives who had roughed me up, were watching through the glass. Two white men in their late forties or early fifties sat on one side of the table. One was in a police uniform, the other in a wrinkled white button-down shirt and loose-hanging tie, slapping a pen against a yellow legal pad.

The uniformed cop, a doughy guy with tiny marble eyes, was the local chief of police, whom I met when I was first brought in. The other man was wide and sturdy, like a former athlete. To my surprise, I actually knew him. Pale with dark brown hair and a wide nose, this was Peter DeMarco, the man with a thousand questions, the prosecutor I met when I signed the release for Gator's car.

Except that's not who he was.

"Mr. Wright," DeMarco started, "you are fucked, my friend. Royally fucked." He nodded to the cop who'd brought me in, who took the cue and left. "First of all, I am not Assistant Prosecutor Peter DeMarco. My name is Richard Thornburg and I'm the Somerset County Prosecutor's Office's Chief of Detectives."

I was as alarmed as you'd be when someone you met as one person introduced himself as someone else. But I didn't let him see that. I dropped my cuffed hands on the table where they hit with a clank. Then I glared back at him, making it clear this was my response.

"OK," he said, glancing over at the local chief. "Look, let's cut the bullshit. We know that you are part of a criminal drug enterprise that spans four counties and—"

"Wait, wait, hold up," I said. "What?" My eyes must've jumped from their sockets.

"—that brings in roughly twenty million dollars a year—" Thornburg kept going, plowing through my protests.

"What are you—" I tried to interrupt.

Thornburg just got louder. "*And* that you keep half a million in cash in a safe in your house."

"Drug enterprise?" I protested. "A half a million where?"

"In a safe in your bedroom," the police chief said.

I don't know what I expected them to say, but it wasn't that. There was indeed a safe in my bedroom, but it held documents, passports, and some sensitive work papers—not money. Like any citizen with a legitimate job, and nothing to hide, I kept my money in the bank. *Who do these people think I am?* Sure, I partied with questionable people and befriended some unsavory ones—that was my life, and frankly, just part of the music business—but last time I checked, that was no crime.

"We know the money's there," the police chief said. "And the state of New Jersey allows us to confiscate anything of value we believe—"

"I don't understand," I said. The speed, amount, and sheer ridiculousness of the accusations were throwing me off-balance. I didn't even know where to start.

"The money was *yours* but it's dirty, so it's *ours*," Thornburg said. "Get it?"

I tried to push my contempt across the table to him, but I could tell he fed off it, like a vampire.

Thornburg fired questions to me about people I knew, some I didn't, names I'd heard, and what I knew about their criminal activity. I didn't respond. He was just trying to throw me off, trip me up, disorient me enough that I might let slip information he could turn into something incriminating. My best move was silence, so I just stonewalled until Thornburg, clearly frustrated, walked out. He slammed the door as he left, the sound echoing through the room.

I stared at the blank wall while the police chief fiddled with his Styrofoam coffee. There was something pathetic about this one, sweaty and desperate. It was like a smell coming off him. The room was stuffy and I could hear the buzzing of the fluorescent lights. The light was clinical, the air stale. I felt like a science experiment being poked and observed.

Thornburg came back in and sat down again. "OK," he said, "so, we have a team at your home right now."

I exhaled, shocked at where this was going. "You have people at my house," I said, a statement of disbelief more than a question.

"Correct. All we need is the combination to the safe."

There was no way on earth I was opening that safe for them, no matter what was in it.

"Forfeit the money," Thornburg said, "and this goes away."

"What exactly is it you're going to make go away?" I asked.

"What about the cocaine at Carlos's?" he asked. "That wasn't yours?"

Protesting my innocence wasn't getting me anywhere. You can't correct someone who doesn't want to be corrected, who doesn't *care* if they're correct or not.

I tried to turn the tables on him. "Why'd you tell me you were a prosecutor when I met you?" I asked. "Why'd you say your name was DeMarco? That even legal?" The police chief seemed shocked at this. He looked over at Thornburg, his brow wrinkled in horror, his face slowly reddening.

Thornburg ignored me. "You want us to pursue a case against you? You want to go to prison?"

"*What* case? Y'all are just making—"

"Enough!" Thornburg slammed the table with his open palm. "Enough with the bullshit." He took a breath, trying to calm down. "You gonna turn over the money?"

I was shocked by the sheer directness, the unsubtle nature of it all. When anyone but police officers did this, they had a name for it: *extortion*. I rotated my body away from the table and stretched out my legs, put one foot over the other in a defiant pose.

Thornburg picked up the phone and dialed. "Forget it," he said into the receiver. "No, he's not talking. Yeah, just get it open."

We sat in tense silence for a while. Through the cinder block wall, I could hear some voices rising and falling. After a few minutes, a uniformed cop came in and whispered to Thornburg; his face dropped. Thornburg turned to me. "Where's the fucking money?"

I thought that their coming up empty might help my cause, drain the air out of their certainty. But it just pissed them off even more.

"I told you," I said. "I don't—"

"You're gonna do twenty-five years," Thornburg said. "You hear me? *Twenty-five.* Either you tell us right now where the money is or—"

"So you pretend you're a prosecutor," I said, gaining some confidence. "You pretend I'm a drug dealer. Then you encourage me to entrap other people, my friends, people I've known for years just because you've seen them in my company. And now you're gonna try to extort me for money that doesn't even exist. If you were me, at what point would you ask for an attorney?"

The word hit the room like a firecracker, setting both of them off. Thornburg said they had witnesses lined up to testify against me, that I wouldn't even get to see my wife. At the end of every false accusation, I responded flatly, with one word: "Lawyer." Over and over again: "Lawyer." I wouldn't even give them my anger, which they could use against me. I stopped listening until I heard him say something about coconspirators in the other room.

I must've flinched. *Coconspirators? What coconspirators?* "I don't believe you," I replied.

"You wanna see?" Thornburg asked.

"Yeah," I said, trying to game out where this was going.

They brought me down the hall to a large office where about six people—all Black men in their twenties—were seated, cuffed in front of a desk. A uniformed officer sat there paying them no mind, processing paperwork. Two officers flanked each side of the line of men. I scanned their faces, people I had never seen before in my life. Then I saw a dark-skinned guy in his twenties with bubble eyes and a stocky frame. *Gator.* He looked worried, panicked even.

Right next to him was a tall heavyset guy with a plump face. He was wearing a checkered plaid shirt with jeans. *Ron.* The same Ron who grew up with Gator, who I knew had been arrested by these same cops a few months back. When Ron saw me in the doorway, he quickly looked down at his feet. Before I had a chance to process them being in there, the police chief grabbed me by my shirt and took me back to the lineup room.

I now knew this was no bluff. This was considerably more involved than my answering questions in a room, more serious than some cocaine found at Carlos's house.

Once that hit me, I shut down completely. They got nowhere after that. At some point, exasperated by hearing me say "lawyer" so much that the word began to lose all meaning, Thornburg brought me back to my cell.

Seeing Gator back there, looking helpless and scared, got me worried.

Growing up in various places in Europe and America, I became adept at being the new kid, finding what to do and who to do it with. As Sunshine and I got settled in our new home in New Jersey, I could see there was nowhere nearby to play basketball. After hunting around, I found a park in Franklin Township and a gym nearby in New Brunswick.

One night in the gym parking lot, I struck up a conversation with a guy on the other team who introduced himself as Gator. His BMW was parked next to my Volvo and we got to talking about our cars and then about what I did for a living. Maybe a month later, I ran into him at a park after another pickup game. As I was getting into my Mercedes, he ran over to me.

"Hey," he said, catching his breath. "Could I talk to you for a minute?"

"Sure."

"Cool, cool." He had a schoolboy shyness, his eyes darting around. "Look, I'm having some issues and I can see—looks like you're doing OK."

"I get by," I said with a slight smile.

"No doubt, no doubt. So, uh, remember that BMW I had outside the gym that time?" I nodded. "They repossessed it," he said. "Just fucking took it."

"Shit, man," I said. "That's rough. That sucks."

"Yeah, yeah," he said. "OK, so no bullshit, I'm just in a rut, like having a really hard time. And maybe there's something I can do for you, like a job or something, helping out . . ." he trailed off.

People knew about my success, so I was accustomed to getting approached like that. When it happened, I tried to be magnanimous about it.

"All my work is across the river, though," I said. "In the city. And if you have no car—"

"I can take the train in," he offered.

"Well, you sing? Dance?"

"Nah, man," he said, sheepishly.

"Listen, I'll be straight with you. I don't think there's anything right now but maybe we can talk down the line?"

I didn't want to blow him off completely. I spent a chunk of childhood down South, among countryfolk, where taking care of each other is embedded in the culture. If people asked me for help, I'd do a quick scumbag test on them, and if they passed, I would help. I had started from nothing myself and knew that sometimes people just needed a break. After that day at the park, Gator and I met up to chat and he seemed like a genuine guy who was just in a rough patch. When we said goodbye, I gave him a couple of dollars.

A few weeks later Gator called me up, telling me how impossible it was for him to get anything going without a car. He said his credit was trashed and what he really needed was a cosigner for a car, which I eventually agreed to be. After that, he was back on his feet and never asked me for money again.

I knew Gator to be an easygoing guy, but at the police station that day, he looked terrified. When I saw Ron was also in that room, I pinned it all on him, since he would not have passed the scumbag test. I assumed Ron was in some more trouble on top of his recent arrest, and Gator had been pulled into it as well. And now, so had I.

Up against the cinder blocks, I slowly rested my bruised back. There was a soreness in my bones and a deep howling in my ribs. I closed my eyes and drifted off.

"No!" A woman's voice cut through the black. "I want to talk to Isaac!" The sound was startling—it had been quiet for hours—and I popped up at the sound of my name. "Stop!

Please! I want to speak to Isaac!" she yelled. "No! No! Let me speak to Isaac!"

For a split second, I thought it was Sunshine, but the voice was higher, younger. Then it hit me: Raquel. Raquel was a young woman I became friendly with when I moved out to New Jersey. She lived with her grandmother and young child in a house Gator let her stay in as a favor to me. She didn't even know Gator or Ron or any of the people the cops were asking about. She only knew me.

"No! Stop! I want to talk to Isaac!" Her screams were piercing, heartbreaking. There was a depth to the sound that was so distressing, like her soul itself was crying out in horror. It bounced off the cement walls and echoed down toward my cell.

"Hey! Hey!" I yelled out in the dark. "Hey!" I started smacking at the brick and trying to rattle the steel bars with my hand, but the sound was deadened, swallowed up by the room. I looked down for anything to rattle the metal, but my belt and boots were gone. I felt like the victim of a cruel, elaborate joke that had gone way too far.

Ever after they stopped, Raquel's screams hung there like a presence. I dropped my head back onto the brick. I'd been in something of an emotional lockdown all day, survival mode. But hearing my friend scream my name, *beg* me for help, dredged up everything I had kept tamped down. Then it just started pooling out.

I thought about my wife, crying above me while cops forced her to witness my beating like some twisted spectacle. I thought about my daughter, wondered who was watching her and what they were telling her about where I was. I thought about my parents down South, who'd be devastated to hear of my arrest and on the first flight into Newark. It was an extra blow knowing how they would take this.

When I was a kid, I used to lie awake at night listening to the sound of my mother crying herself to sleep. My dad's military job meant we moved around every couple of years: Florida, New York, Georgia, Alabama, South Carolina, different parts of Germany. But because of the size of my family—there were six of us children—there was no room for us to live on the base. So every time my father got relocated, which in the military is just life, we'd have to wait for off-base housing to be found and approved, if at all. That meant long stretches of my mother having to parent all of us alone, which took its toll on her.

My mother carries a warrior spirit. She kept us all protected but also in line, at times when that wasn't the easiest thing. Our neighborhoods weren't the best and there was sometimes a lack of basic security in our home. One time my mother got up to take us to school and as she opened the door, the knob fell off in her hand. Someone had sawed off the other side and it was only the dead bolt that kept them from coming in. I can only imagine how she kept it together, getting the six of us off to school, with that kind of stress hovering over her.

Even with all my mother took on, the burden she carried, she never let the strain show. But pain like that doesn't get locked away. It finds its way out like smoke through a vent, curling under doors, around hallways, and into rooms. Late at night, lying in my bedroom, I'd hear her cries. I don't know if anyone else was awake to hear her, and I wanted to save her. But I was just a scrawny kid. There was nothing I could do.

From my cell, I listened to the quiet summer night chirping through the high window, the whoosh of cars from a distant highway. Coiled onto that hard metal bench, I thought of that iron one in Columbus Circle, where I'd slept my first night in New York City. I felt my body deflate, like a balloon let out of its air.

"Wright!"

It was pitch black when I was jolted awake by the sound of my name. As I came to, my head hammering, my body groaning, a light flicked on down the hall.

"Wright!" I heard again, the voice getting louder as someone approached the cell. In the darkness, I could see a figure in shadow trailing behind the turnkey. I thought maybe it was a lawyer someone had sent for me, so I got up to greet him. When he reached my cell, I came to the bars and got a better look at him.

"Nicholas Bissell," the man said, putting his hand out, which I took. He was a diminutive and heavyset white man with a square face and receding hairline.

"I'm the Somerset County prosecutor," he said in a grating voice. He had the pointed nose and rictus grin of a comic book villain. "Just wanted to stop by to let you know I'll be trying your case personally."

It was the middle of the night and the county prosecutor was coming to the local precinct to let me know I was a priority of his, that he'd be leading the charge to put me away.

That's when I knew I was fucked.

Chapter Three

SOMERSET COUNTY JAIL WAS LIKE a medieval dungeon, a horror story come to life. Built at the turn of the twentieth century, the place was four stories of cement floors, solid metal walls, and steel bars, imposing, hard, and dark. The morning after my arrest, I was thrown in there with over three hundred people, all crammed into a place built to house less than a quarter of that. The ceilings were too low, the hallways were too narrow, and everything was shrunken down. It felt like the walls were literally closing in.

The place was a warehouse to cage men making their way through the system, some in pretrial detention but unable to make bail, others serving shorter sentences that didn't merit state prison. It was hard to breathe, harder to move, and everyone seemed one provocation away from exploding. Two, sometimes three inmates were housed in tiny, closet-sized cells, sleeping on the floors, even under the beds. It was a cauldron that summer, with no air-conditioning or airflow to speak of. The sweat pasted our blue khakis to our bodies, and the sticky air hung dead in front of us. Inmates passed around garbage cans filled with ice, and everyone stuck their heads in there to keep from fainting. Those few seconds with my face down in there was like a refuge from hell itself. There was something biblical about that heat, like we were sentenced to sweat away all our sins.

Pain was still radiating up through my rib cage and shoulders whenever I got up in the morning. A few days in, I was cuffed at my wrists and ankles and chained to a line of other prisoners with court appearances. Then we were marched through an underground tunnel to the courthouse, the synchronized metal clinking like a rhythmic percussion.

After days in the grime of jail, the courtroom was overwhelming, like being in a stage show: bright recessed lighting, gleaming wood paneling, the turning of heads and flashing of cameras. When my case was called, I looked over to see who came up to the defense table with me: Carlos and his brother; Gator and Ron; a few faces I recognized from the park or gym in Franklin; and a handful of other guys I'd never met in my life. It was the first time I saw everyone charged in my case, so I probed each face, trying to piece together who knew what, who was connected to whom, who had been lying to save themselves. Their eyes scanned the floor, reluctant to meet mine. Some, like Gator, looked petrified; others, like Ron and Carlos, were dead of all expression.

Gazing into the flood of faces in the gallery, I spotted my sister and one of my brothers, both of whom had come in that morning from New York City. We knew each other well enough that we could have a whole conversation with our eyes.

This is bullshit, I told them. *I didn't do a thing.*

We know, they replied. *Of course we know that. Stay strong.*

In the gallery, I also caught sight of a few eager white faces scanning me up and down: reporters. *You* try looking innocent in a court of law wearing an orange jumpsuit and your hands and ankles in cuffs. The reporters chewed on pens, held out recorders, jotted on notepads, and cracked jokes to each other. It was just another day at work for them. Each one scoped me out with that removed stare: I was more idea to them than person.

In the weeks and months after my arrest, Bissell would use the media as just another arm of the prosecution. He'd already given a press conference announcing the bust, in which he shared a tale about how he took down one of Central Jersey's largest drug traffickers. Meaning me. The media lapped it up like eager puppies, treating him like the heroic lawman, while the truth was so much more insidious. At the time I had no details, just the overpowering sense that there was something seriously wrong with this man.

I watched Bissell closely at the prosecutor's table, slicked hair and high-priced suit, carrying himself more like gangster than public servant. He was chatting with a thirtysomething female in neutral-toned business attire: Veronica Nolan, the assistant prosecutor. She was a slender five foot nine or so, with dark hair and almond-shaped eyes. With a narrow face, pointed nose, and thin lips, Nolan had the bland politeness of a flight attendant.

Then the creak of the side door and another line of defendants, all female: Raquel, looking frail and exhausted; my friend Rhoda, who grimly met my eyes as she passed; Carlos's wife, who had the same impassive stare as her husband;

and in the back, her face swollen and red from crying, Sunshine. I couldn't believe it.

The sight of my wife, in leg irons and an orange jumpsuit, was devastating. Sunshine, always full of vitality and beauty, a woman who lit up rooms and brought crowds to their knees, was deflated, the life drained right out of her. I wanted to run over and hold her, find out how she was, ask about our daughter. But she didn't even look up. We might as well have been miles away. After seeing Sunshine, a hazy filter dropped over me, like I was underwater or in a dream.

"All rise," the bailiff broke in. "Court is now in session, the Honorable Michael R. Imbriani presiding."

I recognized the judge's name. At my cell, Bissell had mentioned that my case would go to him, as though it were a threat in itself. One of the detectives also said Imbriani was a madman, that he'd convict me whether I was guilty or not. "Iron Mike," they called him, though he was less like an imposing presence than a cartoon drawing: a squat, Joe Pesci–looking guy in his fifties with jowly cheeks, thick eyebrows, and a bulbous nose. If he didn't hold my future in his hands, I might have found him comical.

Bissell went through the charges for each defendant and when he got to me, you could have lifted my jaw up off the floor. Incredibly, I was the grand prize. While most of my codefendants were charged with one or two counts, I was charged with five first-degree offenses, ten total counts. The most serious: being the leader of a narcotics drug-trafficking network. Known as New Jersey's "kingpin statute," it came with a life sentence, as Bissell said, almost in passing.

Life. The single syllable hit me like a bullet in the stomach.

Then the weight, pressing down on me, my legs heavy like concrete. *Life.*

I could feel Bissell's eyes on me, boring a hole right through me. The barrage of charges was an intentional maneuver to get me to plea. Now I'd have to beg for a deal, turn over any money they asked for, say whatever they wanted me to say. That's what I was expected to do.

The hearing was quick, cold, and bureaucratic. Court officers going through the motions, muddling through their own workday. I felt like an afterthought to the whole proceeding. The legal jargon, complex and difficult to parse; the speed of the hearing, like they were trying to get through as many cases as they could before lunch; the discussion of my life as though I wasn't even there; the shock of seeing my wife and the mother of my child paraded through in chains. It all separated me from the reality of the case. My life was no longer my own; it was a bargaining chip, a thing to be sacrificed at the altar of an ambitious prosecutor.

And my response? *Not guilty.* That's all I was allowed to say.

Each defendant in the case pleaded not guilty, but my bail was the highest: a million dollars.* Even if I could have rounded that money up, I figured it was a trap. New Jersey had lenient laws about what the police were allowed to confiscate. All they had to do was claim something was used or

---

* Carlos, who was accused of being my supplier, also got a million-dollar bail. How my supposed supplier wasn't also a "kingpin" was never explained.

obtained in the commission of a crime and it was theirs. A cop's word was enough. I'd learn that it almost always was.

So, after taking away two of my cars, they were already looking into my bank records and business finances. I knew that if I produced that money, they'd confiscate it as "drug money," and come back at me with a higher bail amount. Thornburg wasn't exactly subtle at the time of my arrest. It became clear to me that my wealth, relative to that of the other defendants, was one of the reasons they painted a bull's-eye on me. Never mind the fact that when they arrested me, I had $96 in my pocket, and they found only $600 more in my house.

Some kingpin I was.

After Imbriani gaveled us out, I told one of Thornburg's deputies that I wanted to meet with him. Later that day I was escorted in cuffs and shackles to the chief detective's office in a building adjacent to the courthouse. Two officers sat me in a chair across from his desk and stood beside me like a pair of soldiers.

"Mr. Wright," Thornburg said, dropping a stack of papers onto his desk. The smarm wafted off him like a rank smell. He was more aggressive than Bissell, more externally confident. He carried himself like a guy who was used to acting with impunity. "I heard you wanted to meet. What can I do for you?"

I struggled to keep it together. "What is Sunshine doing in court?" I asked, my voice breaking. "What crime is she even being charged with—conspiracy to do what? Sit in a car on the side of the street?"

Thornburg smirked. "Well, I guess you can say that's the

cost of being your wife." He gave a slight laugh and looked up at one of the officers. He was ribbing me on purpose, testing me to see if I'd break. I think he assumed I had just about reached my limit.

"But she didn't do anything," I said, trying to stay calm. "She was just sitting in a car with me. What is she doing here?"

"Sorry if I wasn't clear the other day," he said. "A guilty plea and cooperation can make this all go away. Bring us some cases, tell us where the money is and—"

"What money, you fucking moron?" My frustration flowed out like a boiled-over kettle. "You want an innocent person to bargain for the life of another innocent person? You want me to do to other people what—"

"Look at it this way," he said matter-of-factly. "You're gonna be somebody's bitch when you get to prison anyway. You might as well start by being mine." Then his smile was gone. "Looks like we're done here, then," he said.

He nodded at the officers to take me out, and right as they touched my shoulders, I lunged for him across the desk. They snatched me back as I screamed at Thornburg, calling him all kinds of motherfuckers, anything that came to mind.

"Get him out of here!" he screamed as I was forced out of the office. "You can make this all go away, Wright!" he yelled after me. "It's up to you!"

It took both brawny officers to drag me onto the elevator. And I cursed out Thornburg the whole way down.

Rule number one: everyone breaks.

The engine of the American criminal system is not truth or justice. It's threats. And the fear that results from those threats. The government dangles incarceration over the heads of vulnerable people and produces what we call law and order. It's why 95 percent of cases don't ever go to trial; the system just isn't built for that. "If the vast majority of defendants did not plead guilty," writes former federal prosecutor Paul Butler, "American criminal justice would grind to a halt."[1]

Detectives and prosecutors don't just hope that you fold, they *need* you to fold. Everything crumbles if you don't fold. So they press, provoke, trick, and threaten until you cave and take what's behind door number one. When door number two could be five times that amount of jail time, door number one looks pretty good. For the prosecutors, it's also a thousand times easier than putting a case together through hard evidence. Hard evidence can't be convinced or threatened to do anything. People, however, are malleable.

It's a barbaric system, a type of institutional extortion where human beings are used as leverage to trap other human beings. They take your freedom and then offer to give it back if you help take away someone else's. Not only is this legal, it's the foundation of the criminal justice system in this country. If every single person arrested were guilty, this process might be brutal but efficient. But of course, that's not even remotely true. My wife, for one, was arrested as a ploy to get me to plead, and my marriage and family would end up being collateral damage.

Incredibly, the state of New Jersey was going to turn me into a drug kingpin as a punishment for not admitting to being one. Their plan was to bury me so deep that I couldn't ever dig my way out.

★　★　★

Once you are in danger of serving life in prison, you become a different level of inmate. For one, you are automatically considered to be a security risk. The facility holding you assumes that, in response to facing forever, you will completely lose yourself. You are likely to do anything: plan an escape, lead a riot, attack a guard, stab an inmate, hang yourself from your bedsheets. You are no longer expected to conform to basic human behavior, even the low standards set by the correctional system. For all intents and purposes, you need to be kept separate because you are a time bomb.

So after being processed into Somerset County Jail in Somerville, I was put in a high-security tier: twenty-four-hour lockdown, no recreation area, no outdoor space of any kind, no common area except for the narrow catwalk that ran alongside the ten steel cells on the tier. Day and night, a guard sat in a chair at one end of the corridor, sometimes with a menacing German shepherd with black eyes. It just sat there leashed, a suggested threat, a tight coil ready to spring.

The jail was built long before progressive ideas of humane punishment and rehabilitation passed into the American bloodstream. The place was made up of symmetrical lines of stone holes to store human beings who were worn down to their rawest nerve. The cell had walls of solid metal painted a ship-deck gray; it was so narrow that I could touch both walls with the palms of both hands. The pull-down bed was a metal rack with a thin mattress that, when down, took up the whole cell. My world, as wide and open as it had ever been, had contracted with frightening speed. Not five days prior I was a successful businessman, husband, and father. Now I was an inmate.

The toilet was an indentation in the corner of the wall with a hole in the ground. Taking a shit required complicated gymnastics. Since all the pipes were connected, the stench—a disgusting, unspeakable thing—roamed everywhere. You had to put clothes or books over the hole to trap the smell or else it hung in your cell like a specter.

Besides the smell, there was something else floating around, invisible but toxic. At first it was just a feeling, but over time I'd learn to identify it: the toll of what being locked up does to people. The claustrophobia, heat, and rage in that place was thick, leading people to hurt others and themselves. Suicides were not uncommon.

I remember an older inmate, a tall and balding white guy, troubled but genial. He had taken his sheets and tried to hang himself in the shower. A few inmates got there in time and pulled him down. When the guards showed up, they were making jokes and laughing about it. One afternoon shortly after, he was on the phone at the end of the tier, right outside my cell. Suddenly, he slammed the phone down and ran full speed in the opposite direction down the catwalk, bowling into some inmates.

"Hey!"

"What the fuck?"

Then I heard this flat *thud* that made my stomach drop. I jumped off my bed and looked down the corridor to see him lying on the floor, out cold, a bright red pool flowing from his head. He had run smack into the concrete wall.

"Lockdown!" one correctional officer screamed. "Lock-down!" We all meandered into our cells. The COs (correctional officers) yelled the code for "inmate down" so any guard within earshot would yell it until it made its way—like a game of telephone—to Central. Central sounded the alarm and repeated the lockdown orders over the intercom. A CO opened a large metal box near the tier gate and pulled the lever that simultaneously closed the cell doors. Then they opened the gate to our tier, rushed in, and tended to the man on the floor. They took him away—to the infirmary or hospital—and I never saw him again.

That sickening thud played in my head for days afterward. Deciding your best option was to run full speed into a stone wall seemed like a crazy thing to do. But I guess it was just a literal version of what we all wanted to do: throw our fury as hard as we could against this godforsaken place.

The boredom in Somerset was fierce too. The stagnation of day after day with nothing to look forward to, nowhere to go, and nothing to do. It'll drive you mad. During the day the cell doors were opened and inmates could wander outside their cells on the narrow catwalk. Outside of the bars, suspended on the wall, was a small television, but to see it you had to crowd at one spot with everyone else to get a peek, so I rarely bothered. There was no exercise, no yard, no programs. Our meals were taken on our laps on our beds or on the floor in front of our cells. The menu was a mix of the disgusting and the suspect: mortar-thick oatmeal, bologna and brick-hard ham, waterlogged mashed potatoes with gray beef, a thin layer of grease reflecting a rainbow color.

Gator was housed on the same tier as me, and early on, because of the overcrowding, in the same cell. We talked every day—me pushing him for answers, him dodging my questions. He swore up and down that our arrests were tied to Ron, and that law enforcement was just trying to squeeze me into cooperating. I didn't really trust him completely, but I was drowning and Gator was my only lifeline.

To speak about the case, I usually waved him into our cell where we were out of earshot. He was hard to follow, a human maze. Every time we spoke, I ended up getting turned around. His answers didn't add up, his story had gaping logic holes, and he had a habit of talking a lot without saying a damn thing.

I didn't tell Gator about the circumstances of my arrest, about Thornburg breaking into the safe in my house, about Bissell visiting me in my cell. But the strange thing was, Gator never asked about my case. That in itself was suspicious.

"Go over your arrest again, G," I said in a low voice. We were crammed in the cell, right in front of each other, breath on breath.

"What do you mean? You were there at the station," he started, like he'd already answered a hundred times. "They brought me and Ron—"

"Nah, nah. The one in February," I said. "The one at my house. What happened there?"

"Oh, that was some bullshit, man," he said, waving his hand in the air, as though swatting an insect. "And remember,

Ike, it was in Middlesex County. Trust me, that's got nothing to do with this. This is all Somerset County shit and I told you—"

"Just go over it again," losing my patience.

I had yet to hear a version of that story that made any sense. Here's what happened:

On a bitterly cold night the previous February, I was wrested from sleep by a knock on my bedroom door, sometime after midnight. I opened it to find one of Sunshine's brothers, Ismail, who was around fourteen. At the time, all three of my wife's brothers (ages seven to fourteen) were living with us, sharing bunk beds in the back room.

"Police at the front door," Ismail said, stifling a yawn. "They're asking for you."

Agitated, I threw on some clothes and found two officers waiting in the doorway. Sunshine showed up right behind me, the tension wafting off her.

There were two cops there who reminded me of Laurel and Hardy. One was taller and slimmer and the other was a little chubby and round in the middle with a mustache. Both were trying to look over my shoulder into the house, a flashlight at their sides.

"Sorry to bother you, sir," Mustache said. "We just made a traffic stop and the suspect ran into your house."

"What? Into my—"

"We have reason to believe someone is hiding in your house," the taller one said.

"What do you mean *ran* into my house? Where?" I opened the door wide and gestured into the living room. Ismail turned from the TV and looked over at us. "It's just the kids and us here," I said.

The cops exchanged a look. "We'd like to search your house for him," the taller cop said. He took a step as though I was about to say yes.

"Hold up, hold up. You're not coming into my house. There's nobody here but us and the kids."

He exhaled, exasperated, and looked at a small pad he was holding. "Do you own a blue 1972 Plymouth Duster?"

"Yes."

"Do you know where the vehicle is at?"

"Should be parked in the front of the house," I said. "In the lot."

"Can you go check if it's there, sir?"

I went over to the front window and saw the car was gone. The Duster was mostly for me to teach Ismail how to drive, though Gator had used it from time to time. Sunshine and I also had a driver who would occasionally service the cars.

"Do we have your permission to search the premises?" Mustache asked. The taller cop was holding the flashlight up, pointing it right at me.

My mind was circling different scenarios, but nothing really made sense. I didn't know what was going on. "Fine," I said.

Sunshine and I followed the two cops as they wandered aimlessly around our home, opening doors and closets, places a person couldn't hide in. When they got to my nephews' bedroom, it was dark, but the light from the hallway spilled in. I could see my two nephews asleep in the top bunk bed. On the bottom bed, the pillow and blankets were ruffled in a mound. Mustache stepped forward and pulled back the covers.

"It's him," he said to the other cop. "Get up." A figure stood and a face came into the light: Gator.

Sunshine stepped in from behind me, about to go ballistic. I grabbed her wrist and squeezed before she could say anything. The best thing to do was stay silent until we determined what was going on. We both were quiet as the cop lifted Gator by the arm.

"Let's go," they said to him, escorting him out without another word. The entire incident was strange, and felt almost like a performance.

When they were gone, I sat on the couch with Ismail to find out what happened. He said Gator showed up asking to crash and he let him in. Gator had slept on my couch in the past, so this in itself wasn't strange. But when the light from the TV bothered him too much, Gator wandered into the back bedroom. "I figured I'd just wake him up when I went to bed," Ismail told me.

When I got back to bed, Sunshine was wide awake and pissed. "What the hell was your friend doing in my brothers' bedroom?"

"I don't—"

"Please don't say anything," she demanded before I could answer. "Just don't. He brought the fucking police to our home."

She smacked me a couple of times on my shoulder before

turning over and going to bed. We never spoke about the incident again.

"What really happened that night, Gator?" I asked him in our cell. "Did you run from the police to my house?"

"What?" he protested. "Hell no. That's total bullshit, Ike. Why the hell would I do that?" He was right: the cops' story didn't make sense. If Gator was driving the Duster, why would he run to my house, the one place they would be able to find him, since it's where the car was registered? But Gator's story didn't add up either.

"But why would they say that, then?" I asked. "That doesn't make any sense."

"You think if I ran from cops they wouldn't shoot me in the back? C'mon, you know how that goes."

"Yeah."

"I told you, I had a fight with my girl and my friend dropped me at your crib to crash. That was it."

"Gator, I was there. They arrested you, man. They charged you . . . Why you? Why did they come in my house specifically looking for you?"

"Ike," he said, waving me off. "That was all in Middlesex. Nothing to do with this." Gator weaved in and out of my questions, tossing in some details that didn't seem to matter and leaving out others that did. "I'm locked up here with you," he said. "Where are we? Somerset. You know one person who was arrested in Somerset before and that's Ron. How come you think they separated him? You see he's not here." Gator opened his arms wide. "What other reason could there be?"

"Gator," I said, "we're sinking in a pile of shit here. You gotta level with me, man."

"I am. I swear."

"But I don't even know Ron. And he doesn't know me. The only connection between us is you. You have nothing to do with this? Did you tell them I was some kind of boss? Where'd they even get that from?"

"No idea, man. And no fucking way," he said. "Ike, seriously, I would never do something like that to you." When he started to walk out of the cell, I stood in front, blocking the entrance of the door.

"Sit down, G," I said.

"What you mean, sit down?"

"If you don't sit down, you're gonna be on your back."

He must've seen the fury on my face because he got this look, like he was scared of what I might do. Seeing his fear caused me to gain my composure.

"Ike," he said. "Ike, we all good?"

I walked off without answering.

"Are you kidding me? You can't be serious."

"I assure you I'm not kidding, Mr. Wright."

The attorney was probably in his forties, though it was hard to tell. All I could see was the bridge of a nose and a pair of tired eyes, bloody veins branching in the whites. In a cramped stall, I was standing up and staring at his face, partially hidden behind the scratched visiting window.

We talked through old plastic phones, his voice tinny and distant. It was eerie; I felt like I could hear the voices of desperate men haunting those phone wires. I could smell the breath of every prisoner who ever spoke into that thing.

"So you're saying you *don't* want to hear the truth," I said, dumbfounded.

"It's just . . . whatever story you tell me, I can't lie about," he said. "I can't argue something in court that—"

"Hold up. Hold up," I said, my patience draining away. "There is no *story*. Does it even matter to you that I'm innocent?"

"Let's just say if you tell me the truth, then I'm stuck with it."

"That's fucking crazy," I said.

"Well," he said, "that's the law." I knew this conversation was headed the same way all the other ones had.

Though I didn't yet understand the law, this seemed insane: Being stuck with the truth was a problem? If there was one thing keeping me together in that place, it was that I was stuck with the truth. It was sewed into me.

I closed my eyes and took a deep breath. When I opened them, I could tell the lawyer was somewhere else, already moving on in his mind. No way on earth I was going to war with this guy. As he went into an explanation of actual versus legal innocence, I slammed the phone down and walked off.

Summer into fall I met with a parade of lawyers: pasty white men who got too many cases and not enough sun. They were as interchangeable to me as I was to them. Some sleek and practiced, others rumpled and disheveled; they shuffled through, all telling me that I had to take a plea, that there were really no other options, that I simply could not beat these charges. I had to go to jail for twenty years: that was the argument they *led with*.

Sometimes we met in the assistant sheriff's office, one of the only private spots in the jail. They'd sit down, introduce themselves, open up their little folder, and launch into a version of the case that was entirely skewed. They spoke with the confidence of someone who had the whole picture, even though this was our first conversation. That's because I wasn't their first meeting: Bissell was. I understood that lawyers could not just blindly trust what their client said, but these guys weren't even listening to me. I felt like a sane person thrown into an asylum. Every word and action protesting my sanity was just seen as further proof that I belonged there.

I was stuck. What were they more likely to believe? A conspiracy of police, prosecutors, and codefendants inventing my place at the top of a drug network or the story that I was a Black man who made his money dealing drugs? I was trapped by my own stereotype, by the racist thinking of the country where I was born, by the limited thinking of every defense attorney in Northern New Jersey.

How do you prove you're not something? You can't. Try it: prove you're not a bank robber. Or the king of Spain. Or the reincarnation of Jesus Christ. You can't because that's not how logic works. You can't prove a *negative*, which is why the system puts the burden on the prosecution. But I was in the upside down: I had to prove that I was no drug lord. I had to prove that cops and strangers were lying about me. Forget about the fact that the state had all the money, resources, and credibility. Even by the standards of basic reasoning, I didn't stand a chance.

"You're looking at life," the lawyers all said. "They're offering twenty years. Take the twenty. At least you get some life back, right?"

I refused to put my life in the hands of someone who thought so little of it. Not a single one of them was asking to hear what happened. Not a single one came through talking about fighting. I was nothing but an equation to them: x evidence times y charges equals twenty years.

I was twenty-eight years old. Twenty years was a lifetime to me.

As part of any deal, I would also have to say that I was guilty. How could I plead guilty to something I didn't do? How could I do *twenty years* behind that lie?

These attorneys were offering to take my money to shepherd me into prison. Then they acted as though I was stupid, stubborn, or both for not agreeing to it.

No way, I thought, *let the state convict me.* But I was not going to do it for them. It was like Thornburg and the safe: I couldn't stop them from breaking in, but there wasn't a chance in hell I was opening it for them.

One night I lay down on my bed and stared up at the gray stone ceiling, the cracks like old rivers, the noise from the tier melting away. I thought back to my first night in jail, in Franklin, woken up to meet this strangely obsessed man. That incident had gotten my attention. The county prosecutor was coming to see me personally? To say he was going to try my case? That was crazy. It was alarming, and clearly indicated I was in serious trouble.

But I started to see it in a new light.

The more I thought on it, the more I realized that Bissell's overzealousness was an opportunity. County prosecutor is a political and administrative job; they supervise but try very few cases themselves. So Bissell had chosen me. He clearly had some animosity toward me, but I'm sure the headlines and high-profile nature of the case lured him to the prosecutor's table. And because he couldn't afford to lose, couldn't risk the gross embarrassment in front of his colleagues, his constituency, and the press, he was going to make convicting me a personal mission.

But that aggression revealed a weakness. By coming to my cell that night, he tipped his hand, showed how personal he was making my case. I knew from experience that those who rise to the top—and are able to stay there—are all business. They don't make things personal, because that's when you expose yourself. By taking the case and coming by to taunt me, Bissell had revealed his soft underbelly. It gave me the opening to turn things back on him.

NORTH CHARLESTON, SOUTH CAROLINA
SEPTEMBER 1981

I ended up in New York City because of a twenty-five-cent phone call. A couple of years after high school I was studying mechanical engineering at a college in South Carolina. Tuition was steep, so I was working two jobs to pay for it: package pickup rep at Sears and DJ at a skating rink on the weekends. One afternoon at Sears the boss called me into the office. Because I needed the job to pay for school, my record was sparkling. I got in early, left late, picked up shifts, and did extra jobs that I didn't get paid for. Even being brought into the office was a surprise.

The manager, a tall light-skinned Black man with a stern jaw, pulled out a stack of phone records and handed me a page. "Take a look at this," he said. It was a strange request so I started scanning through the numbers until I landed on my mom's house number.

"Oh yeah," I said, remembering. "Sorry about that. I meant to tell you I called my parents' house that day when there was that big storm for someone to give me a ride."

"You know there's a policy against personal long-distance calls, right?"

"I know, I'm sorry," I said. I didn't think it was a real problem. "I just had no other way of getting home. I'll pay you the twenty-five cents."

He put the paper down on his desk and then sat back, almost in resignation. "No need for that, just get your stuff and clear out your locker," he said.

I didn't even understand, looking up at the clock to check if it was quitting time. "Clear out my locker?" I asked. "Sorry, what do you want me to do with the stuff in my locker?" I thought maybe there was a cleaning crew coming in or something.

"When you leave the company, you have to take your things."

"Leave the company?"

"Yeah, you're fired."

"You're firing me? For a phone call?" I couldn't even

wrap my head around it. "You know I'm in school, that I need this job."

"I don't really want to talk about it anymore," he said, not even meeting my eyes.

I kept asking questions, which was just me trying to process what happened, but he got indignant. "Isaac," he said, "you either leave now or I'm going to get security to throw you out."

I got my things and left.

A few days of despair passed, followed by a few more of intense worry. Tuition was due soon and I knew how long it would take to work my way up at another job that paid nearly as well. About two weeks later, I was passing through the same Sears on my way to the mall parking lot. I saw a new guy working package pickup, my old job.

"Package pickup, huh?" I said, just to strike up a conversation.

"Yep," he replied.

"How do you like working here?" I asked.

"Man, I just got here. I've been begging my uncle to give me a job for months. He kept making promises but nothing until he called me a couple weeks ago and said he had an opening."

I got that heavy feeling in my chest like you do when your world is upended. The rage grew slowly, then all I saw was red. It was worse than being fired for a quarter. I was fired because of an owed favor that had nothing to do with me. They just needed a reason to get rid of me. I was stunned at first, and then I just couldn't think straight. *He had an opening.*

When the anger passed, there was this remnant, like a

hard kernel of wisdom. I realized how vulnerable I was when I had to depend on someone else for a paycheck. At the time, my goal was to get a degree in mechanical engineering and get a job working for somebody. But getting fired taught me that the last thing I would ever do is work for someone else. Only myself. My livelihood had been snatched away on a whim for reasons that had nothing to do with me. It was a profound lesson, so I made a pledge: I would never again put myself in a position where that could happen. As long as someone else controlled my life, I was at risk. My entire life plan changed.

I withdrew from school that week and took out the last of my money from the bank. As far as my parents knew, I was going to visit a friend in New York City and would be back in a few days. If I told them I had no intention of returning, they would've hog-tied me to the bed.

New York was a big enough place, with enough opportunities. It was an open space where I could find my own way. I knew it was where I could be in control of my future.

And for the next eight years, I was.

Chapter Four

THE UNITED STATES—LAND OF THE free, defender of democracy, birthplace of "all men are created equal"—is the only country on record to ever pass anti-literacy laws. It was illegal for American slaves to learn how to read and write, for reasons that go to the heart of who America was built for. They wouldn't give slaves an education for the same reasons they didn't give them land or guns. *Power.*

After slavery, during Reconstruction, when Black education and political power were first given a chance to breathe, Jim Crow laws swooped in to choke off that power once again. It took a century for those "separate but equal" statutes to get taken off the books too. But the ghosts of such laws remain in millions of ways. One of them is the criminal justice system. The law has historically oppressed the less-advantaged classes, and in the late twentieth century, no group was more marginalized by it than young Black men.

It was marketed as a War on Drugs but the battle raging in American neighborhoods when I went to jail in 1989 was not between the police and drugs. It was between police and Black people. While white mob lieutenants and Wall Street defrauders were peacefully escorted out of their homes and businesses in cuffs, police were militarizing against Black neighborhoods, destroying Black families, and decimating Black homes as though they were enemy territory. Children were ripped from their families to be raised by institutions, while adults—some dealing drugs, some using drugs, some living in a home used by those who had drugs—were forced to turn on each other in order to save themselves from incarceration. The prisons of America filled exponentially during the eighties and early nineties because of this crackdown. The criminal justice system was destroying Black people, families, and neighborhoods with impunity. And they were using what was ostensibly the glue of a functioning society— the law—to do it.

Through complex procedures, deceptive phrases, and indecipherable rules, the law has been wielded like a weapon, sharpened and pointed at those who can't afford to learn or buy it. This is to shelter the ruling class. If all people had equal access to the tools of advancement and protection, the power of the white rich male would be threatened. Everything about the law is designed to keep someone like me as far away from its inner workings as possible.

So I hit the Somerset County Jail's law library with a fair amount of skepticism.

At the time, I was still hopeful that I'd find a lawyer to represent me, and I took that term literally. *Represent* me, as in be my stand-in. I wasn't going to put anyone up there to argue for me unless they were willing to fight as I would. As time passed, my hope began to circle the drain. The law library would begin as a curiosity, but as the months bled together, as my hopes for a true legal advocate dissolved, that place would become my lifeline.

The law library was equal parts inadequate and intimidating. It was a small room with six rusted metal shelves holding thick volumes of old books, regal but beaten down. In the center was a large wooden table with a few plastic chairs; up against the wall was a set of file cabinets and a rectangular desk, where the law librarian sat. He was a tall and slender Black inmate in his early fifties, slightly balding with a narrow face. When I first arrived, he eyed me curiously over his newspaper and I gave him a quiet nod.

My first day in there, I wasn't even sure what I was looking at or for. Scanning the hardcover spines on the shelves, I tried to block out that tiny voice of futility in my head. I thought of all the inmates through the years who had come into this place with aspirations of digging into their cases. I pictured them taking a gigantic tome down from the shelf, opening it on that scratched table. I imagined them trying to parse the difficult jargon, the abbreviations and Latin phrases, the pages where footnotes flooded into the text. I thought of them staring into that daunting gap, and how the gap must've stared back. Its sheer size must've made them close the book right up and head back to television and cards, a little embarrassed that they thought they could make sense of something so vast.

I too stared into the gap and marveled at its size, at how much there was to learn, at how far I'd have to travel to learn it. Then I got to work. I approached the law the way I always did something new, by breaking it down to its elemental parts. I started with the most basic questions: *What was I looking at? What were these books?* I learned the largest books were called *reporters,* and they contained court opinions organized by issue, year, and court system: state, appellate, supreme, federal. I began with the New Jersey reporters, where every case would cite and refer me to others, which would refer me to more, so I was traveling along this interconnected branch system.

The reporters weren't written like any books I'd ever encountered. They contained a complex intersection of rulings, numbered codes, and cross-references, like a secret language I didn't yet speak. I'd find a subject heading relevant to my case, but underneath I'd see a long series of numbers, like: 412.(2), 412.(4), 641.3.(6), 641.3(7), 641.12(2).

The librarian was a passive but affable guy. He showed me how to read a citation in order to find the right volume or case, which was like being handed a key to decode the language. When I started asking him more detailed questions about the law, he didn't seem to know the answers. Maybe reading the citations was the limit of his knowledge; maybe it was all he needed to know to guide inmates. So I was mostly on my own in there. It was fitting because I was on my own everywhere else too.

As I parsed through these texts, I began to understand that what people think of as the law is actually the interplay between two things: statutes (the law as written by lawmakers) and precedent (authoritative interpretation of the law by courts). Because of *stare decisis*—the principle that rulings need to be based on precedent—the law is a living, breathing thing. It moves and transforms through individual cases. An interracial couple's case in Virginia led to the illegality of anti-miscegenation laws; a pregnant woman (pseudonym Jane Roe) fighting in Texas led to the legalization of abortion; a confession in Arizona from a career criminal named Ernesto Miranda is why police are now required to inform those arrested of their rights.

The law's fluidity makes studying it a different experience than learning disciplines like history or medicine, where long-held truths have hardened into place. Those subjects are like photographs slowly coming into focus, whereas the law is akin to a canvas repeatedly covered in paint. The untrained eye sees just a mess of swirls and swipes, while the legal mind recognizes the pigment that created those colors, which brushstrokes created what, and how certain patterns and choices undergird it all.

I brought books back to my cell and pored through them carefully, taking notes on legal terms, statutes, and cases to look up later. Then I'd go to the library and trade those texts out for others, pulled by this insatiable desire to learn more. Those musty books were deceptively powerful. They didn't look like much, lined up like soldiers in an airless room, their covers peeling, their tissue-thin pages torn. But when I opened them, it was like lifting the hood on society itself, like getting a peek at the spark plugs and shafts of the larger system.

As I continued to read the cases, a natural understanding of law emerged from inside of me. It felt like I had been doing it all my life. The process opened up even more when I found a legal treatise titled *Criminal Practice and Procedure* by Judge Leonard Arnold. Arnold happened to be a sitting judge in Somerset County and his book was like a shaft of light slicing into a dark room. The text offered procedural information on how to move cases through the judicial system from the arrest through conviction and sentencing. It helped me fill in the blanks of what I was up against, what I could expect, and how things would unfold. Since the day of my arrest, I felt the world was imposing itself on me without my understanding. Educating myself in the law was my form of resistance.

Being locked up is a scarring, powerless experience. But what exacerbates that feeling is the inmate's separation from the legal process. He doesn't know what's coming, or sometimes, what's already happened. He just waits to hear his name and be told where to wait and where to stand. His decisions are no longer his, yet he is asked like a child if he understands what he's agreed to. From cell to holding cell to court he is paraded like an object, traded like currency, argued over in a language he doesn't comprehend, conversed about in rooms he is not allowed in.

The legal proceedings are so opaque to him, so disorienting, that when a plea deal is offered, it's like a mirage in the desert. In pleading, he feels like he's wresting back control of his life. It's a deception, of course: the plea deal is presented as a way out, but it's the opposite.* A plea is an agreement to serve time and forfeit the right to appeal. But

---

* The plea deal also a) has an expiration date, and b) is brought via a defense attorney, who likely has many other cases to get to, may not have the time for a trial, and will, consciously or not, steer the client to take even a terrible deal.

to the accused, who's been behind bars and lost in the nooks and crannies of the system, it can feel like an escape hatch out of the helpless and hopeless dark.

Once I had a handle on how to use the library, I dug into the specific charges against me. They all revolved around my supposed involvement in a drug-dealing conspiracy, which I was accused of running. The two-year-old kingpin statute that Bissell was charging me with was the most serious—it brought a mandatory life sentence—but it was also the weakest.

The War on Drugs had swept the country in the late 1980s.* In New Jersey's haste to crack down, the state legislature had passed a vague, unjust, and sloppily written law. It *sounded* tough, and in politics, that tends to be what matters. But in actuality, the statute had enough holes to drive a truck through. The kingpin statute was a conspiracy law with a laughably low burden of proof. It required that the government prove only that I had agreed with a group of others, as their leader, to distribute drugs. That was it. As written, the statute gave a life sentence to someone for having a conversation that no one had to prove ever happened.

Incredibly, there was no minimum drug amount required, nor did there need to be proof that the person charged ever made money selling drugs. The drugs didn't even have to be distributed. All the prosecutor needed to convict was to have two witnesses testify that I was their boss and I had agreed

---

* "Over 80 percent of the increase in the federal prison population from 1985 to 1995 was due to drug convictions." (Butler, *Let's Get Free*, 46)

with them to sell drugs. With eleven other defendants being threatened with years of jail time, that would be cake for the prosecution.

Of course, the nonsensical nature of the kingpin statute could also give life to a college kid planning with his roommates to sell ounces of weed in his dorm. But those people were almost never charged with any crime, much less something so serious. That's the second thing that made the kingpin statute ridiculous: its selective usage. Bissell's office had conducted plenty of drug busts in the past two years, but the kingpin statute mysteriously wasn't used—most likely because the drug dealers forfeited large sums of money. So Bissell wanted to get his plaudits for convicting me as a kingpin—the first in the state—while also taking revenge for my not paying to play.

In order to prove I was a kingpin deserving of that life sentence, the prosecution had to strip away my actual identity, my humanity, and paint me as a larger villain in the ubiquitous drug war. I had to be framed as a stand-in for everything wrong with "urban" communities, a figure monstrous enough to absorb the public's rage and police officers' frustration. (One of the drug-trafficking police units in nearby New Brunswick was actually called the "Mad as Hell" unit.) My arrest was for show, a fabricated victory in the larger war—as though I had anything to do with it. As though the so-called War on Drugs was winnable in the first place.

Because Thornburg and Bissell had expected me to roll over and take a deal, there was no actual case against me. They threatened and overcharged, assuming they wouldn't have to compile the evidence, that I would cave like everyone else. But once it was clear I wouldn't plead, they needed time to put a case together. It would be twenty-one months from my arrest to trial, an eternity, even in a backed-up system. The saving grace of that delay was that it gave me time to teach myself the law.

Once I adapted to the hefty and overwrought way things were written, the law was a language I grasped, like I had been speaking it my whole life. One problem I ran into—which was ironic, considering where I was—was time. It was painstaking and laborious to read every case, each of which could run up to twenty dense pages. Every reporter contained an average of three to four hundred pages. But at the back of the reporters, the court's legal findings and reasoning were reduced to a summary paragraph called the court's "holdings," organized by subject. That meant I could cover an entire reporter's contents in around three hours, allowing me to plow through about three books per day.

It was like trading my shovel for an excavator. The change didn't just speed up my education, it broadened it, opening up the possibility of what I could learn. I was no longer confined to studying law related to my specific case. I had a thirst for it all: civil, criminal, administrative, murder, robbery, assault, drugs, SEC regulations, contract law. I would go from book to book, reading the holdings in every area of law contained in state, federal, and supreme court reporters.

The more I understood the system, the more I understood my path forward. I dug in deeper and began studying the structure, organization, and details of motions (various requests made of the court) so that I could know and understand how to prepare my own. If I were to ever need to.

Judge Imbriani was eyeing me suspiciously from the bench, as though I was wasting his time. He gave off the air of an agitated teacher dealing with a problem student.

"Mr. Wright," he said through clenched teeth. "I have called this status conference because I am concerned that, according to my case file, you have not yet selected a lawyer."

"That is correct, Your Honor," I said. I could hear Bissell and Assistant Prosecutor Nolan whispering at the other table.

"You are aware," the judge continued, "that we cannot proceed until you are represented by counsel."

"I am, Your Honor."

"And what's the problem?" the judge asked.

"Your Honor, I've interviewed a number of attorneys and . . ." I hesitated explaining my reasoning. "At this point I have not chosen one." There was not a single lawyer I'd met whom I was willing to go to war with, who even saw it as a war in the first place.

"Well, the court cannot operate at your leisure. We have to move this case forward. I've given you ample time to find an attorney."

"Judge," I said, "I understand your concern and I've interviewed several lawyers to date. I think Mr. Bissell can attest to that since they all seem to have talked to him before sitting down with me."

"Judge," Bissell responded at the sound of his name, "I

won't be attesting to anything related to Mr. Wright. He's had enough time—more than enough time—to find an attorney. At this point he's playing the part of an obstructionist and it is the state's position that it's beyond time to move this case along."

"I agree," Judge Imbriani said. I wanted to tell him that it was the prosecution that was dragging its feet, since they had no case, but I refrained. He stared at me with those beady eyes. "Your time for selecting counsel has passed, Mr. Wright. The court is going to appoint you counsel and if at some time you find an attorney that you find *satisfactory*"—he said the word with thinly veiled contempt—"then we'll substitute that attorney. The court can no longer wait."

The appointed counsel was a man named Paul Amitrani, who had black-and-gray speckled hair, a square face with small eyes, and a round chin. He had once worked as an assistant prosecutor for the county but after the governor appointed Bissell as prosecutor, he fired Amitrani. The reasons were murky, but Amitrani had a debilitating disease, which left him handicapped, and word got back to him that he was fired because Bissell couldn't have anyone who "looked weak" representing his office. By the time I met Amitrani, his disease had taken away complete use of his legs. He refused to be in a wheelchair, so he had his legs locked in braces, using Canadian crutches as leverage to keep from falling.

Since Amitrani came from Bissell's office, I didn't trust him at all. I considered that maybe he was a plant, feeding information back to his former boss. Or maybe he was angling to stay on Bissell's good side in the hopes of getting his old job back. I kept a lot of things to myself because anything seemed possible in a county where Bissell seemed to be the self-appointed king. Whether it was Gator from the inside or Amitrani from the outside, I didn't trust another living soul. So I shut down completely and insulated myself the best I could. At the same time I wouldn't give up hope that I would find a lawyer experienced, aggressive, and courageous enough to take on the fight—a legal gladiator, sword in hand.

As the weather got colder and that first winter approached, some good fortune finally landed in my lap. The law librarian got transferred and the jail didn't want to pay anyone to do the job. I met with the warden and offered to run the law library for free, knowing that it would give me constant access to the room and its books. That's when the floodgates opened because instead of piecing together scattered hours, I now had access to the library seven days a week from morning to night. My entire life—from breakfast to lights out—would be consumed by the law.

Whittling away hours in the law library had another positive effect: it separated me from the world of the incarcerated. For long stretches of time, I was cordoned off from the despair that drove men mad. In a place where nothing made sense, the library was a sanctuary, a dusty temple, a well-lit path. I was free from the oppressive lockdown hours, the crushing boredom, the vast open nothingness of endless days. By immersing myself in the law, in its history, philosophical underpinnings, and complexities, my mind stayed engaged. I was conversing with some of the world's great minds, with the history of my country, with ideas that went back to ancient times, principles that were weaved into the fabric of Western civilization.

I read legal treatises during the day, teaching myself how to defend a criminal case, and I read reporters at night, studying case law. I'd disappear into those arguments, blocking out all the mindless clanging of the prison, the stink rising from the pipes, the shrilling bells and sudden buzzes, the barking of the guards and the staring of dogs, the sound of men raging futilely against the world.

I had an image of myself floating on the sea, holding up my own weight, while all around me men were drowning.

"Wright, court in an hour."

On court days, I'd be woken at 7 a.m., the guard not even stopping as he passed my cell. For any pretrial hearings I'd shower and put on my prison blues. By 7:45 a.m. escort guards would cuff me and escort me to a holding cell on the ground floor next to the intake unit. Once I was placed in there, the cuffs were removed and I waited with other inmates to go to court. Breakfast was brought to the holding cell by 8:30 a.m. Then we were lined up one by one, handcuffed, chained together, and processed out of the jail to go to court. We'd be marched through a tunnel underground, to the elevator in the back of the courthouse, and into another holding cell behind the courtroom. There we waited—sometimes all day—for our case to be called.

When I first had to go through this process, I remained locked inside myself. But over time, I began to see the inmates around me differently. I thought of my situation as extraordinary—and in some ways it was—but in other ways, it was just an extension of what was happening to many of these men. Actual justice was rare, a small sliver of this world. The term "justice" was used to camouflage the true motives of the empowered: the decimation of communities of color. The ruling class was protected by a public who assumed the jails were full of the irredeemably guilty. It took being incarcerated for me to truly wake up to reality.

Before my indictment—the formal charges—could be handed down, there had to be a probable cause hearing. This required that the state convince the judge that enough solid evidence existed for my arrest and charges.

The claim: I was running a four-county, 3,000-vial-a-day, 20-million-dollar-a-year cocaine distribution operation.

The standards to prove it: impossibly low.

The support: the word of four detectives out of the exact same office.

And their proof? *Other people they'd arrested.* People who weren't in court, whose statements didn't need to be verified, whose credibility didn't need to be established. People who, above all, were being threatened with prison time. Probable cause is essentially a rubber stamp from the judicial system given to whatever the cops claim.

All of these statements have a legal term: hearsay. *Hearsay* is the unsubstantiated reporting of what someone else—out of court, not under oath—has said. It is the legal term for rumor. It is generally prohibited at trial, but an entire probable cause hearing can be built around it. Mine was. Since I was still unable to find a lawyer, Amitrani was the only firewall protecting me from an all-out lynching.

The first witness, Detective Andrew Racz, was the mustached cop who drove me to the police station on the day of my arrest. At the hearing he claimed that, after my arrest, I told him, "I got to admit you guys are good." He also testified that I said that "I never thought I would be caught in this business." Of course none of this was true. What kind of idiot would say such incriminating things? What kind of kingpin would just spill that out? It was nonsense. The only thing I do remember saying in that car was "Where we going?"

There was testimony from three other detectives, including a more reserved detective with close-cropped hair named James Dugan. All four men testified that people they'd arrested for drug possession said I was their boss. Back-to-back-to-back, the cops said the same thing, virtually the *exact same thing*—word for word.

". . . brought their money to Mr. Wright . . ."

"Mr. Wright was atop these organizations . . ."

". . . said that Mr. Wright was his boss . . ."

". . . claimed that Mr. Wright was running an extensive drug enterprise."

As the detectives recited their incredibly similar stories, Amitrani's cross-examination was befuddled and weak. Even I could tell it was a disaster. Everything he said only made the cops look more truthful, which is literally the opposite of a good cross-examination. Amitrani went through the motions like nothing but a warm body while I sat there helpless. My mind scoured through various grounds for objection or suppression, but I couldn't say a word. I just sat there frozen.

Since only the prosecution presents evidence in a probable cause hearing, there is a giant logistical hole in the process. Any argument you hear where you are only given one side is going to sound like a convincing argument! An argument can only be measured against its counterargument. With nothing to compare it to, in a vacuum, everyone sounds guilty. That too is by design.

The probable cause hearing was like showing up to a prizefight and, during the handshake, getting punched in the face. It was a necessary wake-up call that also taught me an important lesson: *It is impossible to put away an innocent man without a conspiracy.* Think about it: there are only two ways for a group of people to tell the exact same story. Either it happened, or they got together to plan the story. *There is no third way.**

Another element of my case that came to light that day was how incestuous the relationship was between the police and prosecutors. At the time I didn't know much about police jurisdiction and which cops were out of which precinct or department. I learned at that hearing that all four detectives testifying—and all the detectives who arrested me—were out of the county prosecutor's office. They literally worked for Bissell. It colored the entire case because I was no longer just up against the so-called blue wall of silence that banded cops together. I was up against these men's livelihoods. Bissell was *their boss* and they had to do as

---

* Also consider the idea of false confessions, which are far more common than common sense would dictate. Why would someone confess to something they didn't do? More importantly, if they didn't do it, how can they know the necessary details of what happened? *It's impossible.* You can't confess to something that you don't know anything about. The only way to do that is *if the cops give you the information.*

he asked. For god's sake, Bissell was the one right there in the courtroom questioning them.

Watching Bissell in action for the first time, I could see he wasn't questioning the cops so much as colluding with them. He led them where he wanted to go, clearly having coached them so their stories lined up. So the probable cause hearing was four of Bissell's employees testifying that people they'd arrested said they worked for me.

As I suspected, Ron was one of them.

It was a convoluted story, but essentially Ron had been cheating on his girlfriend. When she found out, she told the cops that he had been dealing drugs. In March, he was caught in a Franklin-area motel with almost eight hundred vials of cocaine that he was preparing to sell. Maybe then, maybe later, he began to cooperate in order to save himself, feeding Bissell lies that I was his boss.

Bissell also claimed in court that Gator's February arrest, the one at my house, was related to the drug conspiracy, though he was still investigating it. I was beginning to understand that "investigating" meant pressing on someone to say what the prosecutor wanted to hear. Gator was getting pressured and cornered, which meant I was right not to share anything with him. He had been taken off my tier at the jail, but I'd see him once in a while in passing, like in the law library. We only spoke a few words to each other, and I got the feeling he was sizing me up the same way I was sizing him up. Jail makes you paranoid, sure, but I felt like Gator had been lying to me from day one.

Whenever Judge Imbriani spoke in my direction, there

was a thinly disguised sneer, almost a mocking tone. Every statement made by Bissell or Assistant Prosecutor Nolan was admitted as evidence; every argument Amitrani made on my behalf was swatted away, every objection of his overruled. Judge and prosecutors were ostensibly representing different branches of the government, a separation literally enshrined in the Constitution. But anyone with eyes could see they were operating in concert.

We got trashed. Not only did the court rule that there was probable cause for my charges, but it was clear how they were going to win this thing—by using everyone else. There were twelve arrests made but there would be only one trial: mine.

As I lay in my cell afterward, the ceiling was spinning. I'd spent all these weeks studying and learning about the inner mechanisms of the law. But what I saw in court was bewildering. Not only did truth not prevail, it didn't even seem relevant. *What was I missing?*

At first, it had seemed crazy that every lawyer was advising me to plead guilty. But as I began to understand the larger picture, I realized it made perfect sense. It was in their interest that I plead out. So few cases even go to trial because a deal is made that serves both parties, and that ends up meaning both *attorneys*.

Sure, a plea gets you less time than you would if a jury found you guilty, but that's just because the justice system punishes those who go to trial. (It's literally called a "trial penalty.") It's crazy if you think about it: if you try to utilize the justice system, they make you pay for even trying. Sure, there's a slim chance you'll walk free, but the smart money says you'll lose and then they'll bury you for it.

This was especially true in a county where one man called all the shots. It wasn't just the people who directly worked for Bissell who had to play his game; it was the judge and the defense attorneys as well. The law is a tight club, an interknit community, and it seemed like in Somerset County, the adversarial relationship was just theater. Of course, there are some defense attorneys out there who go to the mat for their clients, but I hadn't met any of them. Every suit who came through those doors was either wary of or duty-bound to Bissell.

As long as my so-called representative was part of this system, I wasn't being served. The only way to present my side and truly serve my interests was to cut myself off from such a mediator. I had to excise my fate from Bissell's wishes, separate myself, become a true adversary, one who would win if the state lost. I was caught in a game of politics and personal survival. As long as I was represented by someone else, I wasn't a player in this game. I was a *piece*.

It left only one solution.

Chapter Five

THERE IS NO JUSTICE, THE saying goes, *there's just us*. From the moment the cuffs were first put on me, I understood that truth in my bones. There was no one whom I could trust, no one putting my interests first, no one else who was going to rot away in prison if I was convicted. What became clear, in all my motions to Imbriani and hearings with Bissell, all my discussions with Amitrani, all my efforts to get Gator to tell me what was going on, and all the lawyers I interviewed that didn't offer even a glimmer of hope, was that I was on my own.

If I waited around for someone to save me, I'd be waiting my whole life. Unless I took the reins of this thing myself, I was going to die in prison. If that was my destiny, then I was going to die fighting. The desperation of that equation kept me up most nights. I would never find a gladiator. So I had to become him.

In the legal system, when a defendant opts to be his own lawyer, he is said to be appearing pro se. The phrase comes from Latin, meaning "for oneself." *For oneself.* The term had resonance for me because it had been true from the beginning.

I had been for myself from day one. So in the spring of 1990, after nine months in jail, I made it official.

"Wait, what? You're what?" my mom asked. I was on the phone with her and Dad.

"I'm going to act as my own lawyer," I said. I could feel the shock on the other line.

Dad wasn't much of a talker, but Mom's silence was deafening. She had run that family of six kids with her strong mouth and fists. But after hearing of my decision, she went quiet. Dad spoke to fill the space.

"What's wrong, son?" Dad was stern, but confused. He could tell that I hadn't told them everything. They didn't know about the line of prospective lawyers urging me to plead guilty and take twenty years, to cooperate and set up other innocent people. I refused to do to another person and their family what had been done to me—it was against my nature and counter to how they raised me.

I didn't need to walk them through all of that. My parents were going through enough pain as it was; I didn't need to detail for them the hopelessness of my situation, that representing myself was a last resort, that it was bound to fail, and that the system was designed to crush me. There was no reason to put that on them.

"Listen, it's not permanent," I explained. "I can change my mind at any time." I was hoping to put off the conversation for later. "Let's talk about it the next time you guys are able to come up."

"OK, well, keep your options open until we get there," my dad said. "We'll see you soon." My daughter was staying with them, so I asked them to put her on the phone. She kept asking, "When are you coming home, Daddy?" Then my parents said goodbye, but Dad didn't place the receiver directly on the phone. As he fiddled with the receiver to hang up, I could hear the anguish in my mom's voice: "We're gonna lose our son." Then the plastic racket of the phone landing in place and the line went dead. For a brief moment, I had gotten a glimpse: they were putting a face on for me just as I was for them.

My parents weren't the only ones carrying some serious doubt. Acting as your own lawyer, especially in a case this serious and complex, was close to unheard of. Everyone who found out about it thought I was crazy. Maybe. But what struck me as really crazy was relying on the same system that put me in jail to get me out.

My mother's eyes go wide and panic rises in her face. She drops her plate, and runs toward the bank. I follow behind her on the slippery grass. One of the twins wrestles in his father's arms, trying to break free. The boy wrenches free of his grip and dives. I watch the smooth splash of the water, its separating and re-forming. He swims out to his waving brother—it feels like hours, but it is a few minutes. Then both boys are waving. After they go under, there is an eerie silence. No one moves.

I opened my eyes with a start, realizing I had drifted off to sleep. I was sitting up against the wall, papers and notes and opened legal texts covering my bed. I reached over and picked up my pen and some of my papers from the floor. My neck felt like a noose pulled tight, my eyelids heavy. I was getting lulled into a trance by the buzzing cell lights, the mechanical breathing of the gears, the empty dead space of the quiet jail at night. My body was screaming for sleep but I had my cell to myself for a few days—a rarity—and I wanted to make use of each hour.

I gathered all the scattered papers together and read a few of the inked lines: it was a handwritten motion to the judge, the first I had ever prepared on my own. I read it back, but the language was jumbled and confused. Though I knew what it was—my motion to proceed pro se—even I couldn't understand it. I was new to the law's distinctive language, but that wasn't the problem here. In the past few months, I'd read and studied enough motions to understand how they worked. This didn't sound like a new lawyer getting his feet wet; it read like a missive from a drowning man. It was so bogged down with emotion, so explicit about the pain, that it was nearly incomprehensible. I might as well have spilled my blood all over the paper and sent that to the judge.

Instead of a procedural history, I gave a confusing rebuke on the court's rulings and inherent unfairness. Instead of a statement of facts, I gave an impassioned protest against law enforcement. It was a difficult read, revealing a man in distress. Of course, that's exactly what I was, but the court doesn't work on mercy; it responds to logic. It doesn't want a plea for help and it doesn't respond to emotion. It demands an argument.

I dropped my head back against the hard metal wall, banging it a few times. Turning my head, I glanced at the photos taped there: Sunshine leaning back into my arms, the two of us carrying the innocence of youth, the bright eyes of better days; an old black-and-white family portrait, my mother in the center of her orbiting children; my infant daughter, in my arms in a white dress, flashing a missing-tooth smile as I plant a kiss on her cheek. The sights punctured right through to my heart. The pictures had gone from mementos of a time, to reminders of memories, to the only things I had in my shrinking world.

My daughter was staying with my parents in South Carolina, her world upended, her family ripped apart. Sunshine and I didn't have much communication, but I knew she had been charged with criminal conspiracy and released on bail. Bissell was using her as a bargaining chip to weaken me and get me to plead guilty. But that was something she and I had promised would never happen. Unfortunately, we had no idea the extent Bissell would go to in order to exact his revenge.

For a moment, I got a glimpse of myself. Not from outside the cell, nor from above, but from some impossible third place. I was exhausted and disoriented, but the image didn't seem strange to me. I was watching myself watch myself— and it didn't feel like a hallucination. It felt like a message. I began ripping the motion into pieces and crumpling them up before throwing them to the floor.

When I had decided to become my own lawyer, I assumed that my passion and my pain would be an asset. It had gotten me through travails as a kid, gotten me out of South Carolina, kept me alive in New York, helped me rise in my business and make a name for myself against serious odds. But my passion and pain were not welcome in a court of law. If anything, they were a handicap. I needed to find a way to put them aside. Since I couldn't ignore what was inside me, the solution was obvious. I needed to create a new identity: a logically and emotionally balanced person—one holding no irrational bias in my own favor.

I had to shield from emotion, protect against impulse, and present to the court as a man in full control. Isaac the defendant and Isaac the lawyer had to be two different people. That was how I'd win. By splitting in two.

Once again, Imbriani had that look on his face, what could charitably be described as flustered bulldog. I was starting to realize that it wasn't a look; that was just his face. Raised above all of us—me, Amitrani, Bissell, Nolan—he took his time. The judge had the manner of a school principal—every sentence an admonishment, every mannerism an expression of disappointment. He had my motion to proceed pro se in his hands and was squinting at it with a mix of confusion and disdain. When he'd read enough, he put it down on the bench in front of him, making a face like he'd eaten something sour.

"Well, Mr. Wright," Imbriani said, "you have a constitutional right to represent yourself but I still have to make sure this is not a ruse. You understand?"

"Yes, Your Honor," I said. I was prepared for the pushback, fully expecting that the system would close ranks against me. It happened almost immediately.

"Again, I have to be confident that you're not wasting the court's time with this."

No one appreciated my decision to represent myself. Friends and family spoke out against it, Bissell mocked me for it, and Imbriani was clearly going to hold it against me.

As an added insult, the judge wouldn't approve the motion without my passing a competency hearing. This in itself proved the rot in the system; the very idea that I wanted to represent myself indicated some kind of deficit on my part. At the hearing he asked me a whole list of questions about my education level and mental health history. I told him about my college background in mechanical engineering.

"And your exposure to the law?" he asked.

"I've been doing research in jail since I've been there," I said, "and I've obtained enough knowledge to do briefs. I prepared the motions for today. I know how to research the information I need and what I don't know I can ask Mr. Amitrani," I said. Though I had no intention of leaning on him, I figured it looked better if I presented it this way.

Imbriani then went into how complicated my case was, how interconnected it was with the others, how the state couldn't coddle me just because I was new to this. The condescension from the bench was pronounced and I had to swallow it. There was something inherently racist in his assumption, in the way he thought I couldn't possibly know enough to do this. I started to sense Judge Imbriani was speaking this way on purpose just to trigger a reaction from me.

"I have more knowledge of the case than my attorneys and the prosecutors," I said, passionately but not angrily. "I'm no attorney, but this case is so complex that I feel I would do better questioning witnesses myself. I'm a man fighting for his life."

I asked for access to the courthouse's law library, which Bissell argued against, saying it would be an undue burden on jail personnel since a CO would have to accompany me. Imbriani agreed, denying the request and saying Amitrani could photocopy what I needed for me to read "at my leisure in my cell." I also submitted a motion for my own typewriter, to have a visiting booth at my disposal from 8 a.m. to 5 p.m. every day, and—when Amitrani was present—use of the conference room, all of which I would eventually get.

The justice system wasn't supposed to be available to someone like me. Though the court granted the pro se motion, the judge appointed Amitrani to sit in the courtroom next to me as standby counsel. If I started utilizing the freedom to represent myself as a weapon against the system, they were going to have him take over. If going pro se turned out to be a strategy to delay, circumvent the process, or pursue some hidden agenda, he would step in. I agreed because I had no choice, though I didn't want Amitrani there at all. He was not allowed to present, question, or argue at the trial, so his assistance was just a mirage anyway. It wouldn't be there when it counted and all it did was put training wheels on something I had to ride on my own.

I understood that Amitrani was there as a fail-safe not for me, but for *them*. He would be planted next to me so that when I inevitably lost, I couldn't appeal and argue ineffective counsel. Every player in the system pushed against my decision to represent myself. They simply couldn't allow me to succeed. Because if I did, where would that leave them?

The judge's reaction to my going pro se, the prosecution's manipulation of every card, the court's hindrance of my work, and the press's mockery of me in the papers—it all lit a fire under me. I just visualized each obstacle as another log on a gathering flame. The larger the obstacle, the fiercer it would burn. While the rest of the jail's population just counted their days and waited on their hearings, I spent hours in the law library and up late in my cell. I dove back in with focus and purpose, relentlessly immersing myself in the law. This time I didn't just concentrate on issues related to my case. I read everything, treatises and reporters cover to cover, much of which was only tangentially related to my case. I was on a journey to internalize all of this ammunition and on the hunt for anything I could use as a weapon. If I was going to get myself out of jail, it wasn't going to be through the front door: a not guilty verdict. So I went searching for side and back ones.

To be honest, I was never much of a student. I was an intelligent and inquisitive kid, but because of my own stubborn will, I worked to make sure I wasn't seen as too smart, even if it meant deliberately answering questions wrong in high school. Something about exposing my intellect made me uncomfortable. I didn't want people to know that I was smarter than them. I can't totally explain this behavior; it's just something I did. As I matured, I saw it as a personality defect that prevented me from knowing who I really was and what I was capable of.

As a young man on the street, I was successful and thought that I had the world in the palm of my hand. But it was in a prison cell where I discovered who I really was. My survival actually depended on my being the smartest person in the room. I had to rise to an impossible challenge and retain massive amounts of complex information without any background in the material. I discovered a gift that I never knew existed, saw my disadvantages as secret weapons. Unlike most others first learning the law, I had tangible experience in the bowels of the justice system. Unlike every other lawyer arguing before a judge, it was a matter of life or death for me. There was no daylight between my life and this legal system. The two were intertwined, tied together like tightly coiled rope. I either learned enough to get myself out or I would die in there.

The more I dug, the more the law began to reveal itself in all its complexities and contradictions. When I began, I thought of the law as a science of truth, a kind of temple of facts. But this is simply not true. Nothing that happens in the legal realm makes sense through that lens. I came across a case that crystallized this newfound understanding for me.

The case involved a defendant sentenced to life in prison for snatching a woman's pocketbook. After he took the purse, the victim ran after him and, in the process, got struck and killed by a car. The defendant was charged and convicted of murder under a so-called felony murder statute. The statute allowed for what is called "strict liability," which means if you commit a felony and a person is killed during the course of the felony, the prosecution does not have to prove intent and the perpetrator *doesn't have to commit the killing.* You are automatically liable for the resulting death if you are found guilty of the underlying felony. You can kill nobody but be in prison for murder—not because of a mistake, but because of how the law is written.

These results—and there were many others in that vein—stumped the logical part of my brain. I flipped back through the pages and read and reread them. It seemed like maybe I was missing something. If the law was some kind of archeology of truth, how could a person be convicted of something he didn't do?

The implications hit me like a thunderbolt. The law, unlike any other science, cannot operate upon exactness. Its foundation is actually based upon fiction. A judge's ruling is just an opinion with the weight of authority. A jury's verdict is a fiction with the weight of consensus. If the courts were arbiters of truth, innocent people would never be convicted and guilty people would never get acquitted. Since that happens all the time, the law is just a grandiose temple with deceit at its center. Think about it in comparison to medicine—if a doctor says a tumor is benign, but it ends up killing the patient, there is but one conclusion: the doctor was wrong. A doctor, no matter how respected, cannot upend truth. But the law does exactly that all the time.

I had once seen the truth as my greatest weapon and I proceeded on the premise that the judicial system depended on it. Since the truth was in my favor, all I had to do was harness it and free myself. But in practice, the judicial system works despite the truth; sometimes it works in clear *opposition* to it. The search for the truth is limited to the facts of a case as a court accepts them to be. Thus, it is a fiction.

For example, the U.S. Constitution acknowledges that "all men" are created equal and have specific rights. The Supreme Court once interpreted those rights to exclude the enslaved. But male slaves are indisputably men, so how could the court exclude them? *Fiction.* Fiction not only allows the court to manipulate a legal result, it allows both prosecutor and defense attorney to do the same.

As baffling as this all was, once I got a handle on it, it was actually empowering. An individual is not confined to what is written in the law; he is confined to the limits of his own ingenuity. I realized that the power of lawyers, judges, and juries was not absolute but subject to the power the law gave me in creating my own legal result. The meaning of anything that is based upon a fiction is malleable. It can become whatever truth you need it to be, limited only by the extent of your intellect, creativity, and understanding of the law.

The state of New Jersey wasn't just building a fiction in court that I had to counter; they were also building one in the press. During my nearly two years in jail before trial, the prosecution constantly leaked or spoke directly to the media about the size and reach of my so-called drug operation. The papers were filled with details of how they found money and drugs at my house (they never found either), how I had a network of runners working out of various motels in the area (untrue, all they had was Ron's arrest), how they confiscated automatic weapons from me (they were stage props for a music show), and on and on.

Two days after my arrest there was a story in the papers where a few of my neighbors gave all these quotes about what they suspected about me, where my money came from, how I had parties into the night and kept cars on my front lawn.[1] Two days before my indictment, a story appeared in the Newark *Star-Ledger* championing the kingpin law, claiming it had been so effective in bringing down organizations, though no one had *ever been* convicted of it. The coordination was breathtaking. On the same November day, three different New Jersey papers published a story on the successes of the Somerset-Middlesex drug enforcement unit. It read like a press release, or a political ad, but it was printed like news.

The media and the prosecution operated in concert with each other to such an effective degree that I became to the public whatever they said I was. There were plenty of things I first "learned" about my case through the newspaper rather than through the courts, and virtually none of it was true. But Bissell and his team understood the game and I was still learning. My identity was this flexible thing no longer in my control.

When you're buried in charges, one of which labels you a "kingpin" before you've been convicted of anything, it's hard for the average person to believe in your innocence. The blanket respect people have for prosecutors and police— especially thirty years ago—was another towering obstacle. And the press played right into it.

The best example of this was a headline printed before I even went to trial. In the months before Rodney King's name became synonymous with systemic police abuse, there was a hearing where I testified about the beating the cops put on me at the time of my arrest, in broad daylight with plenty of witnesses. The story's headline? "Drug ring leader claims unfairness."[2]

ANNISTON, ALABAMA
1970

I spent most of my adolescence overseas in Germany, where as a kid, I didn't feel any different. Sure, we were Americans in a country against whom we'd fought two wars, but my brothers and sister and I never thought about that. And none of the German kids seemed to care that we were American or that we were Black.*

My family lived off-base, in a military outlet surrounded on all sides by a German neighborhood. The local families there accepted us as part of their community. We learned the language and culture and they were curious about ours. If anything, our differences worked as glue that bonded us together. Having to work to cross those bridges became a way into each other's lives. We showed them how we played marbles and they taught us how to dress in lederhosen and suspenders. The other kids invited me and my brothers to what they called "orchard parties," where we raided the fruit orchards in people's backyards, hopping fences and stealing pears and plums. Then we'd dodge the household items the adults would throw at us. It got hairy once in a while, but we had a blast, laughing and taking off as fast as we could. Once we were free, we'd put our hands on our knees, panting, smiles plastered on our faces. I never felt so invincible.

I didn't feel like a Black kid in Germany, just a kid. But when Dad got transferred back home to America, to South Carolina and then Alabama, I was dropped into a racist culture that shocked and confused me. In fourth grade I returned to my home country, a place where I was treated as an Other, disrespected in a way I wasn't in a country that

---

* In *The Omni-Americans,* Albert Murray notes that Black POWs in Nazi Germany during World War II found their treatment at the hands of enemy captors better than that of the white townspeople back home in Alabama. (Murray, *The Omni-Americans*, 23.)

had long been our enemy. It was baffling. South Carolina's version was more polite and subtle, but in Alabama it was brutish and explicit.

Alabama in the early 1970s was still stuck in the 1950s, embedded in the mud of Jim Crow: whites-only fountains, separated lunch tables and bathrooms, whispers and clutched purses as I passed. Suddenly, my color—something that never mattered before—was all anyone saw. My father had fought in two wars and defended his country. Didn't these white people know that?

At first, the racism was so blatant that I didn't really understand it. The segregation didn't make sense to me and I thought "whites only" was some kind of advertisement. My young mind struggled to make sense of it and I'd ask my mother questions to shed light on what I was witnessing and experiencing. Kids are more attuned to issues of fairness and justice than adults can ever be and the Deep South upended my understanding of how the world was supposed to operate.

The Alabama textbooks showed cartoonish pictures of pitch-black slaves with big white smiles, paeans to the glories of plantation life and the Confederacy, and described how the KKK "restored order in the South" during Reconstruction. It was a warped view of history that messed with my mind. This was the country of my birth. Why did they see me this way?

On the playground outside I experienced the cruelty of it firsthand. One afternoon the kids were doing tit-for-tat on the playground, launching playful insults on the verge of the personal. There was some teeth to them, but nothing over the line. However, one of the kids who wasn't even in the circle came over and launched at me. "Yeah," he said, a dumb smile on his face, "well, Isaac looks like the color of my dook."

"What did you say?!" I asked, stepping right up to him. He had a few inches on me.

"I said you looked—" and I just clocked him on the side of the head. We both went into the dirt, scrambling and rolling around until the teachers broke it up. I kept swinging at him as though my life depended on it. I was seeing red, and when it was over, I wiped the dirt off my clothes. Breathing heavily and enraged, I was at least comforted by the fact that he'd get in trouble. But when I told the teacher and principal what had started it, they just ignored it. In all the discussions about that fight—and the ones after—the adults never addressed the racist taunts that led to them. To them, calling a Black person a piece of shit was just conversation.

Once it became apparent that authority figures weren't going to do anything about it, I began to fend for myself. Every time. Every insult in class, every push in the hallway, every slight on the playground filled me with this flooding anger and white-hot rage. No matter how often it happened, I never got over the injustice of it. I should have adjusted by that point, but I just couldn't. It never sat right and it never would.

My Black classmates, who had spent their lives in the Deep South, handled it all better than I did. They knew nothing *but* this kind of treatment. Either they were more tolerant from experience or they had just learned to ignore it to get through the day. But I was dropped into this dynamic that I didn't understand, more foreign to me than anything in Europe. Any time I got ignored at a store counter or a white person moved when I sat down or I heard a whispered "ni**er," I wanted to attack.

On alert at all times, I developed into an angry kid. Everything became a fight and those years of adolescence were difficult and exhausting. I didn't yet know how those kinds of heated reactions only crack your own foundation. Eventually I learned that you have to pick your battles, that you drain yourself to nothing if you go all-out every time. Your punches will never land if you're always swinging. You have to hold off and watch and strike where and when you can do the most damage. So that became my strategy. Don't react right away. Sit tight. Prepare. Lay in wait until the moment comes and when it does, give them everything you got.

Chapter Six

SOMERVILLE, NEW JERSEY, WAS A small town that felt like an even smaller one. The guards at Somerset County Jail were mostly blue-collar good ol' boys who didn't go to college, ex-jocks gone soft around the middle, washed-up bullies and clock punchers looking to get through the day. Lots of the older guards—who had time in and rank—were ex-military who had completed a few years of service and opted for a career change. On the whole, they really weren't the smartest bunch, but that is essentially who the system wants in that job: order followers.

Most of them were some version of Dumb Donald.

Dumb Donald was a rookie guard whose high-pitched whine of a voice reminded me of the character from the Fat Albert cartoons. He was an oversized, pasty white guy with a sagging middle, acres of face, and a nose like a mountain range. One morning, Donald came to our tier, opened the gearbox, and pulled the lever down to open our cell doors. The key to that box was kept on a large metal ring with about thirty keys, which opened every gearbox, gate, and door in the jail. Somerset was too old to have any automatic machinery, so each guard had these massive key rings that were basically an appendage attached to them.

That morning, after the cells opened, we all meandered about on the catwalk, when one of the inmates—Bo—called Dumb Donald over.

"Hey, can I get a request slip?" Bo asked.

Request slips were needed for an inmate in order to leave the tier, to go to the infirmary or library. When Bo asked for one, Donald looked blankly at him for a moment, and then patted his pockets.

"Fuck me, man," Donald said. "You're going to make me go all the way back to the front desk to get slips?"

"I need to see the nurse," Bo said. "I get migraines. Ask anyone."

"All right, all right. Shit. OK, I'll be right back," Donald said, theatrically puffing out air. "Here."

Then to the shock of every inmate on that tier, Dumb Donald *handed* Bo the key ring that carried the keys to every single door in the jail, including the exit door. We all stood there, in total shock as the rookie guard walked off. No one said a word. It was the kind of thing that, if you saw it in a movie, you'd think it was wildly unrealistic. But it happened.

About a minute later, the supervisor, Lieutenant Clancey, came onto the floor. Clancey was a mean dude with crooked teeth and a forehead like a vast ocean. I immediately smelled a setup; even Dumb Donald couldn't have been stupid enough to hand an inmate the keys like that. Once I spotted Clancey, I turned and walked right back into my cell, anticipating a shit show. Staying out of trouble had become an instinct by that point, though it didn't always work. Inmates were often treated as a single unit, so we usually all got punished when one of us did something wrong.

Bo was standing there holding the key ring, knowing he was about to get hammered. "Yo!" he yelled at Clancey. "Yo, Clancey, what kind of slimeball setup shit is this?" Bo held out the key ring and then dropped it through the bars onto the catwalk floor.

Clancey walked over to the tier and picked up the keys. A gathering storm rushed into his face and he put together what happened. *This was no setup,* I thought. *Donald* was *that stupid.*

"Rookie just *handed* him the keys, Clancey," I said, trying to defuse his reaction. "We all saw it. Your boy just gave him the keys and walked off."

The blood erupted up Clancey's neck and to his face as he barked out his orders. "Lockdown! Lockdown, you motherfuckers! Lockdown now!"

Every inmate slumped their shoulders and robotically reentered their cells as the doors slammed behind them. I could hear other guards rushing into the custody area of the jail and the screams of "lockdown" as they climbed from floor to floor and walked from tier to tier. Then the marching started, the sound of rhythmic stomping. This was the extraction team. We called them the goon squad.

Dressed in full riot gear they marched on our catwalk as other squads entered the floors and went to the other tiers. We were removed from our cells, one inmate at a time, given body and body-cavity searches and placed in constraints. Then each cell was ransacked while every inch was searched. When it was over, we were locked back into our cells, which were each now heaps of havoc. Eventually it became clear that there were no sinister plans for an inmate revolt or mass escape. It was just a guard making a dumbass mistake—which we all paid for.

That was about the caliber of mind we were dealing with. I don't remember seeing Dumb Donald ever again.

I fought to separate myself from the indignities of Somerset County Jail, but some things just found me. After I became my own lawyer, especially after I got permission from the court to get my own cell, a rarity in the overcrowded jail, there was this palpable shift in how I was treated.

I was moved to the far end of the catwalk, in a cell with its own stainless steel sink and toilet. Every other cell in that jail had a hole for a toilet. Apparently, this particular cell used to house a four-hundred-pound inmate who couldn't fit inside the indentation to do his business. So every time he needed to take a dump, they had to escort him to a staff restroom in the administrative section of the jail. It was an inconvenience and security concern that ultimately redounded to me.

I was able to convert my cell into an overcrowded office. I got my own word processor, a sort of computerized typewriter. Personal computers were not ubiquitous yet, but the word processor and its memory disks were considered high end at the time. I also had enough room for all the boxes of discovery files in my case. On one of the gray metal walls, I taped up a collage of timelines, articles, pictures, and notes on my case. To be safe, I had written everything in code so nothing could get back to Bissell. I had no idea what kind of eyes and ears he had in there.

It was strange, to be trapped in a tiny room surrounded

by boxes and boxes of paper, each one a shovelful of dirt over my coffin. But I refused to think like that. I might have been buried alive, but still, I was alive. And as long as I was, I could wreak my own havoc.

Once I got my own cell, I possessed almost supernatural focus and tenacity, working late into the night, when the rambunctious noise of the jail finally subsided. In the calm of those hours, with just the clack of the word processor's keys and the buzzing of the pale yellow light, I could think straight. Sometimes, I could even convince myself I was just another lawyer working in a corner office somewhere in the city. If just for a moment, I could pretend I was free.

I had petitioned the court for regular use of the phones, a dedicated booth to interview witnesses, and access to a private room for confidential meetings, all of which Judge Imbriani eventually granted. The response from the guards to my newfound privileges was gradual but unmistakable. They set about walking a careful line. COs couldn't overtly hinder my ability to defend myself because it would give me grounds for appeal, so they had to find subtle and inventive ways to hassle me. Jamming up my work became a favorite practice of theirs. My requests for items would just vanish into the jail bureaucracy: letters undelivered, messages unanswered, requests denied. The agitation was constant, and I did what I could to neutralize it. Sometimes I was trapped, though, like in the showers.

When it was your turn to shower, the guards would yell your name, you grabbed your soap and towel, and then you walked down the tier to the single shower. It was a narrow stall with metal walls and a gray tiled floor with no door or curtain, exposing your naked body to anyone on the tier or in the cell in front of you. The hot and cold water terminals were located outside of the stall in the back of the wall so the guards were the only ones who had access. The showering inmate had to yell instructions to the guards on when to add or decrease hot and cold water until the temperature was suitable. That turned out about exactly as you'd expect.

Depending on who was on duty, the guard would often intentionally turn the cold water off on me and—with no warning—the boiling-hot industrial water would shoot out like needles and scald my skin. I learned to take a shower by turning sideways and never standing directly under the water stream, like a fighter dodging an attack. Because the pipes were ancient, the guards could always claim it wasn't intentional, but it was pretty obvious. It was the kind of low-key abuse that was just par for the course in there. Exposed and powerless, there wasn't much I could do.

However, as the guards' hassle campaign ramped up, there was a counterresponse: the other prisoners started to flock to me. I went from being a curiosity to a figure of admiration. Plenty of them thought I was crazy for being my own lawyer, but just about all respected it.

The two things—the harassment from the guards and the respect from the prisoners—operated in a feedback loop. Guards saw me helping other prisoners, so they'd ratchet up the aggravation, which brought more attention and support from the inmates. Over time, my business became everyone else's. I can't say I went out of my way to help anyone yet—I was still in self-preservation mode at the time—but I wasn't protective about what I knew.

I remember the moment when everything changed in this respect. I was in the library bogged down in a stack of books, researching the historical evolution of jury trial rights dating back to medieval England. A debate between two inmates at the table went from white noise to a clear dialogue, like my mind had zeroed in on the sound.

"Listen, son, we gotta take the fifteen years," the first guy insisted. This was Muhammad.

"For a pack of cigarettes?" the other, Kayborne, countered. "I can't take no fifteen years for stealing a pack of cigarettes. That's just—"

"It's 'cause you put your hands in your pocket like you had a gun. You know our record is fucked. We're on video, bro. Read the law," Muhammad said, shoving a reporter in front of Kayborne. "It's right there in black and white. The two charges that we have *do not* merge. Which means we gonna get time on both and they have to be kept separate. Ten years for each one. That's twenty years, man. You wanna do twenty years?"

"I can't do fifteen. I can't spend the next—"

"What choice do we have?" Muhammad said. "Listen: *we're on video.* We're gonna get twenty years if we blow trial."

I had mostly kept my mouth shut unless directly spoken to, but the words came out of me on instinct. "You couldn't do no more than five years even if you were convicted at trial," I said.

The two of them turned to me, surprised. Bug-eyed Kayborne said, "But our lawyer said that—"

"He lied," I interjected. "A merger means that the convictions *cannot* come together. But even when convictions on each charge cannot come together, the separate sentences on them can still be run concurrently. Which means that if you serve one day in prison, that one day will be subtracted from both sentences at the same time."

"Wait, what are you saying?" Muhammad asked.

"Technically you're facing a twenty-year sentence, but in practice you can only get ten years," I explained. "But of that ten years you will only do three years. Even in the worst-case scenario, with your record, five years is the most you'll do on that ten to be eligible for parole." I noticed the whole library was silent now. "You don't believe me? Insist that you want to go to trial and see what happens."

When word got around that Muhammad and Kayborne had accepted a new offer of three years, I became a superstar among the inmates. They started to navigate their way over to me to ask questions about their own cases. Word traveled through the cells as whispers, then out in the open:

If you go to the law library, the dude who works there knows some shit.

You need help with your case? Talk to Isaac.

Did you show Isaac your lawyer's letter? Let him see it.

In an environment of the helpless, I represented some kind of counterweight. It got out that the inmates weren't trapped by what their lawyer said. That offered a type of power, which became a type of freedom. There was someone on their side whom they could trust, who knew what he was doing, and who could offer the key.

As for my innocence, I can't pretend that everyone in Somerset County Jail was in the same position as I was. There were plenty of inmates who were guilty as sin and a few who would scare the average person out of his wits. Especially on that high-security tier, it was a volatile mix. There was Hammer, a large Black guy with a narrow face and large, unblinking eyes. He got his name because he beat an old lady in the head with a hammer when she caught him breaking into her house. There was Asmar, a muscular dude with braids in his hair who was a member of the Five Percent Nation, an offshoot of the Nation of Islam. He was arrested on petty drug offenses but was such a menace to the guards and other inmates that he was placed on the tier as punishment. There was Hyok Yi, a buff Asian dude—who was an arsonist and escape artist. The guards seemed to know him there, but it wasn't because he was a problem. He garnered respect without having to say or do much, which in itself drew more respect.

But none of these guys could hold a candle to an ordinary-looking white kid named Matthew Heikkila. With cropped black hair and a square face, he looked unassuming, almost forgettable. You wouldn't give him a second look, but once he opened his mouth, you knew this kid had problems. When Matthew arrived at Somerset, his case was making national news. The twenty-year-old adopted son of a renowned researcher, Matthew murdered both of his adoptive parents, writing "mom" and "dad" on the shotgun shells he used to kill them. On our tier, Matthew would freely talk about the murders and his case, which was also presided over by Judge Imbriani and tried by Nicholas Bissell. He would write Bissell these long letters all the time and have me read them. He called Bissell all kinds of names, like "Dumb Fuck" and "Disgusting Fat Fanny." Sometimes he'd ask about my case and my choice to represent myself. I didn't give him any particulars, but he seemed very curious as to how I planned on going it alone. I'd entertain him with a walk-through of how I would question witnesses, make objections, and address the court.

Matthew wouldn't talk to anyone else on the tier. He only talked to me, and when he did, he would not shut up, especially about his crime. I was literally a captive audience. Although I said very little about my own situation, that didn't seem to discourage his openness. Some people took my quiet as an invitation to speak freely and this kid just liked having to be listened to. He told me the reason he killed his mother was she wouldn't let him use her car to take out his girlfriend. Alone at the house, he called his mom to come home, saying he was sick. When she arrived, he shot her dead in the upstairs area of the house. Then he called his father at work. "You need to come home quickly," he said. "Mom is sick. She's doing really bad." When his dad walked in the door, Matthew had the shotgun out.

"Isaac," he told me, "this is something I'm only telling you. No one else knows about it. When my father came into the house and saw the shotgun, he didn't ask anything about it or me. The first thing he asked was 'Where's your mother?' I told him she was in the basement. I lied because I didn't want him to see her in the state she was in. As he was walking down to the basement, I have the shotgun in my hand and he's not asking anything about it. Then I scream out, 'I hate you!' and shoot him in his head. I don't know how it hit his head; I wasn't even aiming for it, I just shot. The damnedest thing happened—a part of his skull shot off across the basement and hit a picture on the wall and knocked it off the wall." He explained, matter-of-factly, that after he killed his mother, he "had to kill" his father, like it was the most obvious thing in the world.

I've met plenty of hard dudes, both in and out of prison, but Matthew's coldness was as eerie as anything I've ever faced. I just stared at him, unable to respond. I was prepared for the bullshit of jail, the boredom, the loneliness, the cruelty. I was even prepared for the heaviness of being on a high-risk tier where everyone was facing forever, but Matthew penetrated way past that. He pushed my own sense of what humans even were.

The guards used the inmates as pawns, moving them around according to their own needs, one of which was to keep me in my place. They would send people onto my tier to harass me and mess with my head. Jerry, who was placed in the cell right next to mine, was a trusty who cooked in the kitchen. Trusties were serving less than a year, so they did their time in the jail rather than state prison and, with good behavior, were given special privileges. They'd be given jobs like cooking in the kitchen, cleaning the common areas, or cutting the grass outside. They were sent to their cell less often and given a type of freedom that the other inmates didn't get. Sometimes it went to their heads.

Jerry had dark skin and thick eyebrows, a sloped narrow nose on a wide face. From the moment he arrived, I was on guard: his presence there didn't make sense. Trusties are given an inordinate amount of freedom and the high-risk tier was the very opposite of that. It was clear that Jerry was placed with us for a purpose, so I was suspicious of him from day one. I'd learned to be wary of anyone who reached out to me, as they could be a plant from Bissell, a provocation from the guards, or just someone willing to use my words against me.

Jerry wasted no time. Right after he arrived, he confronted me on the catwalk, in front of all the other inmates. "You know," he said, loud enough for everyone to hear, "I see you going back and forth to court. What you trying to do exactly?"

"What do you mean, 'what am I trying to do'?"

He smiled, like he knew better. "You have no clue what these people are getting ready to do to you? Who do you think you are?" he said with a mocking laugh. "You know they're going to take you and they're going to be slinging your shit all across the city. All you're doing is making things worse for all of us here."

There was something unnatural about the way Jerry spoke, especially that "us," which didn't fit from a guy who just got there, a trusty who was halfway between inmate and guard. His words were designed for the guys on the tier to hear. Jerry wasn't too subtle; he was trying to put ideas in everyone else's heads about my motives, trying to cut down whatever influence I was accumulating.

"Listen," I told him, scouting him up and down. "My understanding is you came from the kitchen. I don't know what you're doing here or why you're talking like you know me. But if these were slave times, you'd be nothing more than a house ni**er thinking he has some power."

I saw the shock dawn over his face. "You don't know what you're—"

"I can't go anywhere," I said, steamrolling over his words, "none of us can, so we might as well be living in slave times.

And nothing that you're saying is going to stop me from doing what I'm doing. Whatever they have planned for me, they can bring it. I'm ready for it." Then I took a beat. "You tell them that." And I walked off.

I almost felt bad for Jerry, who was suffering from a type of Stockholm syndrome, sympathizing with his captors. The kitchen was the most desirable of all the trusty jobs. In that role, you waited on and fed the guards. Sometimes they'd literally throw you a crumb, share something they brought in for themselves for you to cook or give you leftover Mc-Donald's. These tiny offers felt much larger than they truly were—such is the deprivation of jail—so that the inmate felt that the guards valued him. But really, it was all about manipulation. Jerry might've been intelligent in his previous life, but he was gullible enough to think he had allies in his captors. I knew better. The next day Jerry disappeared back into the cogs of the jail.

I was always being tested. Jerry brought more of a psychological approach, but usually, if there was a real troublemaker in the jail, the guards would ask him to fuck with me more deliberately. Sometimes it would be in exchange for something tangible like privileges, but other times the inmates would do it just to stay in the guards' good graces. This was a common occurrence that just became part of my daily routine in there.

Then Kyle showed up.

One morning, with the tier already in lockdown, I could hear the clanging of the keys and the opening of the gearbox. I got off my bed and stepped to my cell door, which was right next to the entrance. As the new inmate entered, both hands full with intake baggage and personal items, he looked over at me. "What's up, Ike?" he said, passing me and entering into his cell. I didn't say a word, because we'd never met, yet he was using a nickname like he knew me.

Kyle was 250 pounds of bad-tempered muscle, with a dark and narrow face. His default tone was aggressive and he had the habit of repeating himself as if he was trying to convince himself of what he was saying. Kyle was serving time in Somerset for beating up his girlfriend and had been a trusty at some point, working in the kitchen. One day after a shift in there, Kyle went outside to dump out the garbage and never came back. After escaping (and going right to the same girlfriend's house), he was captured and brought back, this time to the high-security tier. Kyle told me later that when he was returned, he was given specific instructions to make my life hell. *We're going to transfer you over to 1 East and we want you to give Isaac some problems. Then we'll help you become a trusty again.*

But they made a mistake. Kyle had anger issues, but he wasn't dumb. He knew that after escaping, he was in serious trouble, and it was not the kind of trouble that could be easily undone. So he did seek me out once he got there, but not to fuck with me. He wanted legal assistance.

They had put Kyle alongside the one person in the jail who could help him.

At the law library I photocopied the statutes involving escapes, with supporting case law, and gave it to him. I did that with everyone who was on the tier with me, unless I thought they didn't deserve it. Kyle was in a lot of trouble and it seemed natural to provide helpful information.

"You need to read up on your escape charge," I told him,

handing over the papers. "There may be some things there that can help you."

Kyle took the photocopies from me but didn't say a word.

The next morning, he came into my cell. "Those papers you gave me? How they gonna help me? I'll just plead guilty right away so I could do this sentence and that one at the same time."

I was sitting on the bed and looked up at him. He had this strange determination on his face.

"Did you read the law and cases I gave you?" I asked.

"Yeah," he said. "Why do you think I'm going to plead guilty?"

"Did you read the part that says a sentence for escape *cannot* run concurrent with any prior sentence of imprisonment? You have to do it separate."

He glared at me with his blank face and unblinking eyes. Then he turned around and left. Three days passed without Kyle saying a word to me. Then late one afternoon, as I returned from the library, he showed up at my cell door with those same papers in his hand.

He slowly lifted his hand and gave them to me. The arrogance had been deflated out of him. "Can you read this to me?" he asked. "Show me where it says my time cannot run together?" I realized in that moment that Kyle hadn't read the statute and case law because he couldn't. He couldn't read at all. I took the papers from him and read the text aloud, explaining the reality of his situation, including the options he had.

After that, we were pretty tight. He came by my cell or the law library every day to ask questions. That evolved into personal conversations about his life and relationships. Then one day out of the blue, he told me about the guards' instructions for him to mess with me, how they offered him special privileges if he did so. It offended Kyle's sense of fairness that there were murderers and rapists in there but I was picked on because I was learning the law and helping out my fellow inmates.

After apologizing, he said, "They lied to me, didn't they? I'm not never gonna be a trusty again."

"Yeah, Kyle, they lied," I said. "You weren't the first. But don't worry about it. We're cool."

A week or so later, the guards came in one morning and locked us all in our cells. Lieutenant Clancey stood in front of mine, his dead-eyed stare leveled on me through the bars.

"Wright, pack your shit up," Clancey said. "We're moving you to isolation."

"Why?"

"No questions," he said.

I didn't move. "Tell me why I'm being moved," I said.

Clancey met my eyes, with nothing but contempt. "Pack. Your. Shit. Up."

"Not unless you tell me where I'm going." I knew legally they could hide *why* they were moving me but they had to tell me *where*. The fact that I even knew that frustrated Clancey. I'm sure in his mind, it was just another reason to punish me. My knowledge upended the social and racial structure in there, and Clancey couldn't stand it.

"Holding," he said firmly. Holding was an isolated area where inmates were put on close watch. It was a row of single-brick cells and metal doors with a guard desk sitting in the middle of the floor. Clearly, it had pissed them off that sending in Kyle had backfired. Now they wanted to separate me from the rest of the inmates.

Everyone was watching the confrontation. I could feel the eyes on me, on Clancey, on a showdown they had been anticipating.

"What for?" I asked. "Let me talk to the supervisor."

"Cut the shit, Wright. Let's go."

"You're gonna have to come in and get me 'cause I'm not leaving."

"If that's how it's gonna be, then," he said.

A few minutes later the goon squad in full riot gear—shields, batons, face masks—began to swarm like bees in front of my cell. The fact that this level of force was used to take on one unarmed man speaks volumes about the guard-inmate dynamic. It's a type of theater, a performance of oppression. Lieutenant Clancey gave me a standard final order before they came in.

"Inmate Wright," he said, almost robotically, "pack your belongings and exit your cell. Consider this your final order. If you do not comply, we will come in by force and we will remove you. Removal by force could result in additional institutional infractions, criminal charges, and confinement in the isolation room for a period of time to be decided by a hearing officer. Are you going to comply?"

I clenched my body, ready for them to come in. Then, out of nowhere, in the cell next door, Kyle just lost it. "Hey. Hey! You touch that man—if *anyone* touches that man—I'm gonna go to prison for the rest of my life 'cause I'm breaking all of you up!"

The loudness and rage in his voice shocked me, like a powder keg that had gone off. "I'm tired of you fucking people messing with this man! Every day, it's something. Leave this man alone. He hasn't done nothing to none of y'all! You come in here, you gonna have a problem with me now!"

The entire tier went totally silent. I could see that the guards were struck dumb. Even Clancey—whose stone face was part of his persona—looked shocked. I tried to hide my own surprise. Without saying a word, Clancey walked around the corner of the tier and then out. The goon squad stood there for a few seconds, like drones abandoned by their controller. Then they all looked in the direction of Clancey's exit before filtering out on their own.

Once the tier was cleared, I spoke through the walls. "Thanks, man. You didn't have to do that. I could've handled it."

"I know, but I'm just— I don't know, I'm just *tired* of that shit," Kyle said. "They always talking about you, all the time. You didn't have to help me and I asked you a question and with all you have to do, you helped me. I had to respect that."

Kyle's blowup had been shocking, but so was the guards' response. The way they all backed down, just *folded,* stunned me. I recognized it for what it was: it was power. Real power. All anyone had to do was stand up to these people, to this system, and they'd crumble. Their defenses were noisy, a lot of pomp and circumstance. But in reality, they were paper thin. Their strength was just an elaborate and well-funded illusion.

Chapter Seven

I'M NOT SURE WHEN IT became clear to me that I couldn't win at trial. Maybe it was after I learned that Ron—along with some other codefendants I didn't even know—had agreed to take a plea in exchange for testifying against me. Maybe it was when Judge Imbriani allowed surveillance tapes of conversations in my car into evidence despite the expert testimony given about their manipulation. Or maybe it was once I fully grasped how much power Nicholas Bissell actually had in Somerset County. From the night he had come to visit me in my cell, I sensed something that turned out to be truer than I could've predicted: Somerset was Bissell's little fiefdom.

It wasn't just the prosecution office that jumped at his every command; it was the police, the court, the lawyers, even the jail staff. There was this unmistakable need for everyone in the system, from the lowliest guard to the highest-paid attorney, to please him. It was in the way defense lawyers had first talked to me about my case, in the way my standby counsel, Amitrani, and the assistant prosecutor, Veronica

Nolan, made sure to never upstage him, and in the way Judge Imbriani deferred to him on everything.

The fact that Bissell had been abusing his power was no secret. In fact, it was essential to his rise. I wasn't up against an overzealous prosecutor who got ahead of his skis. I wasn't dealing with a "law-and-order" man who wanted to clean up the streets. This was a corrupt self-dealer who had a reputation throughout the state of doing what he needed to do to win, to get ahead, and—as I'd learn—to line his pockets. When Bissell sat across from people, they recognized that their own career, freedom, or very survival were at stake. And things unfolded accordingly from there.

Bissell was an ambitious guy who loved the press, played the political game like a violin, and had made a name for himself as one of the state's toughest lawmen. Hailed as the "forfeiture king"[1] of New Jersey, Bissell brought in the highest dollar amount in the state (and allegedly, for himself), even though Somerset is one of New Jersey's smallest counties. This was why Chief Detective Thornburg was so wholly focused on the half a million I supposedly kept in my safe after my arrest. Bissell instructed him to go after it.

In order to deflect any heat away from his activities, Bissell presented himself as the one thing stopping Somerset County from devolving into an open-air drug market. He gave plenty of interviews designed to make white readers fear Black people and make himself look like the one who heroically protected them. For his whole charade to work, he just needed a target. That's where I came in. The deck was stacked far too unfairly for me to win at trial: between the tainted jury pool, the threatened witnesses, and the judge solicitous to the prosecution, I didn't really stand a chance. I was going to prison. The only question was whether or not I would stay there for the rest of my life.

Even as my world was crumbling all around me, I never considered giving in. I just had to reconsider what winning would look like. The plan began to form: I would build a case against Bissell himself. Strike at the roots of the poisonous tree. And I was fortunate enough to get a boost from an unlikely ghost from my past.

In the summer of 1990, about a year after my arrest, an inmate was placed in the high-security tier. Charles was a pale white guy with dark hair that had spots sloppily bleached with hydrogen peroxide, which gave it this orangish-yellow color. I was suspicious of all inmates moved to our tier, assuming they were plants or snitches. Charles had started a fight and threatened the life of another inmate, which seemed like an intentional effort to get moved to our tier. The day he arrived, he beelined right for me on the catwalk, deliberate and unsubtle with his approach. "Hey, Isaac," he said, "I gotta talk to you about Bissell—"

I met his eyes, making it clear I'd heard him, and then just walked away. From that point forward, I avoided him. If he walked in one direction, I walked the opposite way. Every day he tried to approach me until I ultimately had to threaten him to leave me alone.

Then one morning, while I was eating breakfast on my bed, he passed by my cell and dropped a piece of paper through the bars. I reached down to pick it up. It read:

DON'T LOOK OUT THE WINDOW.

I was stunned. This wasn't a literal instruction—there were no windows to look out—but a message from my past. Charles might not have even known what the message meant. But I sure did.

NEW YORK CITY
1981

When I first moved to New York City as a twenty-year-old, I worked as a bicycle messenger in Manhattan. Every morning I'd stop in a café downtown for a breakfast sandwich before starting my day peddling around the city delivering packages. Like clockwork, this one guy would always be sitting at the same table in the back corner with a bagel and coffee, reading the paper. He was in his early fifties in a nice suit, with an aristocratic, sloping nose, neatly trimmed salt-and-pepper hair, and a chiseled face. Everything about his refined look told me he came from money.

After about a year of this routine, never once speaking to the guy, I took a fortuitous step into his world. For three straight mornings, I had noticed an unassuming car with tinted windows parked in the same spot in front of the café. This was unusual for Manhattan as parking spots are the scarcest real estate in the city. As I locked up my bike and walked into the café, the tinted window of the passenger side of the car rolled down slightly and a cigarette was flicked into the street. It was just a glimpse, but I noticed in the car that the driver was pointing a camera toward the café. When I went inside, the man was sitting in his usual spot and I could see the car was clearly positioned to get the best view of him.

The next day, same car in the same spot. This time, I took

note of the license plate. When I entered the café, I took a napkin and wrote a note about the car, along with its license plate number. The note started out in bold letters: *DON'T LOOK OUT THE WINDOW*. I walked over to him, placed the napkin on his table, and left without saying a word. The next day, the man in the suit had disappeared, as had the car with the tinted windows. Other patrons took over his table and eventually I forgot about him.

A couple of months passed. One morning I was delivering a package to the mailroom at the World Trade Center. The desk clerk in the lobby took a look at the package and directed me to the office for a hand-to-hand delivery. This was a little odd, but I didn't question it. When I arrived at the office, the receptionist took a look at the package and stood up. "Come with me," she said, before leading me down the hall to a spacious corner office with floor-to-ceiling windows facing the Hudson River; it was one of the most beautiful views of Manhattan and New Jersey I had ever seen. She directed me to a seat and left.

Then a voice boomed into the room: "Did you know who they were?" I turned around, and there was the man, whom I'll call Patrick, confidently walking through the door in a tailored dark suit. My eyes followed his movements as he came around, unbuttoned his jacket with a practiced hand, and took a seat at the oversized desk. I didn't say a word; I just stared at him, trying to figure out what was going on. He continued, calmly and directly, "I presume you had no idea."

"I don't understand," I said. "What is this? I'm just here to deliver a package." I laid the large envelope on the desk, stood up, and turned around as though to leave.

"I wanted to thank you for what you did and—"

"You're welcome," I said.

"And to offer you a job."

The words surprised me and they hung there for a second like smoke. "Thanks, but I'm good with the job I got now. I make my own time and work when I want, so—"

"Listen," he said, leaning forward, "you have no idea how important your note was. Those guys in the car were federal agents."

"So, what happened? You spent the last few months in jail?"

He smiled and shook his head. "Putting out fires that I didn't know existed until your note. You saved me and a lot of people you don't even know. As a show of appreciation, I'd like to offer you a job."

I decided to humor him. "Doing what?" I asked.

He gestured to the package. "The same thing you're doing now. Delivery. Except, you'd be a runner, not a messenger. And you'd work for me."

"What would I be running?"

Patrick opened a drawer, pulled out a slip of paper, and dramatically slammed it down on the desk. "Tickets," he said.

"To what? Baseball games?" I asked, confused. "That doesn't look like a ticket to me." I leaned forward to get a better look at the paper on his desk.

"It's not that kind of ticket. It's a stock order."

The prospect got my attention, so I sat back down. I had been nibbling at the edges of this city of opportunity; Patrick was offering me an entrance through the front door.

We stared at each other for a moment as I thought about how to play this. I figured I'd ask for something ridiculous. "OK," I said, "I want a thousand dollars a week. Plus expenses."

"Deal," he replied. In 1981, this was a substantial amount of money for a twenty-year-old, almost four times as much as I was getting as a bike messenger. I had the feeling I could have gotten more if I'd asked.

"Off the books?" I asked.

"All cash," he replied.

The decision was a no-brainer; I was a college dropout being offered a chance to step in to the biggest money-making scheme on earth. Patrick hired me as his personal runner, bringing tickets, which were buy/sell orders, to the floors of the New York Stock Exchange. Everything moved fast and I was thrown into the middle of it. I learned a wealth of information from Patrick about trading, public offerings, acquisitions and mergers, financial sheltering tools, and how money was really made on the market. Patrick was an intriguing, intelligent guy with charisma to spare; people just flocked to him. He freely talked with his colleagues in my presence and answered any question I asked. He invited me to sit in on his meetings and briefed me afterward about who was who and what was what.

Patrick was hyper-strategic, calculating, and patient—to a degree I hadn't even considered possible. He made millions by trading in information, which is wealth and power in that world. I didn't even know how he got all his information until he confided in me one day.

I was in Midtown when I got a page on my beeper from

Patrick. As always, I found a pay phone to call him. He told me to meet him in his car outside a store on 42nd Street. Back then, 42nd Street was a ragged and notorious strip of pimps, pushers, and porno theaters. And right there at the corner of 8th Avenue, the Port Authority Bus Terminal, a place where I myself had slept when I first got to New York.

Patrick pointed out the window and tapped his finger on the glass. "That bus station is the best thing that ever happened to me," he said.

"Yeah?" I said, figuring he had a story to tell. He had a few.

Patrick then shared with me the origin story of how he built his empire. He and his friends graduated from Ivy League business schools all looking for an edge in finance. At a young age, Patrick came up with a brilliant scheme that had paid off handsomely, a kind of unorthodox mentor program.

At the Port Authority one afternoon, he struck up a conversation with two recent college graduates, just off the bus from the Midwest. Like so many others, they came to New York looking to become something and Patrick offered to help out. One of the graduates ended up going back home soon after, but the other stayed. Patrick got him a place to live, funded his MBA, and when he got a job at a Fortune 500 company, he began feeding information back to Patrick. After successfully placing one spy in the financial sector, he did it again—befriending a college graduate just starting out, putting him in a luxury apartment and through business school. Then again. He did this over and over again; sometimes they didn't pan out, but he hit the jackpot enough to make the scheme worthwhile.

By the time I came into Patrick's life, he had swaths of people scattered across the financial industry who felt a deep loyalty to him. All those routes feeding back to Patrick made him one of the most prolific information brokers in Manhattan. He thought he had been operating under the radar until a bike messenger unknowingly revealed an undercover investigation—simply by writing on a napkin.

Patrick gave me a peek behind the curtain, among the string pullers and stakeholders and snake oil salesmen. It was a real-world business school: not textbooks selling the lie of free market capitalism, but the on-the-ground, dog-eat-dog nitty-gritty. I learned the ins and outs of the market and how it is kept running by two forces: the filthy rich, who benefit from it; and the suckers, without whom it couldn't exist.

My ending with Patrick came about as abruptly as its start, about a year into our time together. We were at a private gathering he was throwing to celebrate the graduation of one of his protégés. In Patrick's downtown penthouse, surrounded by the beautiful and powerful, among billions of dollars in cumulative wealth, I dined with Patrick and his inner circle. He introduced me to everyone with an almost fatherly pride.

As the night progressed, the alcohol began to loosen tongues. It was getting late when, sitting next to Patrick and me, a friend of his suddenly switched to speaking German. *"Warum sitzt die untere Ebene am Tisch?"* the friend asked him.

Patrick knew my father was a military man, but he had no idea I'd lived in Germany all those years. I still remembered enough German to understand the question: *Why is this nobody sitting at our table?*

It was a startling insult, but it was Patrick's answer that

left me stunned. *"Dieser Affe hat einen besonderen Platz in meinem Herzen,"* he said.

Affe. Monkey.

I have a special place in my heart for this monkey.

I was so floored I couldn't even speak. Minutes passed as I tamped down this desire to explode. I refused to meet Patrick's eye. Calmly, I excused myself from the table, left the party, and never saw Patrick again.

I went back to life as a bicycle messenger, a little wiser about the world and a little more wary about everyone I met. It was another lesson in a sad truth: you never really, truly can know or trust someone. There was always going to be a gap.

And what went on in that gap? That had the power to knock you out cold.

Charles's note, dropped through the bars of my cell, was a message from Patrick. Hearing from him almost a decade later, in the most unlikely of places, was surprising but not shocking. Patrick knew everyone and had access to anyone. I don't know if he was keeping tabs on me all these years or if maybe he read about my arrest in the newspapers. In his inimitable way, he found a way to help me using his network of people, without revealing himself at all. Charles likely had never even met or heard of Patrick.

The day after I got that note, I invited Charles into my cell.

"You wouldn't believe what I got on this prosecutor," he told me, meaning Bissell. "For real: he's a straight-up criminal."

Charles and his brother had both worked for Bissell, who

had business interests all over the state, many of which collided with his job as a top prosecutor. Since owning and running a private business was not condoned for state lawmen, it must've been worth it for Bissell. The money, influence, and partnerships of his two jobs were tied up in a tangled mess.

Charles had worked at one of Bissell's gas stations, and had evidence of many of Bissell's transgressions. As Charles got to talking, I took out a pencil and wrote down on a piece of scrap paper everything he told me. The key facts were:

1. Bissell owned a gas station and business with Detective Thornburg's brother.
2. Bissell was stealing from his partner and forcing him to lie about the true receipts.
3. Bissell was manipulating gas sales in order to get rebates from the gas delivery company. He and one of the delivery drivers in particular hated each other because the delivery driver caught on to the scam and refused to give the rebates.
4. Bissell threatened to plant cocaine in the driver's rig.
5. Bissell was not reporting a lot of the cash receipts (along with the money he stole) to the IRS.

The information Charles gave me about the inner workings of Bissell's finances was a mix of fed information and personal knowledge. The first-person accounts gave him an air of credibility. I concluded that the facts were far too devastating for Bissell for it to be some kind of setup on his part.

I couldn't investigate on my own, so I got word to Gator to meet me in the law library. Gator came through in the evening right as the library was shutting down. He'd been moved to another tier, so I hadn't seen him in many months. In the empty room, we sat down at a table—a little wary of each other. I figured he was out for himself, as anyone would be, and this Bissell information could help both of us. I didn't really trust him, but I assumed we had a common enemy.

As I started going down the list of what I'd discovered, Gator said, "Yo, Ike, you serious?"

"What do you mean?"

"Do you realize what you're saying?"

"Yeah, why?" I asked.

"How did you get this information?"

"Is that what's important to you? *How* I got the information?"

"Nah, man, it's just . . ." Gator searched for the words. "That is not the kind of information just anybody can get. How did you get it?" It seemed so beside the point that I got annoyed.

"I got it," I said. "How I got it is something I cannot talk about. What does it even—"

"Then how do you expect me to buy it?"

"I'm not gonna bring you something that I don't think is true, G, why would—"

"I don't know, Ike," he said. "It's a little hard to believe. That's all."

"Listen, you got people in Somerset," I said. "Send someone over there and have them ask who owns the gas station. If it's Bissell, then you'll know the information is reliable."

He asked me again how I got the information and then

gave me this perplexed look. "If you can't tell me where you got it . . ."

"I just can't," I said, shutting him down. "And don't ask again."

There was a pause and then abruptly, Gator changed tack. "This shit is powerful," he said. "I'm gonna go call my lawyer right now. I don't even know why we in this county." Gator stood up and I grabbed his sleeve.

"G, be careful on the phone."

"I know, man, I'm just—"

"Actually, don't even say anything," I said. "Have him come see you. In person."

"You know they can listen there too, Ike."

"Get them to let you use an office," I said. "They have to."

"Sure thing," he said, then left. I had a wary feeling, but I had been so suspicious for so long that I wasn't sure what was paranoia and what wasn't.

I closed up the library and was escorted back down to my tier. In my cell, I hid the Bissell information between the pages of one of the law books. Then I began my routine of reading reporters and treatises related to my cases. About fifteen minutes later I heard that familiar buzz and then footsteps. Police officers were outside my cell, detectives from the prosecutor's office, escorted by a couple of guards.

They threw me out, handcuffed me, put a knee in my back, and held me down as they searched it. Then the officers went crazy on my belongings as though they were taking out a personal vendetta on the cell itself. They tossed my mattress, turned over and shook all my books, knocked down my toiletries, and emptied every box they found.

One of them bent over a stash of papers that fell onto the floor. He started scanning the pile; I knew exactly what he'd come for. When he found the list about Bissell, he picked it up. "I got it," he said. Then they all left, without taking anything else.

Fortunately I had memorized the Bissell facts. But after the ransack, and the timing of it, every puzzle piece snapped into place.

Gator. Fucking Gator. I kicked myself for not seeing it, not trusting my instincts. Gator had been the answer to every single question from the beginning:

What connection did I have to Ron? Gator.

How did the cops know about the safe in my bedroom? Gator.

Who were the cops searching for that night in my house? Gator.

What even brought them there? Gator.

And who was the only person with whom I shared my information on Bissell? Gator.

Gator had been on their side—maybe from the beginning.

Soon after, he and Ron were both transferred to another jail. I wouldn't see them again until they were up on the stand at my trial, testifying for the prosecution.

As I prepared my case, and got discovery materials from the prosecutor's office (police reports, witness statements, evidence reports), I was able to piece it all together. Even with the police hiding more than they revealed, the whole sequence came into focus.

Here's what happened: Detectives in the county where I

lived (Middlesex) had been following an unidentified man (Ron) regarding his work packaging and selling drugs. They trailed him to a club in Bergenfield I regularly partied at. The detectives wandered out front of the club, marking down license plates and using those to chase leads about whom Ron consorted with.

One reason I stood out among that group was that I had the most money and was not inconspicuous about it. Neither was Sunshine. I also knew a lot of people, both major players in the music business and others who made their money in the street. So I was at a nexus of all these people, the nucleus of the well-off, the famous, and the local hustlers. It put me on the radar of a joint drug unit that Middlesex County formed with neighboring Somerset County. Specifically, it put me in the sights of the prosecutor in charge of the Somerset County office, one Nicholas Bissell.

Middlesex cops investigated me and found nothing. I had only lived in New Jersey for a few months and had met Gator about a month after moving there. All the other suspects were from the same area and had known each other for a long time. The Middlesex cops decided they were going to focus on Ron and his associates, including Gator.

But Bissell didn't care what the clues pointed to. *I want to bring a case against Wright,* he insisted. Maybe he thought Ron was small fish; maybe he really thought my money must've come from drugs. But he saw me as the big whale and wouldn't back down. I had the flashy cars, the profile, the celebrity, and the influence. Bringing me down would garner some headlines and some cash, because forfeiture laws said the county could keep whatever was confiscated.

Because he was dirty, Bissell himself would get his hands on this money too. He would not let it go. His office of detectives had to find something on me. But they had nothing.

Then came that night in February 1989. Gator was pulled over driving my blue Duster, supposedly for a broken taillight. According to police reports, after asking for his license and registration, the police shined a flashlight into the car and saw bags of cocaine vials—some filled, some empty—on the back seat. Not even on the floorboard, but *on the seat*.

The cops asked Gator to step out of the car. "Those aren't mine," Gator said. "This isn't my car. I'm just using it."*

"How did you not know these were here?" a cop asked.

"I just got into the car and started driving," he said. "I didn't see them."

They started questioning him and ran the car's plates, seeing it was registered to me. "Why are you driving this guy's car?" one of them asked.

"Just borrowing it."

"Well, what are we gonna do here? How are you going to get out of this? As far as we're concerned, this is yours."

Gator continued to insist he knew nothing about drugs on the back seat.

Within the hour, Gator would be found hiding in my nephews' bedroom in my house. None of it made sense. How can someone get pulled over on the highway, be found in possession of large amounts of drugs, and then wind up in my house? No police document would ever attest to it, but there's only one logical explanation: the cops *told* Gator

---

* This dialogue is a paraphrase of what was available in the police reports.

MARKED FOR LIFE | 123

to run to my place as an excuse to search it. They told him that in order to get out of trouble, he had to offer something or someone up. Maybe they knew Bissell was looking to get me. Maybe it was just their dumb luck. But because he was in serious trouble, Gator did what they said. And from that point forward, I believe, he kept doing it.

Ron's arrest the next month at a Franklin motel—ratted out by his spurned girlfriend—put both him and Gator in hot water. To get out of it, they had to play ball with the prosecutors and detectives, saying that they were my drug lieutenants. They claimed that I insulated myself so thoroughly from the rest of the organization that they were really the only ones who had contact with me. This helped make their lies airtight; they were the only ones who could prove I was in charge because *I had designed it that way.*

By the time I found all this out in late 1990, Ron had already pleaded guilty in exchange for testifying against me at my trial. And though he waited until the eve of the trial, in the spring of 1991—either out of conscience or to get the best deal he could for himself—Gator agreed to do so as well. By the time of the trial, I'd be the only one left standing.

Chapter Eight

"ISAAC, I JUST—I CAN'T. I can't do it."

Raquel was almost unrecognizable. Only twenty years old, she had aged considerably since the arraignment a year earlier. The stress had taken a toll on her youthful face and she carried herself as though weighted down. From the moment she sat across from me, a panicked energy radiated from her. Raquel was slim but curvy, with a light complexion, wavy hair, and hazel eyes. Her voice was still a girl's, but it had this scratchy, rough quality. Her face around her eyes was puffy from crying.

Bissell had been orchestrating the statements required for all my codefendants to take pleas. Most of the statements mandated pointing the finger at me in various ways. When certain defendants refused or had trouble articulating it the way Bissell wanted, he teamed up with their *own* defense attorneys to coerce the statements. Raquel insisted on speaking to me before pleading to anything, so they had me transported to the courthouse to meet with her.

We sat in an administrative office located on the same floor as the courtroom, across from each other at a polished wood table. Rain pelted against the wall of double-pane windows. A guard stood at the threshold of the door, hands at his sides. Raquel's lawyer, an older white guy with thinning black hair and an off-the-rack suit, took a seat behind her along the wall.

Raquel leaned forward, her hoarse voice low and shaky.

"I'm not gonna do it," she said. "I didn't do shit and I'm going to trial." She kept shaking her head in disagreement as she spoke. "I can't . . . I just can't do it."

"What are they offering?" I asked.

"Probation." She turned around to look at her lawyer, who just nodded without a word. "They said to get a plea I have to give a statement about how you were selling drugs, that you were the head of this . . . like network, this gang or whatever."

Raquel seemed enormously fragile, so I spoke very calmly, almost reassuringly. Her face revealed many sleepless nights. "I didn't do anything and you didn't do anything," I said. "You know that, right?"

"I know, I know!" she said. "Shit, Isaac. They're gonna put me in jail and take my daughter. She's only two. She's not gonna know me at all. She's not gonna . . ." Then her voice broke again and she started to cry, tears coming out in bursts. "I don't know what to do," she said. "I can't plead guilty to something that I didn't do!"

We just sat there in the quiet. The rhythmic pelting of the rain, the lawyer fidgeting in his chair. My heart broke for Raquel. She was a young mother, and from what I knew, a good one. Because of her association with me, her life was being stripped for parts.

"I heard you the night of my arrest," I said. "I heard you calling for me."

"You were there?" she asked, her voice cracking.

I nodded. "In a cell in the back."

The memory triggered something in her eyes and I thought she was going to start up crying again. But she caught herself. She told me how the detectives came to her apartment that night and dragged her to the precinct. When they got there, they put her in a room and pressed her for information on me.

"I kept saying 'I don't know anything!' and they kept saying they knew that I worked for you, that you were this big cocaine trafficker and I'd go to jail if I didn't give them information."

Then she told me how far they were willing to go. One of the detectives took out his service revolver and every time she gave an answer they didn't like, he dry-fired the unloaded gun in her mouth, pressing the trigger until it clicked. That was what caused her harrowing screams.

I looked out the window, the gray day barely visible through the wet glass. These were fucking monsters; they weren't going to stop. I raised my cuffed hands and placed them on her forearm. When the guard stepped forward as though to intervene, I pulled away and made a "don't shoot" motion with my hands.

"I won't plead guilty to something I did not do," she said. "They want me to tell a bunch of lies on you. I don't care what this asshole says." She gestured to her lawyer behind her. "I'm not doing it."

I tried to catch his eye. Was he hearing this? Did he know?

Then I realized: of course he knew. He was the one who had orchestrated this meeting. His face showed nothing—no empathy, no indignation. An officer of the court, a *defense attorney*, just sat there like a stooge, letting the state of New Jersey subvert justice and run roughshod over this young woman's life. People like Bissell don't operate on their own: they rely on a network of cowards, conspirators, and enablers. This guy was just one part of a wide-reaching army.

Raquel's plea deal required only that she give a statement, not testify in court; however, it would still be reported everywhere and taint the jury pool, which was exactly what the prosecution wanted. I could see it in her face; she was asking, begging, for my help. All I could do was give her my blessing.

"Take the deal," I said.

Raquel's eyes went wide, the red veins visible. "What?"

The lawyer looked up at me, alert for the first time. I could see he was stunned.

"If that's the only way to stay out of jail and save your child," I said, "then do it. Take the deal."

I had lost my family, my freedom, and I couldn't allow this woman's life to be ruined as well. It was enough. Raquel and her daughter were just going to be more collateral damage. If I could stop it, I had to. It's not like Raquel's statement was going to be the difference maker anyway. They had a long line of witnesses giving statements and testifying.

"Save yourself," I said.

"Are you sure? You know what they want me to—"

"I do. This isn't your cross to bear. Take it."

To Raquel's credit, she fought with me over it, said I was

crazy. Reluctantly, when she saw I was serious, she gave in. Then she got up slowly without saying a word and walked out. I looked back at her attorney, who got to his feet.

"Thank you, Mr. Wright," he said, all businesslike.

"Fuck out of here," I said, my anger barely contained. He walked quickly past and out the door.

Soon after, I got word that Rhoda, another female codefendant and friend, also wanted to see me. What had happened wasn't hard to figure out. Raquel's lawyer must have walked right out of the conference room and gone straight to Bissell. "You won't believe it!" he must've said. "Wright said 'Go ahead'!"

Rhoda, slightly older than Raquel, was a woman I knew from around Franklin Township. Sunshine and I would go out to parties with her and her friend Nikki. They'd crash at the house, get up in the morning and have breakfast with us, and then head home.

Rhoda was actually a key piece of their case because one wall they were ramming up against was that, for all the millions of dollars I was supposedly making as a kingpin, there was no money. So they were pushing Rhoda to testify that she worked as a courier who helped me get the money down South. Rhoda was a tough woman, so Bissell likely was having serious trouble getting a statement from her. He knew that my blessing would carry a lot of weight, so he sent her in to see me as well. Again, I told her to do what she had to do.

But Rhoda was stubborn—in the best way. She continued to proclaim her innocence, as well as my own, until Bissell brought the hammer down on her, threatening her with fifty years in prison. She had a young child too, so she had no other choice but to give in.

Though she would eventually come back on them. She had too much heart to just leave it there.

ORLANDO, FLORIDA
1961

When I was born, my mom and dad had no name for me. In haste to fill out the birth certificate, the nurse suggested that I be named after my father. From the moment I was old enough to understand that he and I shared a name, it had been a badge of honor for me. The fact that we were both "Isaac Wright" gave us a special bond. The fact that I was appended with a "Jr." always reminded me which way was up.

Dad is not a big man, but he carries a rare type of gravitas, the kind that can take over any room. He has a refined manner, walk, and dress that have been cultivated through his thirty years in the military, which included fighting in the wars in Korea and Vietnam. Everything about him is deliberate and commanding, though he's no tyrant. He is a man of all people, fair and diplomatic. Dad has long been my vision of true power, control without aggression, authority without domination.

When he was in the house, things ran with precision. On school days, he woke us at 5 a.m. so that there was time for the six kids to "shit, shave, and shower" (in military parlance) before breakfast. By 6:30 we had eaten and were working on the job listed on our duty roster, in order to relieve our mother of that added burden. All this had to be done by the time the school bus arrived. If we ran late, we knew it was our own fault and we'd have to chase down that bus on foot or walk to school. He ran a tight ship, but he left the disciplining to my mom. My brothers, sister, and I understood that when Mom punished us, she was acting on behalf of my father as well, whom we knew better than to disobey.

Self-sufficiency was a cardinal virtue of Dad's, so he taught us how to hunt, grow, and preserve our own food, some of which we would sell out front in the yard. But along with that sense of independence, he and my mother cared deeply about the community and cooperation of the family. On the weekends, we always recreated together: fishing, picnicking, amusement parks. On Sundays, Dad would gather us together to talk about family finances, go through our weekly duty roster, and provide us an opportunity to engage and ask questions. He taught us respect by showing us respect, a lesson I tried to take into all my relationships going forward.

When I was younger, it was his physical strength that impressed me. I remember him once loosening a bolt on my bicycle that had proved impossible to me. Watching him closely, I concluded that he was able to do it because of this straining face he made. After that, I'd imitate that face in all my physical challenges, figuring it was the secret to superhuman strength. As I matured, I began to understand his strength not as physical force but as a moral one. He taught us to stand for what was right, that there was no price high enough to back down from principle. I learned from him that what you owned should never determine who you were as a person. Even my understanding of ownership itself came through his teaching.

I remember arguing with my younger brother Reggie, who was two years younger than me and something of a troublemaker. He was a sweet kid, whom everyone liked, but he could talk you out of your shirt. Reggie was so notorious that I nicknamed him Skip, Zaj, and Trub: he would habitually skip the subject when confronted (Skip), exaggerate as often as he spoke (Zaj), and invariably get you into trouble (Trub). When I refused to allow Reggie to play with my BB gun, my father stepped in. He took the gun out of my hands and was about to hand it to Reggie.

"But that's my gun!" I screamed. "That's my gun!" The unfairness of it just set me off.

Dad put his hand out on my chest, to stop me from reaching for it. "Junior," he said calmly, "possession is a figment of the imagination. Control," he said, holding the gun out for me to see, "is the ultimate level of ownership."

I thought about those words. In that moment he was clearly in control of the BB gun. There wasn't much, if anything, I truly owned. That realization fundamentally changed the way I viewed material things and the idea of ownership. Even when I was doing well for myself, I never let the money or material items define me. I knew it wasn't really mine, that it could be taken away in an instant. Which was exactly what ended up happening to me.

My father spent some of his service as an MP, military police. After retiring from the military, he worked as state police. I knew little about the job except seeing him coming and going from the house in that blue uniform. Because of my respect for him, I always held some vision of police as honorable. I didn't have any real experience with police misconduct until I lived in the inner city, where conflict with the cops is as much a part of the environment as anything else. Even though I saw the violence and the harassment, I had very little knowledge about the extent of police power, in terms of your possessions, your freedom, your rights. I thought of them as bullies, but I had no concept of how far they could reach in, how much they could take.

In so many ways, my time behind bars was a wake-up call to my understanding of the world. It taught me the role that had been prescribed for me as a Black man, the way that I was a victim of a power struggle older than this country itself. That time also gave me the tools and the focus to carve out a new role for myself. I would have to chart my own path, conceived from the ashes of my former life.

My parents had been present for most of the major pretrial hearings over the previous year and a half, as had some of my siblings. But interactions in court were limited to nods, smiles, and small gestures of connection. Contact or verbal communication was prohibited. My mom was a firecracker and Judge Imbriani threatened on several occasions to remove her from the courtroom for her outbursts, which were usually directed at Bissell.

My parents would come to visit me at the jail from time to time and we'd talk through the phones in the visitor booths. My mother, who has been in a wheelchair since an accident in 1983, could not reach the phone in the stand-up pod. So she just sat there next to my father, smiling through the glass at me with those worried eyes, and relayed messages through him. It was painful having her so close, but so distant. It was like she had been silenced. On top of everything else, they had taken away my ability to communicate with my mother.

In the spring of 1991, about a week before the trial, my parents came with Amitrani on a specially approved contact visit where we all sat in an administrative office of the jail. Most of the communication with my parents was tinged with sorrow, but that meeting was characterized by a tenseness. As he often did at these meetings, Amitrani got up to use the restroom to give me some private time with my parents. My mother watched Amitrani step out, keeping her eyes on the door until it was closed.

"Are you sure this is right?" she asked.

"What, going to trial?"

"No," she said. "We're with you on not pleading, son. Your brothers and sister too. We're proud of you. I mean—" She let the word hang there.

"Representing myself?" I asked.

She nodded.

"Yes, Ma. I've never been more sure of anything in my life." She looked over at my father. "I know it doesn't seem like it," I said, "but this is the only way I'm going to get out of here."

I could tell she was worried—it was in her eyes—but her words belied that. "OK, we trust you, son," she said. "We're in this together." That had become one of her regular phrases, the thing she said for my comfort, but also for her own. *We're in this together.* No mother wants to picture her child alone in such a hellish place. My father didn't speak unless he had something to say. So when he began to talk, I paid attention. His words would ring in my ears throughout the trial and for years afterward. I can still recite them from memory.

"It is not necessary to win every battle," he said, "when the only thing that matters is who wins the war. All of Alexander's enemies were larger, more powerful and more destructive but they all fell at his feet, not because they weren't prepared for war; they were more prepared than he was. They fell because they were not prepared for *Alexander*. Whatever you do, son, never let them see you coming."

Chapter Nine

ALMOST TWO YEARS AFTER MY arrest on a hot New Jersey street, I was finally brought to trial. Of the original twelve codefendants indicted in the summer of 1989, I was the only one who didn't plead. The only one who didn't take a deal. The only one willing to see this thing through.

The trial itself should have been an opportunity for me to face my accusers, present my evidence, and prove my innocence. That's what a trial is supposedly for, what the law books lay out, what the movies portray, what the Sixth Amendment of the U.S. Constitution enshrines.

But that's not the reality because utilizing the judicial process is treated as a criminal act. If you lose, they are going to make an example out of you, punish you exponentially harsher than if you hadn't put up a fight. In this country, if you exercise your rights, they nail you for it.

On the trial's first morning—April Fool's Day, 1991—I sat and waited in the holding cell at the back of the courthouse with a handful of other inmates minding their own. I thought about the phrase "doing time" and how backward it seemed. I searched the faces and thought about how we were just passive vessels that the hours were passing through. Time was doing us.

I looked over at an older man lying out on the bench on his back, eyes closed, hands neatly folded on his chest. His face was peaceful: I wondered if that was because he was heading home or if he was just resigned to his fate. Footsteps echoed down the hall. With that familiar key jingle and then heavy clang, the caged door opened. A court officer handed me a hanger with a dry-cleaned suit, dark with pinstripes, which my parents had brought from home.

As I slowly got dressed in that cell, I was surprised at how tangible the transformation felt. The smooth texture of the pants, the starched firmness of the collar, the tailor-made fit of the jacket—they made me feel like a person again. The new clothes washed away that film of despair that covers prisoners like a coat of grime, removed that interchangeable feeling that comes with being a faceless number in the same khakis. I felt, in a word, *visible*.

My hair tied back in a neat ponytail, my shoes shined to a gleam, I was no longer an object being acted upon, but a subject taking control of his destiny. I would enter that courtroom not just as a defendant, but as an officer of the court.

A guard opened the holding cell, snapped ankle cuffs on me, and led me to court. As I walked through those double wooden doors, passed the judge's bench, I felt eyes on me like tiny daggers pressing into my skin. The gallery was full of spectators with the first few rows taken up by reporters and personnel from the prosecutor's office. Taking those awkward, short steps, I spotted my parents and siblings and gave them a curt nod. My father returned the nod, his words echoing back to me: *Never let them see you coming, son.*

To my left sat County Prosecutor Nicholas L. Bissell Jr., his hair unnaturally black and shiny, his jowls dangling. Beside him was the assistant prosecutor, Veronica Nolan. To my right sat my standby counsel, Paul Amitrani, alongside an empty chair. Amitrani would sit next to me throughout the trial, though he could not participate. The first chair, as they call it, was mine alone.

The jury box was empty because the law forbids the jury from seeing a defendant handcuffed. Once the shackles were taken off my legs, the jurors filed in. The jury foreman, a bespectacled white male in his forties with light curly hair, was a corporate lawyer. The sole juror of color was a Black woman in her early thirties with large eyes and thin lips. I was scanning each face when I heard Imbriani's familiar voice: "This is the case of *State v. Isaac Wright, Jr.*, indictment no. 07–0478–89–I. May I have appearances, please." All seated at both tables stood to their feet.

"Good afternoon, Your Honor. Nicholas L. Bissell Jr., on behalf of the State of New Jersey."

"Good afternoon, Your Honor. Veronica Nolan, Assistant Prosecutor for the State of New Jersey."

"Good afternoon, Your Honor. Paul Amitrani, assisting the defendant, Isaac Wright Jr., who is representing himself in this matter."

"Good afternoon, Your Honor. Isaac Wright Jr., defendant, pro se."

★　★　★

Opening arguments are about selling a story. The prosecution tells their story and the defense tells theirs. Then twelve citizens, with no more expertise than that of a random person off the street, are granted the power to decide which is the better story. That story is then filed away as truth and a life is either saved or destroyed.

But the process is corruptible—both by circumstance and by intention. It is not uncommon for the truth to sound fantastical and for the fiction to seem plausible. My story—an organized conspiracy of cops, prosecutors, and witnesses—was true, but far less plausible than Bissell's: *You see this young Black man with the guilty friends? He's guilty.* So that was strike one against me.

Strike two was the sheer volume of charges—a total of ten counts against me. Each charge strengthened the others. The average juror may think, *I can see one mistaken count, but ten? He must've done something.* This is not some accident of the process, but an intentional maneuver by the prosecution. The power prosecutors have, and the built-in trust they automatically possess (especially with a white jury), buries defendants from the get-go. Research shows that a large percentage of jurors make up their mind very early in the case, a fact that also benefits the prosecution, who have the power and trappings of the state behind their story. Bissell was the chief law enforcement officer of the county. Who the hell was I?

In addition, my opening argument was a story that wouldn't sit well with the average citizen. My arrest was not a bureaucratic error or a case of mistaken identity. My story? *The state is lying. These public servants you've entrusted to keep your family and community safe are deceiving you. The system that allows you to sleep at night cannot be trusted. Your government isn't interested in neither truth nor justice.*

Nobody wants to hear that.

I had to make the jurors accept something that would rattle their foundation. Author and social reformer Upton Sinclair once wrote, "It is difficult to get a man to understand something when his salary depends on his not understanding it."[1] I'd argue it's even more difficult when their peace of mind and sense of security depend on it.

Bissell's opening argument crafted a story around my litany of crimes, the scourge I was on my community, the threat I posed to their neighborhoods, the message that needed to be sent by putting me away. He played up the theatrics, railing with the false certainty of a movie lawyer, and it seemed to me like he was too invested. Bissell rarely tried cases anymore but he had chosen to do this case because he wanted to make a statement. It made him overly emotional. As I watched him perform his opening, I looked for ways in which I could exploit this.

"Mr. Wright," Judge Imbriani said. "Your opening statement."

I stood up slowly and buttoned the top button of my suit. Everything around me seemed to come to a halt. The world reflected through the high windows got blurry, the faces in the gallery fuzzed into a pool of color, the quiet buzz of the courtroom shrank to a silent pinpoint. I turned toward the jury box and the twelve faces came into crystal focus. I made eye contact with each of them, and tried to pause at the young Black juror's face, communicating beneath the words, sensing in her something that bound us together beyond color.

"Their entire case is based on a lie," I explained, slowly and precisely, punctuating the right words to create a natural rhythm. "They have created that which does not exist. It's a case of jealousy, vindictiveness, hatred, political ambition, and premature actions. It's all second- and third-hand information, brought about from political motives."

Though I had been preparing and practicing for months, I wasn't reciting a speech. There is something inherently unnatural about a memorized opening; it is precise in a world that is not. I wanted my words to flow out of me as naturally as my breath, to have the natural tenor of common sense, so I improvised around the key points of my argument.

I explained how the prosecution had to portray me a certain way in order for their story to make sense. Then I zeroed in on a point that seemed so obvious that it sometimes got missed: it was a *story*. The prosecutor tells this story like he has witnessed it, but of course, *he was not there*. He does not know because he was brought in long after the events of the case have occurred. He has to take the words of police and witnesses and codefendants as though they were fact. *But you, the jury, do not.*

"What you must pay close attention to about the story of guilt the prosecutor just described to you," I said, "is not the story itself but the fact that he *has no personal knowledge of it*. Everything he told you came from someone else. Everything. He has no direct connection that would allow him to confirm the story's truthfulness. He's decided to adopt it as the truth and then tell it to you. Why is that important?" I paused, to drive home the point. "One lie, one exaggeration, one misrepresentation, one half-truth and an innocent person goes to prison."

A sign of things to come happened on day two of the trial. One juror wrote a letter to the judge complaining that she overheard another juror saying how I "looked like a drug dealer." The judge called the offending juror out in open court. She admitted saying that and apologized before Imbriani dismissed her. Then, Imbriani *got rid of the juror who told on her*. I objected: there was literally no reason to dismiss this juror, other than the fact that she was *un*biased. But in a rigged game, that was enough.

Some of the rigging had already been set up in advance, at pretrial hearings.

The first one was about the tapes. As I suspected on the day of my arrest, there was indeed a listening device hidden in my car. The police had installed one at the car dealership without my knowledge. In fact, the dealership worked with the cops to get me to pick up the car early. The police had a wiretap order to record for only a limited period of time and with the car just sitting there, they weren't getting a thing.

The prosecution had hours of tapes—static and indecipherable conversations—from what they claimed was my car. Judge Imbriani himself admitted only a small bit of the tapes was "audible and understandable." He even joked after a particularly inaudible one: "Well, I heard the work 'fuck,'" which was met with laughs from the gallery. At the hearing, I called an FBI expert who testified that the tapes were inauthentic and altered. There were spaces, time jumps, and even a beeper call heard on the tape that didn't match up with the actual phone log.

Bissell never even countered my witness. He didn't call an expert to testify that the tapes were authentic, which could only mean one thing: he couldn't find one. Nevertheless, Imbriani refused to throw out the tapes, so they were admissible at trial. I wasn't even allowed to mention in front of the trial jury what the FBI expert's conclusion was regarding the tapes. When I tried to get it in, Imbriani gave instructions to the jury to disregard it.

Another key pretrial hearing—called a Franks Hearing—was about my motion to suppress the drugs found at Carlos's house. These were seized on the day of my arrest, and were the key to their whole case. The police reports specified that Carlos's house was secured for a couple of hours in the late afternoon while the police sought out a search warrant. The problem with that claim is that was a lie; they seized the drugs hours earlier and I knew it. Detective Racz, who drove me to the police station, told me about the seizure of the drugs when I was in his car, hours before any search warrant was signed: *Looks like we found a bunch of coke at your man's house.*

Of course, in court, Racz denied saying this; his partner—Buckman—backed him up; and Imbriani denied my motion to suppress, finding that the cops' words held more credibility than mine. This was a common pattern through both pretrial and trial: cops lied for the prosecutor, backed each other up, and orchestrated their stories in advance. If I could prove this, the entire case would unravel, but I'd need a cop to come out and admit it. This was about as likely as a comet landing on the courthouse. By law, police are allowed to lie to you during an interrogation. The idea that they somehow then shift to being pristine truth-tellers in court goes against common sense.

At the trial, detective after detective told the same story. I was the leader of this drug organization, the drugs found at Carlos's house were part of my supply, the seizures of drugs during Gator's and Ron's respective arrests were part of my operation, and I was the boss of all the other codefendants. Bissell had lied to the press about recovering guns and rubber-banded rolls of cash from my house, about beepers I bought for other codefendants and about why I paid cash for one of my cars, and on and on. It honestly became hard to keep track of the sheer volume of the lies, which inured to their benefit. I simply didn't have enough time to disprove them all.

And day after day, Imbriani struck down my objections and disallowed my witnesses.

"I won't let you turn this trial into a vehicle for a fishing expedition," Imbriani said from the bench, rejecting another one of my witnesses.

"Your Honor," I protested, "I am merely—"

"No, no, no, Mr. Wright. You won't convert a one- to two-week trial into a two-month trial."

The judge knew a shorter trial benefited the prosecution. They had already implanted their story—in the press, in the volume and severity of charges—and I had to use the trial to take it apart. Yet, I wasn't even allowed to call witnesses to rebut direct charges. In one nearly comical example, Bissell claimed my music company was actually a front for my drug operation, an easily disproven charge. But the judge prevented me from calling any witnesses to show how I made money, so the accusation just lay there like a heavy, immovable stone.

For all the restrictions imposed on me, Imbriani gave Bissell free rein. He sustained every objection, allowed every motion, and let the county prosecutor litigate the case against me with no constitutional restraints. It was a hard lesson in the difference between the law on the page and the law in the courtroom.*

Bissell relished in painting a portrait of me as a so-called kingpin. He was playing up to the media, trying to get the first kingpin conviction in the state. Meanwhile, Assistant Prosecutor Veronica Nolan came off as well-mannered and polite, but she seemed gravely scared of Bissell. In his presence, she could not talk or even look in the direction of the defense table. Once I realized this, I went out of my way to talk to her, as lawyers across the aisle often do.

For instance, each piece of evidence in a trial is marked for identification purposes. There has to be a clear account of which evidence has gone before a jury. One time I was prepping for the next witness when I turned to Nolan. "I have Carlos's pager identified as state's exhibit 45 but no indication whether it's been entered into evidence," I said. "Has it been entered?"

---

* As an added handicap to my operating as my own lawyer, the sheriff's office refused to bring my materials back and forth from the jail to the courthouse each day. They left the dolly with my boxes of documents overnight in a room in the courthouse where anyone with a key could rummage through my files.

Nolan checked her file to look up the answer. "I believe it—"

Bissell whipped around like he'd been bitten. "What the fuck is wrong with you?" he screamed at her. "Don't talk to him!"

Nolan's face turned crimson and she went entirely silent, just mortified. I stepped away from the table to get in Bissell's line of sight. "You know, you're a dickhead," I said, as calmly as if I were stating a plain fact. He pretended not to hear.

It ate at Bissell to have to sit across from me, to have to argue against me, to have to stand on an equal footing with me. We had one out-and-out clash at the pretrial hearing about the tapes over the fact that I had kept the police officers in court testifying all day.

During a short break, Bissell walked up to me and Amitrani, totally ignoring my presence. "Listen," Bissell said, "the detectives have been here since this morning. They're supposed to be out in the field, for surveillance. I'm going to direct them to leave if you're not going to use them."

Amitrani looked over at the row of them on the back benches. "OK—" he started to say.

"Whoa, whoa. Wait a minute," I jumped in. "What do you mean, 'OK'? There's no OK here. They're not going anywhere. They're gonna be here all damn day if I want them to."

"Listen," Bissell said, "these guys work for me—"

"Well right now, they're working for me," I snapped back. "I got them on subpoenas, so they're *my* detectives. I'm gonna keep them until I'm done. And if I want to keep them overnight, I'm gonna keep them overnight too."

I turned to Amitrani, incredulous. "You know this man

is trying to put me in prison for the rest of my life, right?"
Amitrani and Bissell had been acting like coworkers scheduling a meeting.

Bissell looked at me with this bottled-up rage, just pure disgust. Then he turned around, walked to the back of the courtroom, and told all the detectives to leave. As they filed out, I could do nothing but shake my head. But it didn't matter. I had them back the next day.

I hadn't seen Gator in over a year. At trial, he looked different up there on the stand or maybe it was just my eyes that had been opened. I thought back to the anxious guy at the park who came hat in hand to ask for my help and how far we'd come.

Gator was testifying against me as part of his plea, though the deal itself was still under wraps. On direct examination, he told Bissell stories about how often I brought him cocaine to sell, how much money I took from him, and how on the February night he was arrested, I had instructed him to transport drugs in my old blue Duster.

Though I knew it was coming, the whole thing left me dumbstruck. This was a guy I'd helped out of the kindness of my heart, who had come to me when he was down on his luck, who stayed in my house, ate at my table, and watched television with my nephews. Now he was tossing my life away in order to save himself.

On the stand, I noticed that Gator needed to present himself as the smartest cat, like nothing went over his head. He kept turning the conversation toward how he knew how to be in the streets and how nobody could get past him. It was clearly a point of pride with him. So when it was my turn to cross-examine him, I swiped at his Achilles' heel.

"Mr. E__," I began, "on the night of your arrest, you were driving my car, in my name. Correct?"

"Yes."

"My name was on the paperwork?"

"Yes."

"And you knew this?"

"Yes."

"You're saying to the jury I gave you the car to drive?"

"Yes."

"You're saying I gave you that car to sell drugs?"

"Yes."

I nodded and took a beat, looking over at the jury. Then I stepped closer to Gator. "You were the smart one and I was the idiot, right?"

"That's the way it winded up, didn't it?" he said. Some quiet rumbling from the gallery, but I didn't break eye contact.

"You knew the car was registered in my name?"

"Yes."

"And running to my house," I asked, "that wasn't something you set up with the police?"

"You know it didn't happen like that."

"You just ran to my house?"

"Yes," Gator said.

"You want this jury to *believe*—with your intelligence— that you were pulled over in a car in my name, selling drugs for me, and you were going to get rid of the police by . . . running to my house?"

No answer. Gator's eyes shifted to Bissell.

"According to your testimony," I continued, "you have this sharp judgment and unparalleled intuition? And you believed you were going to get away from the cops"—I let out a slight laugh, to punctuate the absurdity—"by running to the very place where that car was registered?" Giggles from the gallery. "Literally the one place the cops would be able to find you in a matter of seconds. That's what you want this jury to believe?"

"Well," he said, annoyed, "you know that's what happened."

"Yes, I know exactly where you ran to and where you were arrested and so does this jury. But that is not what I asked you. So, let me ask again: You want this jury to believe—as smart as you are—that you *chose* to run to my house? That running to my house wasn't a setup. That you were just too dumb to know my house would be the very first place the cops would look?"

Gator didn't answer; his stuck stupid grin slowly melted off his face.

"That was a question," I said.

"As I said, that's what happened."

"That's what your unparalleled intellect told you?" My voice rose to a comical pitch. "To run to the house where the car was registered?"

He stuttered a few words out. "Nah, it wasn't like . . . Well yeah, but—"

"No further questions, Your Honor."

Ron was large and heavy, with a round face, beady eyes, and wide nose. His face revealed a childlike gullibility that both Bissell and Gator had used in their favor. On the stand, Ron echoed Gator on every detail, in some cases word for word. (Incredibly, they had been allowed to share a cell.) Just as Gator pinned the drugs from his February arrest on me, Ron did the same for his own arrest the next month.

During direct testimony, Ron claimed he sold cocaine for me daily and turned over $70,000 a week to me. When I got up to cross-examine him, I started with the inconsistencies in his own story, just to throw him off-balance. To police, he claimed he sold drugs three to four times a month and turned over $200,000 a month. I rattled off the numbers and times and statements just to put him on his back foot. "Which was the lie?" I asked. "What you said then or what you're saying now?"

Once I had him in knots, I struck out at one of his more ludicrous claims. Ron testified that I had actually paid to bail him out of jail.

"Did you see who bailed you out?" I asked him.

"No," Ron said.

"Were you present when this person passed over the money?"

"No."

"You have no personal knowledge of where the money came from?"

"No."

"So when you claim the money that bailed you out came from me," I said, "you are not talking about something you have personal knowledge of."

"No."

"So who told you that?"

"Uh, Gator, I mean Mr. E__ told me that."

"You know Gator is cooperating with the government?"

"Yes."

"Would it make sense for your stories to be different if you're both looking to convict me?"

"Objection!" Bissell was up on his feet.

"Sustained," from the bench.

"We are not friends, correct?" I asked, a little more heated now.

"No, we're not," Ron said.

"We don't know each other well, if at all."

"Right."

"And you and Gator, you grew up together, right?"

"Yes."

"You're childhood friends."

"Yes."

"Did Gator have enough money to bail you out?"

"I'm sure he did."

"But I used my money?"

"Yes."

"And you're comfortable saying that to this jury even though you have no personal knowledge that it's the truth?"

"I believe it's the truth."

"Because you wouldn't dare knowingly represent a lie to the court, would you?"

"Represent?"

"You wouldn't tell a lie in court."

"Absolutely not," he said.

"When you were arrested for drug possession in this case, did you appear before this very court to plead to the charges?"

"Yes."

"And what was your plea?"

"Not guilty."

"Well, Mr. D__." I paused for dramatic effect. "That was a lie, wasn't it?"

Ron sat silent, stuck like a wounded animal.

"You did the very thing you just swore under oath you'd never do, correct?"

His eyes glazed and he looked over my shoulder. "I guess so," Ron mumbled.

"I'm sorry, what was that?" I'd heard him but wanted to extend the moment.

"I guess so," he said.

In the 136 tapes of Gator-Ron conversations from each of their cars, discussing drugs and money, my name—their so-called boss—was not mentioned once. *Not once.* Ron's beeper records showed exactly *zero* calls from me. But throughout the trial I ran into a conundrum: all this absence of evidence could look—to a suspicious mind—like I had covered my tracks. Ron's lack of proximity to me played into Bissell's narrative: as the boss, I was careful about isolating myself, working only through one person: Gator. Gator had been the middleman, for the money, for the drugs, for communication. And Bissell had Gator by the balls.

Bissell wasn't satisfied with the number of cooperating witnesses he had, so he found ways to dredge up some more. One of them backfired on him in spectacular fashion. Will S__ was a member of a rap group I managed called Wise Franchise and the younger brother of a friend of mine. "Chill Will," as he was known, was a light-skinned, impressionable teenager

with a short-top fade and a handsome face. Will had been sixteen when he was stopped by police for driving a friend's car
without a license. Officers claimed that he tried to escape and
run them over with the car. They charged him with assault
of an officer—in addition to drug charges—and put him in
juvenile detention. After my arrest, the detectives went back
to Will and pressed on him to "give up Isaac." Then Bissell
swooped in and threatened to charge him as an adult.

Will's mother, who was at the interrogation, pushed back.
"My boy don't know nothing about Isaac Wright," she said.
"Why are you trying to get him to tell these lies?" Will and
his mother later said Gator offered Will a thousand dollars
to turn on me, but they held firm.

Will was subsequently charged as an adult, facing twenty-
six years in prison. Bissell offered to knock that down to ten
years if he would implicate himself and me at a plea hearing—
which he did, but only after I sent word to his mother that he
had my blessing. If it meant losing the prime years of his life,
he should take the plea and do what they asked.

There was no discussion about his testifying at trial, but
Bissell didn't need to spell that out. He just had to subpoena
him. As an inmate serving time, Will was brought to court
and put on that witness stand. Bissell had set a trap and then
ambushed him.

Either out of anger at Bissell for making him testify or
plain exhaustion at being made to lie, Will ambushed him
right back. On the stand, when Bissell began to lead Will
toward implicating me, Will unleashed on him. "I never did
anything with this man," he said, gesturing to me. "They
were talking about twenty-six years, but say Wright was your

boss and you'll only serve eighteen months or whatever. I kept saying I didn't know anything about him but they kept pushing. I said it to get out of serving that time. I'd do anything to get out of serving all that time."

Bissell stomped over to the prosecution table and took some documents from Assistant Prosecutor Nolan. Then he started reading back Will's plea deal statement.

"Mr. S__, do you remember saying these things about Mr. Wright?"

"I remember them clearly," Will said. "They are all lies." Murmurs from the court.

The embarrassed look on Bissell's face—in his courtroom, with his own witness—was priceless. In frustration, he started to read back more statements from Will's plea agreement, but Will cut him off. "I don't care what that says," he said, defiant. "None of that is true. In this place, all you have to do is say 'Isaac' and you can get whatever you want. I was just saying that stuff. It sounded good. I told the judge what I had to tell him."

"It's disturbing that you would say those things," Judge Imbriani interjected. "This is not a game. I am going to write to the bureau of parole and tell them you will lie and say anything necessary to get out of jail. You've lied before a judge. You said you lied many times today."

Imbriani's threat was far beyond his judicial responsibility. As the judge knew, Will's plea should've only concerned his own guilt. However, Bissell made it mandatory that those pleading guilty had to implicate me, a requirement that bred inconsistencies and lies. And during Will's testimony, it blew up in Bissell's face.

Will was bold up there, almost relishing his chance to upend the cocky prosecutor. Later in his testimony, Bissell asked if it was true that I had taught him to be careful in how he transported drugs.

"If he taught me that," Will said, "I wouldn't be serving time today, would I?"

"Well, maybe you're not a good listener," Bissell said.

"I don't see why not. I've been listening to you run your mouth all day."

Bissell's face went red and the entire courtroom broke out into laughter.

There were other prosecution witnesses whom I didn't know or barely knew testifying that I was their boss, that they got drugs from me, that they collected money for me. There were witnesses like John, a friend of Gator's from New Brunswick with whom I played basketball. He was not part of the original bust, but he showed up at the trial to claim he regularly sold up to $30,000 worth of cocaine for me. I can only imagine what Bissell had over him. I did what I could to establish that these witnesses had no proof, that we had no relationship, but if someone is going to get up on the stand and lie like that, Clarence Darrow himself can't do much about it.

The climax at the trial was Carlos, whom I hadn't seen since the day of my arrest. High-top fade haircut, droopy face with a mustache, sports coat with a wide collar, Carlos looked defeated up there. Gone was the confident operator I knew and in his place was this docile man with stooped shoulders. I knew that Carlos was testifying and pleading in order to help out his brother and wife, who had both been arrested with him.

Of all the witnesses paraded before the court, Carlos made me the angriest. On the day of our arrest, when I sensed cops surveilling the area, I could've bolted. I probably should've bolted. But I stayed there—with my wife in the car—in order to warn him. To save him.

Through questioning I established our business relationship, the cabinet company we were partners in, and the reason for our meet-up that day. He admitted that he had told me to go there in order to give me furniture blueprints. "Those plans are still in my truck if they still have my truck," he said.

I also addressed Carlos's supposed role as my "supplier." If I was the leader of this twenty-million-dollar organization, why was I arrested allegedly buying a half kilo off of Carlos? How could I be charged as a kingpin if the man above me, the man who provided me with drugs, was not? How could this be a drug deal when there was no money to be found anywhere? Carlos had no answers, refusing to go any further into the lie than he had to.

"So according to the prosecution," I said, "you're my supplier—"

"No, no. I'm not your supplier."

"Well, you do know the state is saying that you're my supplier?"

"Yeah, I know, but I'm not your supplier."

"So what was going on that day, then?" I asked.

"I sold you drugs."

"Just that day?"

"Just that day."

"So, I had bought these drugs from you," I said, almost thrown off by Carlos's refusal to take things further. "Then why'd you throw a package of cocaine at me when the cops arrived?"

"Well, because you were walking away."

"You threw a package of cocaine at me because I was walking away."

"Yes."

On the stand, Rhoda took the opposite tack that Carlos had. Knowing that she had my blessing, that I had told her to do what she had to do to save herself and her son, she went all in. She was a victim as much as I was, but it was strange, surreal even, watching her up there, telling a fictional version of our entire friendship.

A serious problem Bissell was having was how to account for the fact that no money was found on me or anywhere else. Throughout the entire investigation, including all of the arrests, no money was ever found. This was where Rhoda was most effective. She testified that she once took me to the bus station with "a bag of money," which I took down South. There was absolutely no corroborating evidence of my taking a bus anywhere. The whole story was ridiculous. Why would I need her to drive me to a bus station? Why would I ride a public bus at all? Why only one bag of money for a ten-hour trip when Bissell claimed I was generating $30,000 in cash per day? Why would a kingpin be taking all of these risks himself when he has this elaborate organization of willing participants? It was all nonsensical, but Rhoda did what she had to do to sell it.

The one issue I tried to get out of Rhoda was the secret deals. All the codefendants who became prosecution witnesses pleaded to lesser charges for less prison time. But these were still second-degree crimes, serious crimes that required prison time. However, incredibly, there's no direct enforcement to make sure the sentence you actually receive meets the legal requirement of the charge you pleaded guilty to.

Rhoda was the one who first tipped me off about these deals. When she and I had met in that office before the trial, she said, "Listen, I'm pleading guilty to a charge that carries time, like five years. But my lawyer tells me I'm not going to do any time, is that true?"

"What do you mean?" I asked.

"Can they do that?"

"*Can* they? Yeah," I said. "They can do anything they want until you're sentenced."

On the stand, I brought this up to Rhoda. "Was there a secret deal you made with the prosecution?" I asked.

"No."

"So, you're definitely going to prison after this?"

"Yes," she said.

"But you're not sentenced yet, correct?"

"No, I'm not sentenced yet, but my plea agreement says I will."

That's the loophole. *My plea agreement says I will.* Technically, that was the truth. The reason the secret deals work is there is no way to catch them. Besides Carlos, none of the defendants did any time—though their plea agreements all claimed they would. And who was the judge who would sign off on these deals, making sure none of the testifying defendants spent a day in prison? Imbriani. When the judge himself is part of the conspiracy, there's not a damn thing you can do about it.

Even with a fully rigged trial, the nearly all-white jury in the conservative county couldn't find me guilty. It took almost a week and pressure from the judge to force through a unanimous verdict.

On the third day of deliberations, the jury sent a note to the judge: they were having trouble reaching a unanimous verdict. One unidentified juror felt the kingpin drug law was unfair. Essentially, the juror—whom I would learn was Deborah, the young Black woman—disagreed that someone should be put in prison for life for the crimes that other people committed. Of course, it was a valid point. The kingpin law was incredibly broad and a lifetime conviction could be based merely on the words of other people, which in my case, was exactly what was happening.

The judge read the jury's letter to those of us in court. He placed the piece of paper to the side of the bench and then turned to the jury box, livid. "You took an oath to apply the law," he said, trying to keep his composure. "I do not make the law, and you do not make the law. The law is made by the governor and the legislature. You must accept the law as I charge it to you."

This is actually not true. Though they are rarely notified of this, jurors have recourse to disagree with the law: it's called jury nullification.

The next morning, when the jury claimed they reached a unanimous verdict, I was suspicious. I asked for the judge to "poll" the jury, asking each individual juror if he or she agreed with the verdict. When he reached Deborah, she said, in a low, muffled voice, "I disagree."

Stunned, Imbriani looked over at the foreman. "I thought you said we had a verdict," he said.

"Yes, I thought we did too," the foreman said, a sweaty embarrassment seeping through him. This exchange between judge and jury foreman, conversational in nature, was highly inappropriate. Imbriani sent the jury back in—with the anger of a parent grounding a child—and told them not to come back out until it was unanimous, a highly prejudicial threat.

After that, the deliberating room of the jury got loud, penetrating through walls into the courtroom. A few times the sheriff's officer had to go in there and stop them from fighting. Deborah wrote a letter to the judge saying she felt pressured by the foreman, who was a corporate attorney. She wrote that he claimed the jury could not leave the room without a unanimous verdict, which is not true. Under the law, this type of coercion is a highly inappropriate influence on a jury full of laymen. At one point, they had even been 7–5 in my favor.

When they wore Deborah down and ultimately came back with a guilty verdict on all ten counts, it seemed like the entire courtroom breathed a sigh of relief. Even Amitrani seemed glad it was finally over.

SOMERSET COUNTY COURTHOUSE
MAY 22, 1991

I leaned back to rest my shoulders against the holding cell wall, always cold, no matter the season. Like the outside world didn't penetrate in there. Like you were so closed off that you were in a place that overrode the laws of nature.

"You g-gonna eat that?"

I turned in the direction of a stuttering voice. My eyes scanned men all dressed in the same blue two-piece khakis, like clones littering the room, until I came upon a particular Black male. His eyes were glassy, his face was puffy, and his dark complexion highlighted the discoloration of his large nose. His dingy hair was matted to his head like a cap with large, long lumps of knotted hair hanging to his shoulders. He seemed like a ghost. Maybe an apparition, a vision of myself from the future.

I had been staring at him, not answering.

"If you not g-gonna eat that . . ." he said again.

I looked down to the paper container at my feet, at the dry baloney-and-cheese sandwich in there. The baloney was more like a strip of leather, topped with hard welfare cheese between two slices of cardboard. I handed it to him. As he savagely gobbled it to nothing, I studied him. While the others slept or had intense discussions about utter nonsense, this man's world was contained at that moment into a single thing. I couldn't help but envy him.

"Wright, you're up," the sheriff's officer bellowed.

Then the heavy familiar sound like a coffin opening. I stood to my feet and duck-walked along the polished cement floor, past several other men sitting on the stainless steel bench. The chains on my ankles bounced around, clanging against each other and the floor.

"Good luck!"

I turned toward the voice. It was the guy I gave my sandwich to, his eyes twitching in the morning light. I gave him a nod.

Cuffed at my ankles and wrists, I was led down a long wide corridor for a walk I had taken many times before. But this time felt different, almost like a death march.

Scanning the gallery, I was relieved not to find my parents' faces. I had asked them not to come, did not want their grief to be a spectacle. I couldn't bear something so private being put on display for public consumption. In the court, I took a seat next to Amitrani. Normally a talkative person, he was eerily silent. There was a different energy charge to the room after the suspense of the trial. It was a cold and empty feeling that sank down to my insides.

As Amitrani leaned over to whisper something to me, he was interrupted by the bailiff and the announcement of my case.

After I stood, Judge Imbriani fixed me with his steely-eyed gaze. "Mr. Wright, you are here today to be sentenced," he said, businesslike and efficient. He had a docket to get through and I was just one item to be disposed of. "This is your opportunity to address the court. Do you have anything to say before I impose a sentence?"

"I understand that a life sentence is mandatory and nothing I can say or you can do here today will change that," I said. I just wanted this part over with.

"I am bound by the law, Mr. Wright."

"Then do what you have to do," I said.

"Very well, then. A jury has found you guilty of all ten

charges against you in an eighteen-count indictment . . ." As the judge spoke, I noticed Bissell out in my periphery, moving from his table to in front of the judge's bench.

"The evidence against you was overwhelming," Imbriani continued, "and this court has no doubt that you were, in fact, a major supplier of drugs throughout the New York–New Jersey metropolitan areas . . . Who knows how many lives you ruined and how many deaths you caused by the poison you peddled in our communities. In light of these uncontroverted facts, this court has no problem handing down the following sentence."

When Bissell reached the judge's bench, he turned his back to Imbriani so that he could face me. We looked into each other's eyes as the judge continued. "For your conviction on count one of the indictment, charging you with being a drug kingpin, this court sentences you to life in prison."

The moment those last words left Imbriani's mouth, a smile slowly stretched across Bissell's face. Imbriani read through the rest of the counts, but his voice began to fade into a high-pitched static, white noise. The sound in the room dropped out and everything blurred over, like paper being burned at the edges.

I was found guilty of all charges against me in the indictment and the judge gave me life on a never-before-used kingpin statute, plus seventy years on the remaining convictions. Life *plus* seventy years. I was twenty-nine years old.

My world shrank as though in a keyhole, with only myself and Bissell standing amidst a complete white background.

His smile was all I saw. It was the same thing that he had revealed when he came to my cell that first night: he had made this personal.

He just didn't count on me doing the same.

Chapter Ten

AS A YOUNG KID, I scared easily. If I did something wrong and was waiting to get disciplined for it, I'd be shaking. You didn't have to do anything to me; you'd just have to look at me real hard and I'd be terrified. Especially if I was about to get in trouble, that fear of the unknown and lack of control terrified me. Unlike most childhood tendencies, which fade over time, this one didn't go away gradually. I can pinpoint its vanishing to a single moment, on a blistering summer afternoon in 1968.

When I was seven years old, my family moved to New York City. My father was stationed at Fort Hamilton in Bay Ridge, Brooklyn. Our apartment was located in a building at the foot of the Verrazzano Bridge, which rose in majestic steel behind us. My family was always too big for easy accommodations, so to fit all eight of us, the military would approve us for two apartments and knock down a wall and construct a doorway through the living rooms in order to convert two two-bedroom apartments into a single four-bedroom apartment. We moved as an unwieldy unit, putting our stamp on every place we called home.

Even at a young age I was already resourceful, with an entrepreneurial spirit and roving eye. Moving around from place to place, I looked for different schemes to make pocket change. When we moved to densely packed Brooklyn, and I realized how many people we lived on top of, I quickly saw how this could translate into an opportunity.

Recognizing the volume of glass bottles discarded in the city, I organized my brothers and friends into a consortium of collectors to redeem the bottles for money. We were so efficient, our wagons of clattering glass such fixtures of the neighborhoods, that the grocery store clerks referred to us as the "Bay Ridge Bottle Mafia." We made about twenty dollars a week, a fortune for a kid back then. After payoffs, I'd have somewhere between five to seven dollars. Not bad at a time when White Castle hamburgers were only ten cents each.

One scorching afternoon, after paying off my crew, I had around six dollars in my pocket. Skipping down the sidewalk to the corner store, I heard a dog barking incessantly across the street. I recognized the bark and the dog: it was a ferocious German shepherd who belonged to Peanut, a friend of my oldest brother, Wendell. In the hazy sunshine, I saw the dog chained up to a link fence in front of his building. I paid him little mind and the barking soon blended in with the scenery as I made my way to the corner. A few steps from the store, I noticed it was a little too quiet. The air had gathered this storm of silent menace. It took a moment for me to register why. Then I pinpointed it: *the dog had stopped barking.*

I looked back in the direction of the fence and the dog

was gone. When I turned to the right, I startled as he leaped atop the hood of a parked car. He was a black-and-brown shorthair shepherd with dark lead eyes, snarling and salivating, his tongue unfurled like a sopping carpet. Then in a single stride he was in the air—like in slow motion, all legs fully extended. Before I could scream or run, he was on me, knocking me to the ground with the force of the jump.

He pinned me onto the pavement and tore at my clothes and arms, slinging my body back and forth like a chew toy. All I heard was the clenched growling, the gnashing teeth, and the sound of my own cries. In my panic I just started flailing my arms, swinging with closed fists. It felt like an unbearably long time, the fear pounding in my chest, the total loss of control or thinking.

Then, suddenly, a high-pitched yelp.

The dog stopped and I wasn't even sure what had happened. I just lay there, staring at him, bloody and confused. But my hand had felt it: I had punched him square in the eye. I felt the wetness in my hand, the pain in my scraped knuckle, the exhaustion in my limbs. It startled both of us. *I had hurt him.*

Once it clicked for me what I had done, a force was unleashed inside of me. I started punching and kicking the dog with every ounce of myself. My middle finger got caught in his mouth, and his teeth ripped it open, but I barely felt it and kept going. It was like I was possessed, driven by a rage that fed on itself. The adrenaline coursed through me like a rushing wave.

As I punched and kicked for my life, someone grabbed the dog's collar and pulled him off of me. I looked up to see

Peanut, who was probably around thirteen, tall and skinny with dark skin and a head that scrunched in at the middle like the nut that gave him his nickname.

"Hey!" he screamed at me, hooking the leash to its collar. "What the hell are you doing?!"

"He jumped on *me!*" I yelled, wiping the snot from my face. "He fucking attacked me!" I was still trying to hit the dog when Peanut grabbed me by the arm.

"Leave my dog alone!" he said, pushing me away. "Stop it!" The words were just sounds to me and I kept kicking. The dog wailed, lowering his head and wiping his eye with his paw.

"Isaac!" Peanut yelled. "Stop or I'm gonna tell Wendell!" That got me to stop. My brother had that kind of power over me. Peanut walked the dog down the street, but I felt somehow unfinished and didn't want to let it go. "Bring him back here!" I yelled. "Where you going?"

Once they turned the corner out of sight, I stopped yelling. With my mouth bleeding through heavy breath, I went into the store and got Band-Aids to wrap my finger, a couple of hard candies, and a soda. As I stepped onto the curb and popped the drink, a calm flooded over me. Instead of fear I felt something new, an intoxicating force. I had discovered something elemental. Not only could I fight back but I could win.

That was the last day I ever felt fear. I would never be afraid of anything or anyone, ever again. I had gotten in touch with my own power.

In my mind it was quick, a forty-eight-hour span that passed in a blink. The echo of the gavel slam, the cuffs pinching my skin, and then I was packing up my possessions, which was mostly legal documents. My life had been distilled down to a few photographs and the contents of my case. The reason for the quick transport wasn't hard to figure out: jail officials don't like inmates with knowledge, and they definitely don't like ones with power. Even with a life sentence plus seventy years, I still possessed both. Everyone from the guards up to the warden wanted me out of there. But not without coming clean first.

The day before my transfer, the warden at Somerset had me escorted to his office with no chains and no handcuffs. He was a middle-aged white male with short cropped brown hair and a large round nose, not too different from a TV sheriff from the shows of my youth. His face seemed flushed all the time as though he drank heavily, although I never smelled alcohol on his breath.

Over two years, we had built something resembling a relationship; not personal, but based on respect. I had run the library like a professional place, and saved him money by doing it for free. He also recognized that I had become a fundamental aspect of the inner security of the jail, solving and squashing inmate problems on my tier. We sat down across from each other at his desk, an approximation of man-to-man. It was a stilted and one-sided conversation, with me saying little and him trying to keep the balance between apology and deniability.

"Listen, Isaac," he said, like we were a couple of colleagues. "I know you had a hell of a time here."

He waited for me to respond, but I didn't. I didn't know what was safe to say, whether his office was bugged, or what this was all about.

"Now to be fair," he continued, "I have to admit that I'm the cause of some of that, some of the guys that came on your wing—that was"—his eyes wandered the room as he searched for the word—"by design. To cause you some problems."

I nodded. I wasn't surprised at all at what he said—just the fact that he said it.

"Anyway, I just want to apologize for that and wish you well," he said, his eyes direct and serious. "Good luck."

I don't know if he was pressured into doing it, but I gave him credit. At some point a grudging affinity had sprouted between us. He wasn't a bad guy, just a man doing a thankless job. I think he admired the way I fought, the way I refused to back down from an impossible situation. Maybe he had his own sense of justice and appreciated what I was doing for other inmates. Maybe he just wanted me to leave without any issues.

No matter how much status I gained in there, there were things to remind me of how little control I had over my body. You never get over not being in charge of your own movements, of being grabbed and handled by other people, of feeling like an object belonging to an authority like the state. After being processed out, I passed into the custody of the transport officers. One, a thin-lipped white guy with a substantial paunch, had my commitment order. He looked through the papers, and handed them to another officer who escorted me through the back double doors onto the transport van.

It was a dingy cargo van, retrofitted with a caged wall to separate the driver and backseat passengers. In the back were torn upholstered benches along each side, with bolt hinges along the walls to fasten the long chains that allowed arm movement. The van could hold at least twelve prisoners, but I sat there alone in my orange jumpsuit, on a high-security escort with marked patrol cars leading and following us. The display was overkill, like I was some kind of master criminal or caged wild animal. The whole procedure was ridiculous, a tail-wagging-the-dog situation. I had to be a threat to society; after all, look at the level of security required just to bring me downstate. Like so much about the world of corrections, it was a charade, something that made no sense dressed up to look like public service and safety.

As we headed onto the highway, with Somerset County vanishing in the distance, the passenger officer shuffled through my file. He was a lanky Black guy with wiry limbs and a high-pitched voice. "Drug kingpin, huh," he said, sounding out the words in his mouth like they conferred status. I thought about how this title was desirable in some worlds, though it was like a boulder chained to my foot. "Damn, they got you for a long-ass time," he said, setting the file down on the middle console of the van. Then he half turned to look at me. "Guess your parole officer hasn't even been born yet, huh?"

I stared at the back of his head through the mesh cage, but didn't answer. I had nothing to say. What I thought: *He'll probably never be born.*

That ride for me had a dreamlike quality, like a short stay in an in-between space, a visit to purgatory. Not free, but not inside. Frozen in place but whizzing down the interstate. Alone, but surrounded by my own cadre of security officers.

I stared through the metal cage, past the officers' heads, out the dirty windshield into the world.

Jail is a colorless place and being locked in had left me in a literal and psychological darkness. My marriage was slowly breaking, my family grieved for me like I was dead, and my little girl was a thousand miles away. But at sixty miles an hour on a four-lane Jersey highway, the world outside revealed itself to me in all its beauty. It felt more vast, more promising than it had been in my mind. The greens were sharper, the blues more majestic. I closed my eyes and basked in the sliver of sun, glorious even filtered through thick and dusty windows. I watched the faceless and blurry go on with their lives, headed for places no longer available to me. My mind flicked through distant memories of a man who once was, a life once lived. The sky was wide like it went on forever, and the trees grew higher than any man could reach. You forget: the world is gigantic.

My childhood had taken me around the world and my business had taken me to the top. But after years of being trapped in that cell, I had forgotten the size and scope of it all.

It was yet another thing they had taken from me.

In the evening, we pulled into Trenton State Prison, the stone fortress stretching out haunted and unforgiving in the dusk. The oldest section of the prison dated back to the late eighteenth century, making it one of the oldest operating prisons in the country. The newer section, taller redbrick buildings along the prison's back edge, didn't look too different from some of the housing projects I knew from Harlem and Queens. It was a resemblance that struck me as far from a coincidence.

Trenton was the state's only maximum-security facility and it housed the most dangerous people—serial offenders, violent criminals, and undiagnosed sociopaths—in the state. It had also been the home of exonerated boxer Rubin "Hurricane" Carter, who was framed by cops and prosecutors for a triple murder he had nothing to do with. He spent nearly twenty years in prison, and was finally freed in 1985. I wondered how many other Hurricane Carters were on the inside whose stories never merited a single mention in the newspaper.

After going through a series of manned gates, the van passed the threshold into the intake bay of the prison. The sound of the garage door closing behind us was like the scattering of dirt across a coffin. The driver passed along my custody papers to a man behind bulletproof glass, like they were exchanging data on a shipping container.

I couldn't hear the resounding noise of the prison but I felt it, like a beast coming awake. It was like an imperceptible shaking in the ground. I can't say I was afraid because I had reached a mental state, back when I was a kid, where I refused to feel fear: it accomplished nothing and singled you out in a place where everyone was trained to smell it. I had taught myself to shut down when the emotion started to develop deep in the recesses of my nervous system. By killing it at its root, it never got a chance to sprout.

The passenger officer swung open the back doors, and unchained me from the van wall without a word. The friendly chitchat had vanished and neither officer even made eye contact with me as I was escorted out. I was put in heavy shackles, cold to the touch in the airless and tepid heat of that garage. The officer behind the streaked glass looked at my photo and then up at the real thing.

"Isaac Wright Jr.?" he asked.

I nodded.

"I need you to speak, son."

"Yes . . . yes, sir." I hadn't spoken for hours and my voice came out unrecognizable, like someone else's. A sudden buzz startled me and I was brought inside into a holding cell. I waited for maybe minutes, maybe an hour. Time collapsed. I felt like a newborn child. I felt a hundred years old.

The word *incarcerate* shares a root with the word *cancel,* to cease an object from existing. That's the government's intention with prisoners. You are an irritant that won't just go away, so you're treated as a pariah. They have to look after you, but they resent it. Society has written you off, but your body is still there and they are responsible for it. You are kind of like a ghost.

Two bulky guards ordered me to strip and then conducted a body surface and cavity search, where they pawed and prodded me to within an ounce of my humanity. Any time I had to go through this, I would disappear somewhere else in my head, never letting the humiliation touch my inner self. It was like an iron gate I put up between their hands and my body.

When it was over, I was handed a laundry bag of everything I'd need: green khaki shirt and pants, underwear, shower slippers, deck shoes, and basic hygiene supplies, including a face cloth and towel. I put on those drab prison greens, carrying the smell of the men who wore them before me. Now I belonged, as interchangeable as anyone else in there, no matter what they'd done and what I hadn't.

I was escorted to a small room where I was interviewed by a social worker regarding my personal and family background and any issues I had that might result in problems for me or others at the prison. I was given a prison handbook, which was dropped in the laundry bag with all my other personals, and was taken back to a different holding cell where numerous other new prisoners—"fish," in the parlance—were being held.

About an hour later, two officers removed each of us from the holding cell and had us stand in single file in the corridor. All the new fish were duck-walked down a ramp, to the bowels of the jail. It was a damp and musty place not fit for rats, much less men. When we could go no further underground, we were marched to a line of stone squares: these would be our homes until someone upstairs got transferred, released, or died. It was an emergency housing unit carved out from administrative segregation (ad seg), the place where they stored the particularly violent or the perpetually misbehaved. We had done nothing to earn this, but prison is not like a hotel. There's no cell waiting for you when you arrive. This was one of the ripple effects of the War on Drugs and "tough on crime" trend from the mid-1980s into the late '90s, which led to the overcrowding of the prison system and the epidemic of mass incarceration. They had so many bodies they had nowhere to put them.

"Turn and face the cell door!" a voice bellowed. Then a

guard pulled a single lever to open all the doors at once. We each stepped in.

The man next to me started panicking, screaming. He ran out of the cell and screamed to the guard, "Where's the toilet?"

"In the back of your cell. Step inside now!" the guard yelled back.

As the scared inmate stepped back in, with one synchronous *clunk*, all the cell doors closed. He yelled again from inside the cell. "I don't see it. I don't see it!"

"It's in the back of your cell," I yelled.

"Oh my god," he screamed after realizing it was just a hole. "Oh my god." Then he went mute before returning with the mumbles of a quiet prayer. I spread out a shirt and a couple of books to cover the hole in the back wall, an action that perversely felt normal.

It was mostly quiet that first night down there, with none of the raucous energy that I'd come to associate with jail. The word *penitentiary* actually comes from the word *penitence*. In the early nineteenth century, Quakers built prisons to isolate the prisoner so completely, to provide such a solitary experience that they would have the time and peace to get right with God.[1]

In the darkness that night, I stewed in the nervous energy of the fish, the thick walls both ordinary and strange, the silence that actually had a sound. The change of scenery had made me restless. As awful as Somerset was, it had become familiar. That jail ran like a machine to which I owned a blueprint. I knew I'd have to do the same thing in Trenton, and trusted I'd get there, but the not knowing—who to trust, who to watch, who to befriend, who to avoid—made it hard to shut my brain off.

As I was finally drifting off, I heard a *tick-tick-tick* from above and then felt a crawling on my face. I smacked it away and turned on the lights of my cell: a swarm of dirt-brown roaches dotting the floor, wall, and ceiling scattered in the light. I grabbed my pillow and moved under the thin metal bed, only to be greeted by an enormous rat running along the walls from cell to cell, startled by my presence on the floor.

I just lay there, staring up at the bottom of the iron bed-frame. Sleep never came.

Part Two

OUT

Prison is a different planet, a world turned upside down. It has its own kind of oxygen and gravity, its own powerful rules and hopeless slaves, its own distinct wars and martyrs, rough morality and sin.

—Michael Morton, exonerated after spending twenty-four years in prison[1]

Prison is the very absence of normal.

—Jerry Metcalf, writer, prisoner[2]

Chapter Eleven

MONCKS CORNER, SOUTH CAROLINA
1977

WHEN I WAS SIXTEEN YEARS old, I nearly lost my life. One evening, my brother Danny was driving us in a passenger van home from football practice. I was a decent enough student, but football and track were really my world. I had made my bones the previous year as a high school star athlete in both the four-hundred-meter and mile relay teams. In football, Danny was the star running back while I played free safety on defense and wide receiver on offense. I took both sports extremely seriously and had plans to ride one or both to a college scholarship.

Danny was the closest to me of my three brothers, in looks, in age, and in terms of our relationship. But we were actually complete opposites. He was very cautious and conservative, a burgeoning young man in the mold of my father, while I was a little reckless and quick-tempered. I was always launching schemes and taking shortcuts, while Danny would reel me in, keep me in line, and set me straight. We were a balanced pair.

On the way home that evening, with the light fading, Danny was about to make a left turn into a juke joint on the side of the street to get a soda. The place was at the end of a blind curve and the traffic coming around it had no conceivable way to see a car stopped making a turn. Right before we turned, a truck plowed into the back of the van. The force of the crash knocked me back into the curtain rod that separated the front and back of the van, ripping it from the metal wall and knocking me out.

The next thing I remember was waking up in a hospital bed with a biblical headache. As I opened my eyes, the nausea came on fierce, like my insides were rushing to come out. I had a fit of vomiting that wouldn't subside until I felt completely emptied. An hour later, the doctor ran a few rudimentary tests on my reflexes, and was upbeat about what happened. "You were hit pretty hard and there's some swelling back there," he said. "But you're OK."

I didn't feel OK, but what did I know? So he sent me home.

A couple of mornings later, I woke up in my bed completely unable to move. My fingers and toes were so numb they felt disconnected from my body, like they belonged to someone else. I could move my arms but couldn't feel or move any of my lower limbs and extremities. The terror of it shot like a lightning bolt through me. In the South there's a myth of a ghostly old woman who enters your room in the middle of the night and sits on your chest until you can't move. It's called "getting ridden by a hag." That's what it felt like. Panicked, I started screaming for my parents, who came running into my room.

My father gathered me up in his arms, carried me to the car, and sped us to the hospital in Charleston. The doctor examined me and, though I still couldn't move, insisted there was nothing wrong with me. As my parents protested, the doctor pushed back, insinuating that the problem was psychological—like I was faking it or maybe mentally unstable. Then he sent us home again. Exasperated that no one was listening to us, my parents could do little but relent. My father carried me back up to my bed, the strain and fear on his normally implacable face so pronounced that I felt like apologizing to him.

When the movement didn't come back and the numbness didn't go away, my parents called an ambulance to the house. When we got to the ER, they wouldn't even see me. "Look," one of the doctors told my parents, "there's nothing we can do because there's nothing wrong with your son."

After that a switch got flipped: my mother went full-on berserk. She caused a scene in the entranceway, screaming for a nurse, a doctor, anyone to see me, to fix me, to do anything but turn us away again.

Then the patronizing started. A nurse came out of the ER and approached my mother. "Ma'am, would you—"

"My name is not ma'am, it's Sandra B. Wright! My son's name is Isaac Wright Jr. Before you say anything else, just understand this. If you came out here to do anything other than help him, don't even bother. We are not going *anywhere!*" The rage in my mother's eyes convinced the nurse to return to the ER without uttering another word.

My mom stepped back over to the front desk. My father was right beside her, remaining silent while my mom continued to unleash. "If a doctor does not come out here to talk to us about treating our son, there is going to be whole lot of people needing treatment!" she yelled. Her voice was cutting through the chaos of the busy emergency room. Nurses and administrators filtered out to manage her, but she refused to be calmed. The looks and whispers in that ER were unmistakable and the hospital staff came off looking like monsters. Security showed up to escort us out, but right then, another ER physician walked out to talk to my mother.

"Mrs. Wright," he said, struggling to remain calm. "We ran every test we could on your son in an attempt to find answers. They all came up negative. He did get a little banged up from the accident, but . . ."

"A little banged up?!" my mom screamed. "He can't move, you jackass!" Dad immediately reached for her arm. My mom was a Christian woman through and through, but Dad and I knew she was about to lose her religion. Impending havoc was always precipitated by a curse word.

"Where is your supervising physician on duty?" Dad asked.

"I am the supervising physician," the doctor said. "My name is . . ."

"We don't need to know your name," Mom interjected. "We need to know your boss's name."

"Please call your medical director," Dad added.

"I'll call him down right now," he replied.

As we waited, two patrol cars arrived and four police officers entered the lobby of the ER. They walked by us and the ER security followed them. About five minutes later a distinguished-looking man in a suit entered the lobby, accompanied by staff, and went inside past the front desk.

Within ten minutes they all came flooding out. The police

and ER security surrounded my mom and dad as the man in the suit spoke. He introduced himself as the hospital's chief of staff, explained that there was nothing further the hospital could do for me, and asked that we leave or be arrested for trespassing. As anticipated, my mom went off again.

"Don't tell me you can't help my son!" she said. "Don't tell me that! We are not leaving here until y'all do something!" An officer moved to grab her.

My father stepped in between. "Listen," my father said. "You're about to step on a Bouncing Betty. If you don't want gibs scattered across this hospital, I suggest you stand down." The cop stopped in his tracks, looking perplexed at Dad.

"You're military?" the chief of staff asked.

"Army," Dad answered.

"Nam?"

"Nam and Korea," Dad answered.

The term "Bouncing Betty" was one used by U.S. soldiers at war to describe a mine with two charges: the first propels the explosive charge upward, and the other is set to explode at about waist level. The term "gibs" is used to describe body parts that have been blown apart. Dad was speaking this guy's language. Unlike everyone else in the room, the hospital chief of staff understood him.

"There is nothing more we can do at our facility," the chief of staff said. "However, there is a new medical scanner called a CT scan. It's much more effective and thorough at finding anomalies in the body than anything we have here. Unfortunately, no hospital in this state has one. The closest hospital that has this particular scan is in North Carolina. I'll make the arrangements."

The hospital admitted me. Within twenty-four hours they loaded me onto a helicopter and flew me to a hospital in Wilmington, North Carolina.

What they found in the CT scan was that I had a cerebral hematoma—bleeding in my brain—which had clotted. The blockage was preventing the flow of oxygen, which damaged brain cells, which in turn paralyzed me. Had they let it go much longer, I would've been past the point of saving. I was whisked away in a gurney into emergency surgery where they drilled a hole in the back of my head to relieve the pressure. My mother's outburst—and my father's quick thinking—ended up saving my life.

The accident ended my athletic career and, in my mind, my entire future. To recover, I was sent to a pediatric rehabilitation center in Fayetteville, North Carolina. I was devastated, distraught, and pissed off at the world. I took my anger out on everyone and everything—my family, other patients, doctors and aides, any visitors. My resentment about the unfairness consumed me so completely. I was like nothing but this hard kernel of rage that writhed and pulsated.

After one particularly frustrating session with a physical therapist, where I snapped at her for doing nothing but her job, I saw myself the way she did. My rage was ruining my life more than the accident ever could. It was keeping me stuck in place, on my back counting the holes in the ceiling. I got a glimpse of what the future held and I found it simply unacceptable.

After that, my anger appeared differently to me, not a weight pinning me down, but a fuel that I could use to power my recovery. I began to hate the injury more than I hated anyone or anything else, despising it too much to let it win. Doctors calmly explained to me and my parents that I would never have full mobility, would never again move properly. Unintentionally, they were giving me all the motivation I needed. I'd never been one to listen to other people's predictions about what I could or couldn't do. It could be exasperating to others, and exhausting for me, but that quality was what would get me out of there. And I knew it.

The facility was filled mostly with teenagers with football injuries, paralysis of one form or another. The worst was Dorsey, the only other Black kid there, a high school running back paralyzed from the neck down. Dorsey had no movement at all and could do little but speak and make facial expressions. But he had a brave, warrior spirit that all of us could feel. There was also David, a hulking teenage linebacker who was pushed at a pool party into shallow water and broke his neck.

Despite our situations, we were still just kids and a camaraderie formed among us. On boring days, we had wheelchair races and taught each other how to pop wheelies. I became very close with Scott, a high school quarterback whom I watched fight to get out of his wheelchair with every fiber of his being. Watching Scott day in and day out, struggling on the bars to walk again, elevated what I thought of as my limits. It punched a hole in the ceiling of my expectations.

It took a full year but I finally regained mobility. At first, I had to walk with Canadian crutches, which are cuffed around the elbow, and heel boots, which have a metal guard that wraps around your calves and a spring that kicks the front of your foot up when you lift your leg. I remember when they were fitting me for them, they told me I'd eventually get used to them because I would have to wear them for life.

They didn't know what I knew.

There was this thing inside of me that I couldn't shut off. It was both a virtue and a curse. I carried a resentment to anyone who didn't treat me right, anyone who challenged me. I was driven by a desire to prove them wrong or to win long after they stopped caring. Though I had never been the biggest or toughest kid, very few people messed with me. Even my own siblings—far bigger than I was—refused to fight me. They didn't want to deal with the fact that a fight with me didn't end. I would keep coming and coming until they gave in, which was my secret weapon.

The fight was never over until I won.

Two or three days merged together in a blur. While still in the emergency housing unit with the rest of the new fish, I got a visit from a veteran prisoner who went by the moniker "New York." He was tall and slender with short-cropped hair and the wisps of a mustache. New York had a jittery energy and a savviness that I could tell came from time on the street, hustling in one way or another. He talked rapid-fire about himself, about the ins and outs of Trenton, about his people on the outside. Then he deftly shifted the conversation to what he'd heard about the work I'd done up in Somerset. Figuring he was just making conversation, I didn't respond beyond one-syllable answers.

"OK, cool. Cool," he said, wrapping up. "Yeah but, so, just so you know, I'm with the Inmate Legal Association."

He looked at me as though I was to respond, so I just nodded.

"OK, right," he continued, "so the ILA is the prisoner paralegal group here and we do a lot of work with motions, appeals, courtline hearings, and the like."

I wasn't even aware something like that existed. When he made an offer for me to join, I played noncommittal. "Maybe," I said. "I'll think about it."

I needed the lay of the land before I jumped on anything, and all I'd seen of this place was the dungeon.

"All right, cool," New York said. "Sure, sure, I get it. Just so you know, though, as soon as you sign up, I can get you out of here and into a cell within a few days. You'll also have an office to work out of up on the balcony."

New York dropped this line, knowing it would get me to bite. My cell was a hellhole and I would've signed up for anything just to get out of there. The next chance I had, I joined the Inmate Legal Association as a paralegal. At the time, it was just a way out of the jail's basement, a rope to pull myself out of there. But it would become so much more.

I was moved to the West compound, to a section called 7 wing. Seven wing was part of the original prison complex dating back to the 1830s, when the building was originally a high-ceilinged horse stable. The catwalks were long and narrow; across from the cells was a metal cage that climbed from the balcony to the ceiling. The fencing was newly installed because inmates had been throwing heavy items—sometimes other prisoners—off the balcony onto the floor below.

Seven wing was stone and cement and mechanical, a relic from pre–Civil War America. The new wing, the tall brick buildings I saw when I first arrived, had been modernized to comply with federal law: automatic doors with windows, stainless steel toilets and tables in the cells, individual shower stalls. But the West compound was grandfathered in, built long before modern correctional facilities even existed. In that archaic and crumbling compound we were stuck in time, abandoned in a place where progress itself didn't penetrate. It was like the earth didn't spin for us at all.

My cell was maybe a foot wider than the one in Somerset, with an old ceramic toilet extending from the white stone wall, an aged concrete floor, and a single lightbulb hanging from the middle of the ceiling. It was like every cell I'd ever been in: hard, old, and lifeless.

Most of the inmates there kept their cells freshly painted. Some put throw rugs on the floor and affixed homey ornaments or installed shelves on the walls in search of some level of comfort. But I bristled against any effort to bring comfort to that cell. In my mind, comfort was the enemy, antithetical to my purpose; I *sought out* the friction. I could have put in a complaint to get my cell fumigated, but I opted to kill the roaches myself. Having to stomp and sweep them out of my cell became a ritualistic process, a gratifying reminder that I was in the shit and the only way out was with my own feet.

My cell was ugly, uninviting, and undesirable because I

wanted it to be. I didn't want to ever be tempted to let up. To fall back. To get complacent. In my mind, I had to make sure that I slept in the trenches, on the front lines—where I could keep tabs on my enemy, one eye always open.

The justice system moves at a glacial pace, especially for the already convicted, so I buckled down. I had an appeal in the works and a lawsuit filed against Somerset prosecutors and detectives, but it would be years before those things bore any fruit.

I had to do more than just cross off days. For one, that kind of waiting game, which removed all agency from your life, was a shortcut to crazy. Secondly, my eyes had been opened to what the system actually was. In a place without hope and without the tools that would bring any, I saw I had a role to play. Trenton was home to some of the worst criminals in the country, but like all pens, it was also a place where injustice flowed downstream, mostly pooling around young Black men.

As an official paralegal at Trenton, I had access and opportunity to meet hundreds of inmates and learn their stories. Of course, many were guilty, but they didn't lose their rights or humanity because they'd committed a crime. If a prisoner seemed to have a particularly violent past—especially against women or children—I steered clear, but overall I didn't prejudge them. I knew that there were also crimes being committed against them, by the state, in this very place. And those crimes could be harsher than anything they had done on the outside. This was at the height of the War on Drugs, when nonviolent offenders had come up smack against a cruel and disproportionate system. I saw how little they knew, how some of them were rotting in there for no other reason than poverty, skin color, or the unchecked power of their own Nicholas Bissells.

Early on in my time with the ILA, I had a brief interaction that had a disproportionate impact on me. I was in the law library getting books to bring up to the paralegal office when an inmate beelined for me. He was young but frail looking with big saucer eyes and a front lip that drooped down. In his arms was a haphazard stack of case materials, books, notes scribbled down, and photocopies of case law. He walked up to me and tried to hand me everything.

"Sorry, man," I said. "I gotta head back to the office. But just fill out a slip and—"

"Yeah, yeah. I know," he said. "I'ma do that." There was something childlike about him, an innocence. "But could you just . . . just look at what I got?"

I put down my stack of books and took his materials. As I sat down and read through it, my heart sank for this guy: it was clear he didn't know what he was doing. But more importantly, he didn't even *know* what he didn't know. From what I saw, his plea meant that he'd already screwed himself, but I couldn't tell him this. I wouldn't take away his hope. So I explained to him how to submit his case to my office and told him I'd take a more thorough look.

These men didn't have a chance in hell up against the system; they didn't even speak the language. I had long known it was an unfair fight, but my experience was teaching me how it's *intentionally designed* to be an unfair fight. The Sixth Amendment, which grants everyone the right to understand the nature of the charges and evidence against them, is a bald-faced lie enshrined into our nation's founding. A survey across America's prisons found that only 3 percent of prisoners were even considered "proficient" in reading and writing, much less able to understand the complexities of the law.[1] The law exists on a higher plane to ensure that only a select few can reach it. Prison is filled with people on the ground who can't even get a fingertip on it. My job was to reach in their place, help them seize the constitutional rights that their own nation had tried to strip from them.

No one gives a shit about a convicted prisoner—but *I* was a convicted prisoner, so I knew how meaningless that label was. The rest of the world has given up on them, so a legal representative becomes something elemental, their tether to the world. You are the reminder that they exist. That they matter. That they are human in the eyes of God if not in the eyes of their country. I helped people back in Somerset County Jail because it was no skin off my back to share my knowledge. But in prison I saw God's larger plan behind my predicament and I made a pledge to myself: I would become the man on the inside that I never would have been on the outside.

Without my even realizing it, the ILA had been setting me up for this exact trajectory. It turned out that New York had done a good job of hiding his interest in me. When he came down to visit me in the bowels of the prison to invite me to join ILA, he made it seem like a casual offer. But he had actually been sent there to draft me.

Up at Somerset, I was locked in a court case for my life that had made me feel shut off from the world. But my story had taken on a life of its own, traveling downstate in a way

I hadn't even understood. Prisoners tend to be more avid newspaper readers than the average person because the news fastens them to the world; it becomes their unbreakable routine, their daily visit, their bible.

Throughout the spring of 1991, my name and case were in the papers every day; prisoners at Trenton, at least the legal-minded ones, had been following it with the zeal of sports fanatics. It was abnormal for a defendant to represent himself in such a major case, and up against the county prosecutor, no less. Once my sentence came down and they knew I was headed for Trenton, the paralegals prepared to swoop me up for their team.

The ILA office was located on the upper floor of the custody area of the prison. In order to get to it, you had to pass through the central rotunda and its line of metal detectors. You then made your way up a flight of stairs that took you to an officer's station. After stopping at a window there, you'd show the officer your inmate ID and he'd check your status. Once cleared, he buzzed you into a door that opened onto a wide catwalk. All inmate offices—chapel, interpreters—were in this row. At the end of the catwalk were the two ILA offices. The first office contained the desks and workstations for paralegal staff. The other was the office of the executive director and deputy director of the ILA. The ILA at Trenton was a huge legal and administrative machine, with multiple offices of desks, fax and copy machines, typewriters and word processors, a full law library with updated legal treatises rivaling any you could find in the average courthouse.

The ILA setup there was not the norm at all. At the same

time prisons were filling up in the late '80s and early '90s, the money for educational, treatment, and vocational programs were heading for "virtual extinction."[2] The trend across federal, state, and local governments at the time was "to make prison life intolerable," according to a Florida congressman who pushed forward a bill trying to do exactly that.[3] It turned into an arms race because everyone was trying to prove how tough they were on crime, upping the ante, creating zero incentive for politicians to ease prison restrictions. The societal implications of this were enormous: 95 percent of prisoners at some point have to rejoin society and their experience in prison has been proven to affect their reentry and success in staying out of jail.[4]

Large, insular institutions don't change until *they have to*. Like all progress in the criminal justice system, the ILA apparatus at Trenton was the result of a protracted battle. A few years prior, Trenton ILA members just like me had filed suit regarding prisoner legal access and won. The court sided with them, mandating that the prison's paralegals have a dedicated work space and that inmates have "meaningful access" to the courts.* The very offices I came to every day were borne from the tenacity of fellow prisoners. I owed them my freedom to practice law, so I paid it forward by using it to help others stuck in there, some who would never see the light of day again.

Each morning I'd check my inbox at the ILA office to find

---

* *Valentine v. Beyer*, 1988. Emmitt Valentine was the lead plaintiff, a prisoner and member of the ILA; Howard Beyer was Trenton's warden, who would remain in that role for a year and a half after my arrival before becoming New Jersey's commissioner of corrections.

two piles. The first was a docket of prison cases—infractions that happened in the prison—which were adjudicated in courtline hearings. A courtline hearing was an in-prison inquiry that took place in a mini-courtroom on the premises of the prison. The second pile was from convicted inmates who had requested my help with their various appeals and motions in their criminal cases. The work I did on these was handed off to their attorneys to be submitted to the court.

In addition to my paralegal duties, I also taught classes for the ILA once a week in the visiting hall area. I looked at my position as an instructor as part of my mission. On one hand I was fighting for them to obtain justice. As an instructor, I was also arming them with the tools to fight for themselves. *Teach a man to fish* . . .

Knowledge expands when it's shared, so I did not hold back. Whatever I knew, I gave it to them. I wanted to saturate and overwhelm the prison with sound legal minds. I wanted it to spread to every prisoner I could, in hopes that they would then spread it to thousands of others. I was creating an army of inmates who understood the tools and weapons of the law. As Dr. King said, "Injustice anywhere is a threat to justice everywhere." Justice didn't exist unless everyone had equal access to it. And no one was going to give it to these men. They had to learn how to take it for themselves.

One morning, I went to visit a prisoner in administrative segregation who had requested assistance from the ILA. When prisoners commit a disciplinary infraction, they are separated from the general population in one of two ways.

The first, which is commonly known as "the hole," is called disciplinary detention. It is a brief stay in an isolated cell as part of an in-prison punishment where they're kept until a hearing on their disciplinary charge. The other type of isolation is administrative segregation (ad seg) and it is far more permanent. You could get up to a year in ad seg, but because they could add time for infractions while you were in there, they could restart that clock, keeping you there for extended periods of time, even permanently. Ad seg was a darker, damp, more isolated area of the prison. The ad seg prisoners were locked down nearly twenty-four hours of the day with a random opportunity to exercise or walk around in a small enclosed yard at the guard's leisure. It's a place where prisoners were warehoused as they rotted away.

I went down to ad seg to talk to inmates who had requested my help, go over the basics of their case, outline a strategy. This was a daily routine. First, I'd take the request slip to the control booth and obtain an access pass for ad seg. Once I arrived at the entrance booth for ad seg, I'd provide the names of all the prisoners I needed to see. The officer would cross-check the names with my request slips, note them, and buzz me into the wing. Then I'd make my rounds. Paralegals were not allowed to enter the inmates' cells, so interviews would take place through the cell bars.

On my way out, in an adjacent cell, I caught sight of another prisoner. Tall and silent, with dark skin, scraggly hair and beard, he appeared lost within himself. The inmate was shuffling his feet side to side, babbling to himself in a quiet whisper. At the time, I paid him little mind, as talking to oneself was not strange to see in there. But a few weeks later, I got a slip in the infraction pile with writing like a young child's, crooked and sideways letters that were indecipherable. The only thing I could make out was his wing and cell number in ad seg, so I went to see him. It was this same prisoner.

His name was Maurice and in the few weeks between when I first laid eyes on him and my visit, he had deteriorated precipitously. Time in ad seg is not like regular time. The days are endless, with no light and no contact, and each one feels like an eternity. For Maurice, those two weeks had been a quick and hellish spiral downward.

As I approached his cell from down the corridor, a fetid and sour smell assaulted me. It stubbornly hung in the stifling air. When I reached his cell, which was the source of the stench, I was stunned. Maurice was completely naked, covered in feces, which had dried on his skin. It stuck to his arms and legs, and he was sitting in a puddle of what could only be urine. His skin was ashen, like coal, and there were sores on his arms, legs, and chest, likely from the acid in the waste. It was difficult to approach him because the smell was overpowering and rancid. Clearly he had been like this for a while.

"Hi, Maurice," I said through the bars. "My name is Isaac Wright and I'm with the Inmate Legal Association."

He responded with a mash of quick and mumbly nonsense. He stood up as though he could tell someone was there, but when I tried to ask him basic questions, he would speed up his words way beyond comprehension, the gibberish pouring out of him like a rush of liquid.

When I got back to the ILA office, I looked into Maurice's case. Though clearly mentally ill, Maurice had been put in ad seg for throwing feces at a guard. As his behavior deteriorated in there, he kept getting hit with more and more infractions—including the catchall "refusal to follow an order"—while the guards did nothing to get him the help he needed. None of them bothered to understand what he was suffering from, and no effort was made to humanely address it. All they did was continue to punish him, day in and day out. Maurice was not a case of bureaucratic neglect, which is the norm in all prisons. He had been living in his own filth and waste, right in front of the guards' eyes, and they were doing nothing about it. This was deliberate and it was barbaric. In my mind, it was also criminal.

The severity and ubiquity of mental illness in prison is of a kind and degree you don't find anywhere else in society. According to the Prison Policy Initiative, 37 percent of U.S. prisoners report some kind of mental illness[5] and the APA estimates up to 25 percent of prisoners have a major psychiatric disorder.[6] Sixty-four percent of jail inmates and more than half of state prisoners report mental health concerns.[7] Judges have called ad seg "virtual incubators of psychoses,"[8] and psychiatric experts say it is "known to exacerbate symptoms of mental illness."[9] Any issue an inmate is already suffering from is going to be magnified and worsened in prison, especially in a maximum-security facility like Trenton.

Even if Maurice needed to be separated or punished, he should've been in the medical unit or a specific area carved out for those with mental health issues. It is cruel and unusual punishment, forbidden by the Eighth Amendment, to put someone like him in ad seg. The only conclusion was that the guards—and the administration—just didn't care. I had one brief meeting with Maurice nearly thirty years ago and the smell and the sight of him are still burned on my brain. How could guards pass his cell every hour and just ignore him? It's unconscionable, evidence of a broken and vicious system.

When you abandon a mentally ill person to a tiny stone cell with no human contact, no fresh air, and nothing to occupy his mind, it's natural for him to act out. "If a man in solitary confinement feels himself slipping," Dr. Christine Montross writes, "feels the reality of the world around him slipping, he seeks a response to reassure him, to anchor him to the real."[10] These basic psychological responses end up getting the prisoner *more* time in ad seg.* They're hamsters on a wheel, doomed, never realizing that they are the source of the spinning.

I researched how many prisoners in ad seg at Trenton had mental health documentation, went to the medical ward to investigate, and learned the procedures for how mental illness was handled there. What became painfully obvious was that the prison didn't distinguish the mentally ill from the non–mentally ill when it came to infractions and confinement of any kind. They were tossing prisoners in ad seg no matter their condition. I put in a request for there to be clearly defined procedures for separating and punishing the mentally ill, which was ignored. The administrative staff at the prison wouldn't change the procedure and they wouldn't respond to me. So after multiple requests, I did the one thing left in my power.

I took them to court.

---

* Montross also found that 85 percent of inmates in ad seg were there for nonviolent infractions.

Chapter Twelve

The opposite of poverty is not wealth. The
opposite of poverty is justice.

—BRYAN STEVENSON[1]

PRISON IS HARD RIGHT ANGLES and straight lines. You can
see the measurements, the planning, in each piece of metal,
each brick, each pipe. If light does come in, it's sneaking
in—through a high or small window, just a slice. Like con-
traband. The place is built to be both impenetrable and invisible. Nothing changes, nothing grows. All life in there is
suffocated, all brightness snuffed, all hope smothered before
it has a chance to sprout its head, as though it were the early
stirrings of a riot.

The prisoner's experience is piled up with irony after irony.
You're ignored when you need someone's attention and singled out when you want to be left alone. You are never by
yourself, though you are always on your own. You are completely forgotten yet constantly on display. You have to mind
your business while everyone else's spills out and blends together into a combustible mix. It's either too loud to think—a
cacophonous noise of banging, buzzing, and yelling—or too

quiet not to. You have all the time in the world, but every single minute drips, drips, drips the life out of you.

Prisons are built with a single purpose, to send you the same message over and over again. Everything and everyone inside of it are there to amplify and emphasize this message: *You are nothing.* That's it—day in and day out. *You don't matter. The world turns without you.*

Look how fine the world is turning without your sorry ass.

To some, the only sensible reaction to living like this is violence. Violence is a way to assert themselves, to take a stand, to own the space where they're standing. Everything of theirs has been taken away, tossed, and disregarded. But violence is a counterforce. It allows the prisoner to stand firm, holding on to this last piece of himself because his life depends on it. *Fuck, no. Not this. You're going to have kill me because I'm not giving up this last bit.*

I don't agree with it, but years in prison helps you understand a reaction like that. It starts to seem almost natural.

There are general rules to staying safe in prison. Mind your own business. Keep your mouth shut. Respect others and their space. *Do not* try to make friends. Friendship and camaraderie will come to you without you having to look for it. Do not seek out protection if you're not looking to be used and toyed with. Carry yourself like a man; be willing to take a beating, even a serious one, while standing up for yourself. Stay clear of the vices and rackets of prison life like drugs, gambling, loan-sharking, extortion, and the trade in electronic equipment and weapons. These vices will cause you to spend your entire bid in debt and in danger. Most importantly, never forget that you're a prisoner. Never get comfortable with the guards or the administration. It is the quickest way to lose your life.

Trenton was far more restrictive than Somerset, permanent rather than transient, and the population was way more dangerous. Unless you had special permission, most prisoners were kept in their cells all day except for a single hour in what was ironically called "the yard" and mealtimes.

The cafeteria was like the killing fields. We would line up in front of double barred doors as though entering a gladiator arena. Once we were locked in, there was no guard presence in the cafeteria, as no CO was paid enough to risk his life like that. There was a raised cage attached to the wall where a video camera would record what happened inside, but no one would intervene. That was just so they could punish people after the shit went down. Everyone congregated in groups, like with like, holding tight to those who had their backs: Muslims, Christians, Blacks, Hispanics, Aryans, various rival gangs. The new fish, or those without a group, stared silently into their metal trays, eyes alert like frightened bucks, just trying to get through the meal.

In prison, fistfights were rare. Those might happen among friends who had a disagreement, or dudes from the same neighborhood who got into it. But most of the violence was sudden and sneaky and over in a blink. You didn't square up with someone if you wanted to hurt them. You went at them with a weapon, often a shank, a piece of scrap metal or hard plastic sharpened to a deadly point. No one could even call it a fight. It could happen when you were waiting on line for cafeteria food or in the yard lifting weights. You could be lying down on the bench press, lifting a two-hundred-pound bar up and someone would appear, stab you in the ribs a few times, and walk off into the crowd. Before you even knew what happened, it was over. Only the blood told the tale.

You were navigating your life every second of the day, never knowing who was against you or why or what someone might have said or done. In the middle of the night, your cell door could open and someone could stab you in your sleep. That kind of prolonged paranoia and stress does a number on you. Some men were tight balls of fury, concentrated and wound up: you stayed away from them. Others were zombies, drifting through that space in a kind of haze: they stayed away from you.

Back in Somerset, I put myself on an island, blocking out the world of jail. There was a sense of denial in me: *I don't belong here, so I'm not here.* In prison, I began to do the opposite: I opened myself up to it, tasked myself with fighting the larger injustice that comprised all the smaller injustices like mine. I believed in the cause, but it also became a part of my survival. I worked to make myself valuable, irreplaceable, untouchable.

One evening I came back from the ILA offices a little late, right before count time. Everyone has to be in their cell for the count, no exceptions. I headed to the shower with a towel and a plastic bucket of clothes to wash in there. This was against the rules, but I didn't care; I refused to have my clothes mixed and washed with everyone else's. It was one of those small but necessary things that I wouldn't give in on.

The guard on duty, Fletcher, was a white guy in his early forties who looked a good decade older. His body was thin

(Top left) A family passport photo taken during my family's time in New York City, 1968. (Bottom left) A picture of my mother, Sandra B. Wright. (Center) My father, Isaac Wright Sr., in uniform. (Far right) My parents, circa 1994.

(Top, left to right) Walter D. Wright (8), me (7), Sandra B. Wright (29), Quinten W. Wright (10). Bottom, left to right: Steven J. Wright (4), Sandra J. Wright (4), and Paportia R. Wright (6).

My father, at 18, serving in the Korean War, 1952.

The grand matriarch of our family: My great grandmother, Eliza Hutchinson, Moncks Corner, South Carolina, 1972.

My grandfather, Walter Wright, St. Stephens, South Carolina, 1959.

My grandmother, Mary Gibbs-Wright, St. Stephens, South Carolina, 1945.

My great-grandmother, Myrtle Anderson-Hamby, grandfather Claude Hamby, and grandmother Rosalie Hutchinson-Hamby, 1944.

My grandmother, Rosalie Hutchinson-Hamby, Moncks Corner, 1937.

(Left) Veteran: My father at twenty-seven, serving in his second tour in Vietnam, 1962.

My father, retired from the military, working as campus police, North Charleston, South Carolina, 1980.

(Left) My mother's sister, Claudia (4), my mother (13), and their father, Claude Hamby, 1952.

First grade class photo at P.S. 104 in New York City. I am easy to spot in the bow tie.

Me, at sixteen, two days before the car accident that left me temporarily paralyzed.

Me clearing the bar at a Berkeley High School track meet, Moncks Corner, 1977.

Portrait of a Young Family: Me, my wife Sunshine, and our three-month-old daughter, Tikealla, New York City, 1981.

Me planting a kiss on my three-year-old
daughter in New York City, 1983.

My daughter, Tikealla,
riding a big wheel in
Moncks Corner, 1985.

Me and my daughter, Moncks
Corner, South Carolina, 1983.

Me and my daughter a week before my arrest, 1989.

My dancing group, Uptown Express: (left to right) Willie Cobb, me, and Donald Walker on *Star Search*, the *American Idol* of its day, 1983.

A poster from the Fresh Festival Tour, Chicago 1984, with Uptown Express on the bill alongside big names like Curtis Blow and Run D.M.C.

The Cover Girls, 1987 (left to right): Carolyn Jackson, Angel Mercado, and Sunshine A. Wright.

My RIAA Platinum Award awarded for LL Cool J's album *Mr. Smith*.

My RIAA Platinum Award awarded for *The Nutty Professor* soundtrack.

My RIAA Gold Award for LL Cool J's "Doing It."

Me and Willie, who called Bissell out on the stand after the prosecutor threatened him, Trenton State Prison, 1994.

Me and my daughter, age 12, in the visiting hall of Trenton State Prison (now known as New Jersey State Prison), 1992.

Me and my daughter, Trenton State Prison, 1996.

Me and my sister, Sandra J. Wright-Laribo, Trenton State Prison, 1995.

(Left) Me and a dean at my graduation (with a Bachelor of Science), Thomas Edison University in Trenton, 2002.

(Below) Ooh Ra: My brothers Quentin and Walter, me, my sister, Sandra J. Wright Laribo, my brothers Paportia and Steven, Moncks Corner, 2015.

Me and my daughter driving around New York City, 2020.

My parents, married for over sixty years, Washington, D.C., 2020.

and frail and his face was regularly flushed. Something about him reminded me of a Chihuahua, always snapping and yapping at everyone. Even though he had a desk and chair on the wing, he liked to stand, with legs spread apart and hands at each hip as he bellowed out orders like a plantation owner. Fletcher sat atop the CO hierarchy; he was the string that if you pulled, the rest of the custodial staff came down on you.

"Count time, Wright!" Fletcher's voice carried down the tier. "Get out of the shower!"

I yelled over the running water, "I'll get out when I'm finished washing my clothes!"

The shower was situated at the far end of the wing, below the four levels of tiers that contained cells. It was literally an open space with showerheads lined up side by side. The floors were cement with a few drains to collect the water. It was a completely exposed area where you were vulnerable to attack by anyone with a vendetta, a debt to collect, or a mood swing.

No one showered naked. Underwear and slippers remained on for two reasons. One, if trouble came to you, it did not catch you with your pants down and without something on your feet for traction. The other reason is straight men did not want to be looked at by other men in ways that made them uncomfortable, especially sexually. Contrary to popular belief, being gay is not widely accepted on the inside. In prison, it could get you killed. While homosexual activity exists in prison (as it does everywhere), it was dangerous to outwardly express, show, or expose.

"Wright," Fletcher yelled. "I'm gonna ask you one more time! Get out now!"

"I'll be out in a minute!"

"I'll put your ass so fast in the hole, you—"

"One minute!"

Most of the cells allowed its occupants to be able to see down toward the showers. Like water running downhill, all the inmates came to the bars to watch the showdown.

Back when I first got to 7 wing, Fletcher stood out to me. He had these drastic mood swings and a face that would go beet red without any provocation. So I started watching him more closely. Every day at a certain time, after we were locked in, I heard the distinctive sound of the opening of the metal drawer at his desk. No paper shuffling, nothing being jangled or sorted. Just the quick open-and-close sound of the drawer—*errrrr boom.* Then a few minutes later, again—*errrrr boom.* The routine of the sound told me something was hidden in that drawer.

One day after lockdown, I borrowed a circular mirror from the guy in the cell next to me. When Fletcher passed, I held the mirror out through the bars and angled it to watch him at his desk. I saw him open the drawer, pull something out, and then walk off out of view. A few minutes later, he came back to sit down, putting something back in that drawer.

I couldn't see the bottle, but I knew it was there. Fletcher would come on the tier drunk, harassing inmates for no reason, running his mouth like he thought he was a badass. I could've filed a complaint, but I didn't. If he left me alone, I was going to leave him alone.

But he wasn't leaving me alone.

I finished in the shower, grabbed my bucket, and started walking back to my cell. As I reached Fletcher and the stairs, I could see four other officers entering the wing. They congregated near Fletcher's desk, glaring at me as I got closer. I ignored them and kept walking toward the stairs.

"Wright!" Fletcher yelled.

I looked in the direction of Fletcher and the other guards.

"Get your fucking ass over here," he said. "You're going to the hole."

I stopped and turned toward them. All five officers approached me. "Place your bucket on the floor," one of them said, as he removed the handcuffs from his waist.

I did as I was told and turned around to be handcuffed. "Fletcher," I said, "since you're not going to allow me to put my things in my cell, can I put them in your desk drawer?" I met his eyes. "You know. The top *right* drawer."

He looked dumbstruck, just a wide-eyed flatland of a face. Then I gave him an opening. "Did you forget that you gave me permission yesterday to take a shower and wash my clothes if I came back late from work?"

"Right," he said, coming to. "Right." Then he switched back to slave driver. "All right, stand down! Stand down!"

"What's the problem?" one of the COs asked.

"Shit," he said, "I forgot. I gave Wright permission yesterday to wash his clothes in the shower. Too much shit to remember all the time. Uncuff him."

The officers released the handcuffs and left the tier. Fletcher just walked off. I picked up my bucket and returned to my cell without further incident. After that, Fletcher and

I had a quiet understanding that I could ruin him, so he let me be. If the shift supervisor found out he had alcohol in the building, much less around inmates in a wing he was running, it would've been over for him.

It didn't matter to me what vices the guards had or what kind of rackets they ran. As long as they didn't make trouble for me. As long as their misconduct didn't violate the rights of the inmates, it wasn't an issue. When the lawsuit on behalf of Maurice and the other mentally ill prisoners got going, I knew I was carrying an ace in my pocket.

"For nearly two centuries American courts had largely ignored the legal claims filed by prisoners," criminal justice author Joseph Hallinan writes. "Inmates were considered legal nonentities, devoid of most constitutional rights. They were, as one court put it, 'slaves of the state.'"[2] Things began to shift in the years following the civil rights movement in the 1960s, when prisoners—many of whom were Black Muslims—joined together to protest and fight the federal and state governments for basic rights. There were Supreme Court cases that shifted some of the power balance (especially *Cooper vs. Pate**), but the real catalyst for change in the prison system began in upstate New York in the late summer of 1971.

At the Attica Correctional Facility, prisoners were rotting

---

* This specific case was about a prisoner's right to read Black Muslim texts, but by taking on the First Amendment, the case became a larger issue. One of the court's key findings was that "the Bill of Rights applied inside prisons." (David L. Hudson Jr., "Encyclopedia of the First Amendment," MTSU.edu.)

away under budget cuts, neglect, racism, overcrowding, and out-and-out cruelty. They were denied medical attention and the "minimum dietary standards," given few showers, little water and toilet paper, saddled with unreasonable censorship and religious restrictions, and forced to navigate an "arbitrary" and "capricious" parole process, including a condition that they couldn't leave until they found a job on the outside.[3]

In response, a group of inmates worked to petition the commissioner of corrections for these basic rights. After being repeatedly ignored and punished for their efforts, they took over a yard of the prison. The inmates took guards as hostages, demanded that impartial observers be let in to report what was going on, and drafted a new list of prisoner rights to be negotiated by outside lawyers. One guard died from his injuries during the initial takeover, but none of the hostages were handled violently or even cruelly by the prisoners.

The uprising lasted four days until untrained state troopers stormed the prison and murdered thirty-nine people in a botched rescue attempt, which the state commission called "the bloodiest one-day encounter between Americans since the Civil War." The fallout from the incident, along with the retaliatory torture committed by the guards in its aftermath, was like an earthquake on the corrections system. It shifted the ground on the issues of prisoners' rights and legal access in America. As New York State Senator John Dunne noted at the time, "More has been accomplished in terms of penal reform in the last three days [of the uprising] than ever before."[4] Though they were prisoners, they were still patriots.

They just wanted their country to live up to its promises, even for its most disadvantaged.

I knew I was fighting in their long shadow.

At the ILA, we were ready to take the lawsuit all the way if we had to. Our demands weren't radical: We wanted the prison administration to recognize that there was a difference between the mentally ill and the general population when it came to punishment. We argued that there should be a separate procedure and location in place, so that punishing a prisoner for an infraction didn't precipitate their decline. Maurice, and many others like him, was caught in a cycle that the prison's cruelty and neglect was exacerbating. These inmates were trapped, living in a hell that ignored them until it penalized them for things far out of their control.

Our attack would take place on two fronts. For one, there's corruption in every institution and more so in those organized based on power structures: law enforcement, politics, military, and corrections. Trenton State Prison was home to a great number of illicit activities—among them a loan-sharking business and a gambling pool—run by the guards and known by the administration. A lot of my information on these underground economies came from the old prison network of lifers. Many of them had been there longer than any guard or administrator. They possessed that rare, valuable thing: institutional memory. They didn't go looking for trouble—they just wanted peace—but they knew what they knew. When I went digging, and told them what I was looking to accomplish with their information, they told me: *Have at it.*

The other prong of the attack was through the discovery process. A lawsuit is a powerful thing, even when the plaintiff is a handful of prisoners and the defendant is the state prison system. Because of the laws regarding discovery, the defendant must turn over all evidence; the defending party is laid bare. All the bureaucracy and red tape that holds together an institution is stripped away. I got a look at the sacred documents of the prison: custodial standard operating procedure (SOP) and administrative procedures. They had to turn over the booklet on the chain of command, the obligations of each officer, and the process of handling complaints and reporting infractions. It was like opening Pandora's box.

I learned how the administration was supposed to handle certain things and how they actually did. After I'd gone through it, I knew everything they knew, which put me in the same position as the guards and the administrators. The SOP showed no programs or contingencies for mental health issues when it came to punishment. I also got the histories of inmates charged with similar infractions, those with histories of mental illness and what happened to them, including those who never got out of ad seg. The records were pretty damning.

Probably the most dangerous tool the lawsuit gave me was the right to hold depositions, forcing anyone in the prison to answer my questions under oath. Public officials regularly have to deal with lawsuits, some of which are frivolous, some of which have merit. There are mechanisms in place to separate powerful people from having to deal with those suits. But the threat of a deposition is like a vise. Agreeing to it means opening yourself up to questions that will likely embarrass, trap, or endanger you. I could question them for hours upon hours with no recourse except an objection on the record. Nothing would be off-limits. On the other hand, fighting a deposition causes problems as well. When a normally insulated official seeks to quash a deposition, the plaintiff must explain why in this case and these unique circumstances the deposition is necessary. This would allow me to reveal what I'd uncovered during my investigation. Either way, the information was going to come out.

Improprieties at the prison weren't enough to win a case. I needed to argue that these improprieties—this institutional corruption—*directly led* to the neglect and abuse of prisoners. Here's the argument: As part of an illicit conspiracy—whether that's loan-sharking or a gambling ring—a codependency exists that ties the participants together. Think of the Mafia or even a couple having an affair. They are bound together in secret. It's a special kind of glue that affects everything in their relationship. If members of a conspiracy are colleagues, then the workplace, the job, and those under their care are affected.

For instance, a mentally ill inmate throws his own waste at a guard. Instead of sending him to the medical unit or to counseling, that guard writes him up with an infraction. One of the other guards witnesses it and his supervisor signs off on it. Just like the detectives who put me away, the COs look out for each other, don't question each other, sustain each other's lies, and protect each other's culpability. When those in professional relationships also have an *illicit* relationship, their professional capacity is corrupted. So the criminal relationship affects the work relationship, which in turn infringes on prisoners' health, well-being, and rights.

That was the battle plan, but ideally, I just wanted the warden's office to change its procedures. After putting in a request to the warden, I got no response. Then I called his office, and still, nothing. I left messages and never heard back. I don't know if he was ignoring me, hoping I'd just go away, but clearly they didn't know me. It became obvious that a face-to-face conversation had to happen for me to move the ball downfield. At certain intervals the warden along with a captain or lieutenant did the rounds of the prison. The next time he was due to come by the ILA office, I made sure I was there.

Howard L. Beyer was a tall white guy with receding red hair, a long face, glasses, and tiny little razor teeth. I saw he was chatting with the ILA executive director and I waited in the hall for him. When Beyer stepped out, I was on him. "Warden," I said, "did you get the requests about the lawsuit we're filing related to the mental health issues and disciplinary issues in ad seg?"

He seemed taken by surprise, slightly befuddled. Then he found his feet. "Um . . . yes, yes." The captain was already trying to move him along. "You know," he said, with the practiced nonchalance of a politician, "I just let my lawyers handle that. I don't really have time to deal with that."

His breeziness and his choice of words pissed me off. *Deal with that.* He was making his way down the hall when I called after him. "Well, I'm going to depose you," I said.

The warden pulled up. The captain and lieutenant behind him stopped as well. When he turned around, the glad-hander's glaze had dissipated. A flicker of anxiety passed behind his eyes.

"What's that now?" he said.

I stepped closer in order to speak quietly. "I think some of the things I learned about the administration and custody is going to be of concern to you," I said in my most practiced polite voice. "So before I get you in a deposition, I was trying to give you the courtesy to speak to you first."

I could see the gears working in his brain. "You know what? I'll get back to you." He touched me on the shoulder. "I'm on rounds so I don't have time at the moment. But I'll get back to you."

The warden knew a deposition was checkmate. Now he *had* to respond.

A couple of hours later a guard showed up at my cell to take me to the warden's office. I was cuffed and escorted out of the West compound to the front section of one of the newer buildings, everything shiny and automatic. I was brought up the elevator, down a long corridor, and into the warden's office. It was a space buffered by an alcove with a secretary and a sitting area. Inside the office, the captain was talking to the warden. When I arrived, the warden asked him to leave.

"Close the door on your way out," the warden told him. The captain hesitated, but the warden waved him off and he shut the door.

"OK, Mr. Wright," he said, shuffling some papers, "what can I do for you?"

I took a seat and told him about my visit to ad seg and seeing Maurice, how inhumane his situation was, and how long this kind of thing had been going on. The warden had this blank look on his face. "Sir," I continued, "I believe the reason why it's happening is because of some of the other things going on here. These issues in the administration are directly connected to these problems." I laid out what I found about the gambling, about the loan-sharking, about certain guards' behavior. His eyes shifted away and then back, but he didn't look surprised. Not about any of it.

"If you don't believe what I'm saying," I said, "I'll tell you exactly where Fletcher keeps a liquor bottle in his desk and you can send a guard to get it right now."

"No, no. That won't be necessary," he said. "We don't need to start throwing out threats."

"With all due respect," I said, "this is not an empty threat. I intend to ask you questions about it at the deposition. I intend to depose a number of other officers and administrators until we see changes. You can even—"

He held his hand up to silence me and then chose his words carefully. "I understand this lawsuit gives you the right to depose whomever you think you need to depose, but let me ask you something." He leaned forward, his practiced ease letting out a slight air of menace. "What do you think you're going to accomplish for yourself by doing that?"

I was surprised the warden would go the personal threat route, as I was so clearly not the kind of person that would work on. "If I was actually concerned about myself," I said, "I wouldn't even be here. This isn't about me. It's about humane treatment of mentally ill prisoners under your care. Some of your people may get pissed at you and I know you have to run a prison, but find a way to convince them that this is the right thing to do. This is your prison, which means these are your prisoners."

"I'll take it under advisement and—"

"Look, believe me, I don't want to do this lawsuit. I'd rather peace than war. But I can't stand by while prisoners covered in their own waste are rotting in ad seg, for years, because every response is treated as an infraction. We both know that's a punishment worse than what they can bear."

"Let me—"

"We can get rid of this suit today," I interrupted. "I want you to do right by these people. I just want the changes made. You can dictate how they're done, as long as we do something to fix this situation."

"Listen," he said, "just give me some time. Maybe we'll talk again, maybe not, or maybe this is something we're going to have to allow the courts to hash out. Give me a week and I'll get back to you."

A week passed and I heard nothing. So I started to prepare my deposition request. Early that next week, a memo came through the ILA office without any fanfare, detailing the changes to custodial policy. Officers were now required to record mental health issues they witnessed and report it to the medical unit. They would then refer the inmate to a social worker. The inmate would be given the option of being sent to a mental health professional to be evaluated. Unless the prisoner's infraction was a bodily threat, the guards had to first place the inmate in the mental health unit for evaluation and treatment. Then, a decision on their punishment would be made through the appropriate process.

We won—without ever having to fire a shot.

I never saw Maurice again. They shipped him out to a hospital soon after the warden gave in to our demands. After he left the hospital, he was transferred to another prison and I never got word about what happened to him. I thought about him, though. Anytime I saw a prisoner struggling with the hell that prison put people through, with the noises in their mind too loud to think, I thought of him.

After that, I gained a new level of respect. All the inmates knew who I was and what I could do. They saw I had influence over prison policy—a very rare thing. I was bad now, the one who struck fear even in the COs, even in the boss himself. I was the most dangerous motherfucker in there.

The infliction of physical pain or injury is an incomplete definition of violence. Unlike hand-to-hand violence between prisoners, which changes nothing, I was committing violence against an institution resistant to change. Those who ran that prison could see and feel its impact. It was akin to the violence that the words of a judge can inflict on a human being. We dress it up in elevated language, but the criminal justice system is a forum for the infliction of pain. This makes the practice of law an inherently violent endeavor. Prisoners understood that this kind of power was rarely something they could access. But now, through me, they could. It earned me a new nickname. They started to call me B.I.G.

When the day ended and it finally got quiet and the prison rumbling stopped, I'd think of my daughter. Those times with her had become much more special and precious now: our walks in the park, our trips to the Coney Island boardwalk, holding her hand while we crossed the street, struggling to do her hair during daddy duties. Every waking minute with her was now trapped in the recesses of my mind, which meant I could access them. I could go there. Those moments kept me together, served as my comfort while I slept and during the waking nightmare that was my life.

When I lay down at night and closed my eyes, that's when I heard it. "Daddy Duna," light like a breeze on the face: Daddy Junior. My father was Daddy; I was Daddy Junior, which she couldn't pronounce. So I was Daddy Duna.

I protected those memories and images like gold: no one could touch or take them away. In the dark, that's where I would go. As I fell asleep, I could hear it for real, like she was right there next to me, her high-pitched voice in my ear: *Daddy Duna.*

Chapter Thirteen

THERE ARE SOME WHO BELIEVE that the ends *always* justify the means. As far as they're concerned, the means may even be irrelevant. There's a reason why prosecutors are so dead set about getting that conviction, often to the exclusion of everything else. Once they get the guilty verdict, it's pretty much under lock and key. There are stories you hear about successful appeals, reversals, and clemencies, but those are beyond rare. That's *why* they're news.

The sad reality for most inmates, even ones with a solid legal case, is that it's extremely difficult to get out of prison after you're convicted. The appeals process is a byzantine and bureaucratic maze that is overfilled and understaffed. The convicted carry the heavy presumption of guilt, the very opposite of what they supposedly had at trial. No matter what injustice they've faced, with a conviction they are nailed to the ground. The public believes in their guilt because it wants to. The court believes in it because it must. If the justice system stopped to consider how many innocent people are locked up, it would come to a crashing halt.

My appeal was particularly fraught. It was a high-profile

drug kingpin case led by the head prosecutor in the county, an ambitious man with well-placed friends who helped to make a career out of my conviction. And it happened during a time in America when those convicted of drug charges were slated to stay in prison and serve out their punishment. The War on Drugs had hardened even liberals' views of drug users and dealers and there was little sympathy or recourse for anyone mixed up in the trade.

The kingpin label stuck to me in the most egregious and penetrating way. When I opted to be my own lawyer, my case became even more politically charged, nearly electric. I was a young Black man going against the system on his own, railing against racism, corruption, and conspiracy. I was a raging fire in the halls of justice and it was imperative that I be smothered of all oxygen. The system had to strike me down as an example to anyone else with such audacity.

So like every man in there, I went through the appeals process, though I held out little hope it would be successful. In order to have a chance at freedom, I had to build a second front in my case. In 1990, before I even went to trial, I started the process of suing the prosecutor's office, the detectives involved in my arrest, and the state of New Jersey. On my way out the door of Somerset, literally, I got Amitrani to file the paperwork for my lawsuit. They had succeeded in convicting me and sending me to prison, but I pledged to keep coming back, like a ghost haunting them from beyond the steel-and-stone grave.

The lawsuit was strategic. Though the civil court was not likely to rule in my favor, I didn't see a win there as the only way to win. I understood enough of the intricacies of the law to see that the process *itself* could be my way out. Just like with the suit regarding mentally ill prisoners, a lawsuit would act as a giant fishing net. It would allow me to accumulate as much information as possible on the misconduct, mistakes, and deceptions of everyone involved in my arrest—from the prosecutors to the detectives. Then I would lay all the pieces out, get a look at the board, and figure out what my best move was.

Since my meeting with the mysterious Charles back in jail, I had been collecting information on how dirty Bissell was. My suit against the state, and specifically his office, was a reversal, a way to switch places and put Bissell on defense. It even got me on the radar of the higher-ups in the state, including the attorney general, who was representing the state in the civil suit as well as Trenton State Prison in my suits against the institution. Even though I was serving life in prison, I could still get the attorney general's office on the line. When prisoner #234266 called, they picked up that phone.

Trenton had an incredible law library, a vast open area containing every state and federal reporter, but it was empty most of the time. During that free hour, everyone was in the yard. The guards opened all the tiers and inmates would set out in single file, walking down stairs to the ground floor. As we walked out of the door, we entered a high-ceilinged rotunda—which had a metal detector we all had to filter through, single file like mice through a hole. We'd empty our pockets, go out another door on the opposite end of the rotunda, through a huge corridor out into the yard.

Yard was a misnomer. It was just an open slab of cement surrounded by twenty-foot-tall stone walls topped with barbed wire and armed guards on the corners. On the opposite end was a couple of torn weight benches and free weights. One basketball hoop and a few bolted metal tables sat near the wall. Inmates mostly just stood around talking or walking to get life back into their legs. Sometimes I lifted weights, but usually yard time was my version of office hours: I'd be talking with inmates about their cases, walking in a circle, chatting in a low voice, charting a course out of there. It was like every day we were planning prison escapes—but legal ones.

One day I had just come out onto the yard, the gray forbidding sky like a blanket, when I heard, "Yo, B.I.G."

I looked in the direction of the voice and I saw Ali at the north wall of the prison, trotting toward me. Ali was a slim Black dude with large eyes and an angular face who stayed to himself most of the time. He was in Trenton on a murder rap and lived on my tier. Ali was reserved but hooked into many of the notorious Black inmates in the prison.

"What's up, Ali?" We dapped and embraced.

"Yo, man," he said. "I was wanting to ask you this forever, man. But, you know, it's a situation that's definitely gonna bring you some heat so . . . I'm a little hesitant."

I waved him along. "Let's walk." As we moved, I scanned the yard. "Go ahead and ask, I ain't got no problem saying no."

"OK, sure," he said. "It's like this: You think you can help my cousin, O.D.? You know he's been in MCU forever and nothing's worked to get him out. I know it's asking a lot but—"

"Small thing to a giant."

"Word?" he answered, a little shocked by my nonchalance. Playing cocky worked for me, but it was also a type of theater: it lifted others' spirits, gave them something to believe in. I was not intimidated or afraid of taking on the task; in fact, I invited it.

"I'll go see him first thing in the morning," I said.

"You think you can get him out?"

I chose my words carefully. "I think I'll be climbing a nearly impossible hill," I said. "But you know, if I fail, it's not like I would have done worse than anyone else."

A blank look came over Ali's face. "You think it's a waste of time, right?" he asked.

"I didn't say that."

"You didn't say you could help him either."

"I'm not going to be the one making the decision," I said, "so I'm being conservative."

"Meaning, you're fronting on me right now."

I put my hand on Ali's shoulder. "I'm gonna do everything I can. If there is a way to get him out, trust me, I'll find it."

Ali was elated. It seemed like he wasn't going to stop shaking my hand and thanking me. When he finally let go of me, he patted me on the back and took off running, like a young kid going to play outside.

MCU, the management control unit, was the most isolated and highest form of segregation, utilized for the most dangerous and violent prisoners. No one got released from the MCU; it just didn't happen. The administration had nothing to gain by going easy on a "violent" prisoner, the guards certainly didn't want to deal with him, the public wasn't going to care how a convicted murderer was treated, and lawyers rarely succeeded in changing in-prison circumstances. A maximum-security facility was given a lot of autonomy about which prisoners were deemed dangerous and what infraction they may or may have not committed. Put simply, MCU was a one-way street.

Numerous attempts to get O.D. out of MCU had all failed. Ali saw his request of me as a Hail Mary, and understood that my attempt would be its own Hail Mary. Desperation is the coin of the realm in prison; if you threw a rock you'd hit someone who felt they had a million to one shot. So the downside was minimal. But if I succeeded in getting O.D. out of MCU, both of our lives would change. O.D. would be back in general population after years in a cage and he—and all of his people—would be indebted to me.

Everyone knew O.D., a hefty guy who had a notorious reputation in the street. Before visiting him I read over his rap sheet and complete file. He had been in jail for murder (and numerous other counts) since he was nineteen. Incredibly, he had been in the MCU for nearly ten years and there was no intention or plan to release him back into gen pop. What landed him in management control was a violent incident in the rotunda of the prison where he severely injured several guards, including a female guard whose face was bruised by his blow. It took the riot squad to finally subdue him. Already feared by the inmates, O.D. now petrified custody and the administration as well. As far as they were concerned, he was an angry Black man who had to be put away—if need be, forever.

But O.D. hadn't started a thing; he had actually jumped in to help a fellow inmate who was being abused by a guard. The prison code was that you did *not* stand around and do nothing when a fellow prisoner was being brutalized by a CO. In fact, if you did stand around, you'd be a target of the other prisoners who heard about it. So he acted—and he paid the price.

MCU was a pod located in the North compound, which was part of the new area of the prison. It had the feel of a high-tech lab experiment, with the prisoners as subjects. The officers' booth faced the entire pod, which was visible through a huge glass wall. As I walked into the pod, two tiers of cells curved toward me in an oval shape. The inmates lived in cinder-block cells with stainless steel toilets and automatic metal doors.

Dotting the floor of the pod were cages with nothing but a single table and chair inside. In order to eat, MCU prisoners were required to leave their cells and enter into an isolated cage to individually eat their meals at the table. Providing access to food trays and utensils could facilitate the manufacturing of weapons, especially if they were allowed to eat in the privacy of their cell. The cages enabled MCU inmates to be watched and recorded while they ate.

O.D. was in his late twenties, a stocky 250 pounds, with hooded eyes and short-cropped hair. When I met him, he walked with a demonstrative swagger, shoulders out, even around his restrictive cell. He approached the cell door with a hard look on his face, like a mask that had frozen into place. When I introduced myself, explaining that I was an ILA paralegal, he looked at me, at the papers in my hand, and then back up as if to say: *What the fuck do you want?*

"I'm here to discuss your MCU status," I said.

He heard me but was completely unresponsive. I began to give him my take on his situation, how he was in MCU for far too long without due cause, and that I thought I'd have a chance to rattle the cages, talk to the warden, and maybe get him back into gen pop. It was obvious he wasn't going to respond. After each thing I said, I would make an assumption about whether or not he agreed or disagreed, and said so aloud. If I thought he disagreed, I'd address it in a way that was designed to satisfy his concerns.

"It looks like you've had around four reviews since you've been here," I said. The wrinkle in his forehead suggested that I look again. I quickly flipped some of the pages in his file and saw that there were footnotes indicating that it was actually *six* reviews. "I'm sorry, six reviews." He didn't respond, just kept looking at the folder.

"You've attempted to get released a total of five separate times. And . . . it looks like you had attorneys at least three of those times."

I was starting to read his silent language. His raised eyebrows said: *Yeah, and?*

"And I can see," I continued, "that no one ever raised a 'cultural defense' in mitigation of your time here." He looked down, his head slightly tilted, clearly having no idea what I was talking about. He wasn't alone.

A cultural defense is a foreign legal phenomenon, almost completely absent in American jurisprudence. I came across it in my extensive reading of legal holdings and treatises, and the moment I learned about the fight that put O.D. in MCU, I recalled it. There was a 1985 unpublished case titled *People v. Kimura*, which involved a thirty-three-year-old Japanese woman in California who learned about her husband having an affair. In response, she took her two children and walked into the ocean, in accordance with the Japanese practice of *oyako shinju* (parent-child suicide). Though she was rescued, the children died and Kimura was charged with two counts of first-degree murder.[1] The Japanese community rose up against the charges, protesting that her response was a common cultural reaction to infidelity in Japanese culture. After getting so much heat from the Japanese community, the prosecutor gave Kimura a deal of one year in prison and five years' probation.[2]

Picking up on O.D.'s confusion, I explained: "Helping or protecting your fellow inmate when being assaulted or mistreated by a guard is a necessity of prison culture that could carry a death sentence if violated. You had no choice when you made the decision that landed you here. That was never addressed, probably because no one knew to argue it. I will." I could see some light pass over his face.

As I wrapped up, I asked him if he had any questions. He took a beat before silently shaking his head no, turning, and lying back in bed. He was so stoic and confrontational when I first arrived that I saw that head shake as progress.

I came to see O.D. two more times, updating him on my efforts, what legal recourse he had, what I'd try to negotiate with the warden, and he never said a word to me. He barely even registered my presence. MCU had done a number on

this guy. They had built walls around him, and out of necessity, he had built one around himself.

Some prisoners—especially those never getting out—have
no choice. In order to survive, they have to lean into their
identity as prisoner. There's no alternative of who or what
they can be, so they become something inhumane, someone who can exist—even thrive—in prison. Like an animal
adapting to a habitat, they become who they have to be.

The public has no idea how many people lose their minds
in prison. I watched dozens of people, some of whom came
in after me, slowly go insane. They'd arrive, seem fine in the
yard, talking and lucid. Then a few months would go by and
I witnessed the progression—their hygiene fell off, their hair
went unkempt, their skin became dirty. Then some more
time would pass and I'd see them in the yard, bleary-eyed,
gaunt, and mumbling to themselves, picking up half-smoked
cigarette butts off the ground. They disappeared completely
into themselves and never found a way out. Then they'd get
an infraction slip for not following a guard's order and end
up in ad seg, pacing in a box, slowly losing their mind.

When the outside world gets a glimpse of these inmates,
they assume that these are just the kind of people who wind
up in prison. Though there are those who come in mentally
ill, from my experience, observers got it backward: *it's the
prison that does it.* Yes, the people in prison are broken, but
it's prison that breaks them.

Prisons are dehumanizing places because they have to
be. The machine couldn't function otherwise. The more inmates are seen as people, the less that system can roll freely
over them. The prisoner's humanity is sacrificed, stripped

away, out of convenience. Dehumanization "is a psychological process whereby opponents view each other as less than human and thus not deserving of moral consideration."[3] It helps alleviate the dissonance between what we know about a human being and how prisons are forced to treat them. As reformed former prosecutor Mark Godsey notes, criminal defendants become stereotyped as "'evil,' 'guilty,' 'all the same,' and not worthy of individual attention."[4] This starts the moment they enter the system and can continue for decades. It's easier on the system, but also easier on everyone's conscience. There is no upside in seeing a prisoner under your care as human. In fact, it's likely to eat at you, keep you up at night. Best to deny them their humanity altogether.

The Attica Uprising was over fifty years ago but its resonance remains. All of it—the cause, the uprising itself, the violent retaking, and the aftermath—permanently shifted the ground of how we talk about prisoners in America. It also revealed that given the authority to do so, white law enforcement would freely massacre Black men. Predominantly upstate white cops put on helmets, took off their name tags, dropped tear gas on the unarmed, and then slaughtered predominantly Black men from New York City with such verve and abandon that they murdered some of their own.[5] That butchering, and the retaliatory torture of prisoners in the weeks after, is only one of the most famous examples of mass abuse inside the correctional facilities of America. But Attica was no outlier. It just shined the brightest light on a systemically abusive system, one that remained twenty years later when I was in prison, and continues to this day.

*   *   *

The fourth time I went to see O.D., there was a noticeable change in his demeanor. It had taken those first three meetings to strip away some of his armor. The moment I approached his cell, he rushed to the door, and his first words to me, the first he *ever* had said, were, "What's really up with you?"

The warden had come to see O.D., who—as was his way—refused to talk to him. By this point, Beyer had moved on to become commissioner of corrections, so his former assistant warden, Willis E. Morton, was now in charge. As Warden Morton walked off, O.D. heard him tell one of the escorting officers, "Have Wright call my office." O.D. had been suspicious about my motives and my chances, but those words from the man in charge let him know I was for real.

"I'm gonna get you out of here," I told O.D. at the start of that meeting. He leaned against the cell door, exhaled like he was burning off a layer. Then he regained his composure, stood erect, like he was dropping the resistance. "OK," he said. There was a whole world inside those two syllables. Looking at his eyes, I caught a desperation in him that he'd been trying to hide. I understood O.D.'s reluctance. He couldn't give himself over to the idea of hope. He had to protect himself.

"I'm gonna sit down with the warden and speak with him personally about your case," I said. "I think I maybe . . ." At that, O.D. turned around, walked over to his bed, lay down, and looked toward the ceiling, his hands behind his head.

I understood. *Enough talk.* Now I had to get it done.

On O.D.'s behalf, I filed a Notice of Claim against the prison, essentially a warning that a suit was coming regarding the unconstitutional imposition, execution, and indeterminate status of his detention in MCU. The threat of the suit alone would no doubt get their attention, especially because of my successes with Maurice and other cases. One of the major hurdles was that the female assistant warden, who was deathly afraid of O.D., was absolutely adamant that he needed to stay in MCU.

Through my network, I learned that the assistant warden was secretly Warden Morton's girlfriend. My intuition told me that the female warden was the emotional lever, and ultimately the main reason Morton was keeping O.D. in MCU. If O.D. were released and hurt someone else, Morton would be finished. He stood to lose both his woman and his job. I had to find a way to balance the ledger, to make letting O.D. out worth something to the warden.

Warden Morton was dark-skinned and a bit overweight, a slow mover who got tired on his feet. He had a broad face and large eyes that popped when he was angry or amused. When I sat down with him, I told him that were he to release O.D. to gen pop, he would no longer have any direct problems with me, legal or otherwise. He'd be free to administer the prison without the threat of legal ramifications or resistance against him, both personally and professionally. I would also keep him out of any future lawsuits.

Essentially, I traded my reputation on O.D.'s behavior. I gave the warden my word that O.D. would never participate in violent activity or get into any serious trouble again. As assurance, I put my job on the line, offering to resign as a paralegal indefinitely if O.D. screwed up. The prison would be free of me and my crusades for justice on behalf of the inmate population. I knew that Morton would take the offer to his staff, who would find it too good to resist.

O.D. was just one man, and the solitary man has no power in prison. So I advocated for O.D. by attaching him to everyone else. I made his case not about a single deal for a single prisoner, but about *everyone*. Morton told me he'd think about it, but I could see in his eyes that I'd gotten to him.

I gambled on O.D.'s hard-won wisdom that the embarrassment and diminished respect that would result from any fuckup would not be worth it. After I explained to O.D. that I had put everything on the line for him, he gave me his word. If released from MCU, he would be a model prisoner and protect my reputation with his life.

About three days later, I was in the yard when I heard someone screaming my name from the other end. "Yo, Wright!" I looked up and all 250 pounds of O.D. was rushing across the yard toward me. "Wright!" He gave me a giant hug and actually picked me up off the ground, as the other prisoners watched in awe. It didn't endear me to them—most seemed terrified of O.D.—but the respect for what I'd done was undeniable.

Prison is a complex interplay of rackets. The guards have their rackets, the other inmates have theirs. And I had mine. I was part folk hero, part gun-for-hire, paid in endless cartons of cigarettes, the hard currency of prison. After a while, I didn't have to indulge in the poison served up in the cafeteria. I'd put in an order with an inmate cook and my meal would be placed on my tray or brought to my cell. I was also given a cast-iron pot for my own cooking and snuck what I needed through the kitchen.

As a paralegal, I had access to areas in the prison most of the COs could not go, including death row. I knew about everyone's case, every beef between the guards and administration, and every prisoner gripe about both. I knew which cooperating defendant was being snuck out of the prison for secret conjugal arrangements, which informant was being paid on the sly, which guards owed money and to whom, who was helping Fletcher with the loan-sharking, which administrator was looking away from the gambling ring, whom Warden Morton was watching closely and who had free rein. I possessed the knowledge and, more importantly, the understanding of how to use that knowledge. That gave me power.

By my third year in Trenton, I had become untouchable, more protected than even the gang leaders because no one was looking to take me out. I floated among everyone. I sat at the cafeteria table and ate with Muslims without reprisals, even with pork on my plate. They didn't like it but they didn't lose respect for me because of it. Sometimes I sat across from the Aryans with their shaved heads and Nazi tattoos—some would leave, others would stay, but none would attempt to expel me. I mixed it up with the different groups who split up that prison like their own territory. My safety was secured by that ancient wisdom: *The enemy of the enemy is my friend.* At the end of the day, no matter how angry or violent a prisoner might be, he never forgot that we were all against the system itself. And I was the system's worst nightmare.

I thought of myself as a fighter, but also a corrective. By bringing the power of law to the dehumanized, I was working to rebalance the system. Everyone in jail saw the benefit in having a legal representative in their corner. It was only a matter of time before they'd have an issue with their case or would get charged with an infraction and sent to ad seg. On the outside, people who can afford to have a lawyer on retainer; it's no different in the prison system. I just got paid in my own protection and safety. But it was a two-way street. I needed them too.

The legal work I did in prison gave me a refuge during a time that didn't make sense, in a place I didn't belong. It gave me an identity and a purpose removed from that of just a lifer. I found a way to separate myself from my emotional baggage, my indignant rage at the world, and my heartbreak over my broken family. The work allowed me to be a version of myself that gave me strength, along with something I felt I'd lost, something like hope.

My parents, who were raising my daughter down in South Carolina, drove up to visit regularly. Mostly these were window visits, talking through a hole, unable to even touch. However, there were a few in the visiting hall in the prison, an open room with cheap linoleum-tiled floors and cinder-blocked walls painted a light blue. To give some life, or the approximation of it, paintings of flowers and nature decorated the walls. Rows of plastic seats lined together were reserved for inmates. Facing those were parallel rows of seats for visitors, with no tables in between.

At the end of the hall in the right corner was an area with a television where visitors could sit and watch while other family members conversed with the inmate. Beverage and snack machines stood alongside the opposite wall. There was an area where photos were taken (for a price) where you could sit on a long bench in front of a serene nature backdrop. Two to three guards were positioned at strategic locations in the hall so that they could observe all areas in order to eliminate blind spots. The entire room had a sterile feel, like a movie set or showroom. It was cleaner than most areas of the prison, and it carried a stilted air, the remnants of all the broken lives and families that had passed through that room.

My parents carried their increasing age and weariness on their faces. When they came to visit, we would talk about everything *except* my case. It was the oxygen we breathed, the lives we were living, so there was really nothing to say. I didn't have any answers for them, just my own plans, which everyone told me were crazy. The last thing I wanted to project to them was that I was losing my mind in there.

To an extent, I had been the bedrock of the family; each of my siblings at one time had lived with me and I knew my parents had depended on me for emotional support. If I dropped any more pain or fear onto them, it would only keep them up at night. I thought of my mother crying herself to sleep when I was kid from the strain of raising us all. Now I felt like I owed it to her, to both of them, to project normalcy. Our conversations were as regular as we could make them under the circumstances: about my siblings, births and marriages, celebrations and occasions. I had missed it all, so this was my chance to get an inkling of what was happening in my years away. The world had been turning without me and their visits were like messages from the beyond. It hurt to know I was missing it, but even experiencing it all secondhand made me feel tethered, a hugely important thing to someone behind bars.

My daughter was six years old when I went away. When she first came to visit me in jail with my mom and dad, her face would light up the second she saw me. She'd break away from them and come running to me, screaming "Daddy Duna!" She was every bit daddy's little girl. On the phone, she'd fight over getting to talk and ask over and over, "When are you coming home? When are you coming home?" I sent her birthday and holiday cards, gifts from the inside and through people on the outside, and she'd send back her kiddie pictures and scribbled cards. Back then, I felt like I was some kind of presence in her life, if an absent one.

But time goes in one direction. Every year is a lifetime to a child and I watched as she inevitably grew up and away from me. She got older and stopped sending things, or responding to what I sent. She didn't want to get on the phone as much, wouldn't even sit down with us on visits. She'd say hello, give me a quick hug, and then go sit in front of the television.

That was the most difficult thing for me, watching myself become a stranger to her. That distance accumulated as she got older, and it tore at my insides, to watch my only child walk away, grow apart, and not know me. She was an adolescent and then a teenager and I just wasn't there. I was her father but, at the same time, I was just someone she visited when they all had a chance to come up to New Jersey. I'm sure this was a survival mechanism on her part, a way for her to cope with the reality of her family. It's not like it came from a place of anger or blame. She was a child, and I was trapped in an institution designed to strip away bonds, encourage distance and disinterest, and turn loved ones into strangers.

I tried to be hopeful about it, but it weighed so heavily on me. In my darkest moments it was enough to break me down. In my stronger moments, it became motivation for me to get out of there. The fact that she always inquired about the next visit and always insisted to be there was revealing. She loved me and never gave up on me, but she didn't know how to act around me or what to say. The teenager left the little girl behind, but I didn't want her to completely forget who I was.

I pushed with everything I had to get a chance to mend what had been broken.

Chapter Fourteen

GROWING UP, I HAD A healthy respect for authority, the implicit dignity that came with it. The matriarch of the family, my great-grandmother Eliza Hutchinson, was the nucleus around which we all orbited. Eliza was a short and thin dark-skinned woman with silky black hair. She had graying blue eyes with a darker blue ring around the iris. Those eyes ran deep. When we got in trouble she'd have us go to a tree out front, grab a branch, peel all the leaves off, and hand it to her. She'd whack us with that switch and we understood that we had done wrong and promised to do better. The pain of the stick hurt, but the pain of disappointing her hurt even more. This was our understanding of justice.

Eliza was a pillar of the community in the literal sense of the word: she kept it standing up. Decades earlier she had taken care of the prominent white men (they were always white, and always men) in the community when they were young. Years later, once they'd been established atop the community's firmament, those same men would come to her porch to pay their respects. As a kid I saw people like the sheriff and the mayor come over and sit down with her, have a cold drink of tea, check in on her. Those images stuck with me. I understood what respect for authority meant: it first came from Eliza.

As I got older, and we moved around, that same understanding came from my parents, and from the way the military colored our home environments. My siblings and I spent most of our childhood just off the various military bases where my dad was stationed. The term military "brat" comes from the British acronym—British Regiment Attached Traveler. It doesn't mean "brat" like we use it in America, to mean spoiled. If anything, military children have to deal with an instability that makes them grow up faster.

As a social introvert bouncing around to different towns and schools, I had to teach myself some things that came naturally to others, like when to turn on that social mechanism. It was difficult for me to make friends because I'd learned they were fleeting. This was a painful thing to recognize for a time, but then it became a numbness. I was a little isolated, sticking mostly to myself or my brothers and sister, who often seemed like enough.

We called Wendell, the oldest, "the Gestapo" because he acted like he was in charge, especially in my father's absence. We all resembled each other, but Wendell had a darker complexion and was much bigger than all of us. Artistic, athletic, musical, and intelligent, he was the consummate general with prima donna tendencies. Before breakfast Wendell would hide all the forks but one for himself and lay out only spoons for the rest of us. It was his way of reminding us of his status. As we all grew up, he loosened his grip, though I always admired him and looked up to him. We all loved each other, took care of each other, but if there was a disagreement, we fixed it—either physically or diplomatically. In a big family, there's always infighting and competition. Those conflicts actually turned out to be positive things when I moved into adulthood, kept me sharp.

With three brothers close in age, there was a sense of protection and insulation in school. Being one of the Wright brothers gave me strength. We'd put our arms around each other and recite this military chant we'd heard around the base and adopted as our own. *Ooh ra.* We had each other's back, no matter what the cause, and stood together like a shield, knowing nothing could touch us. We drew strength from each other, and with my brothers tied to me, I could never be lost. I would never be alone.

Ooh ra.

The years flowed by and blended together, something that I had no idea years were capable of doing. When you are young, years take their sweet time, develop an identity, assert themselves. As you age, they slowly merge together. In prison, they just dogpile on top of each other, blending into one hazy blur. It was a maddening repetition of each day that could drive even the most stable person crazy. You know what's going to happen because it's already happened. You've already heard it. You've already seen it. The days mashed together into one long and painful single day, weighty and unrelenting. My life was walking in circles, over and over, day in and day out. I had to push hard to make it feel like forward progress.

Prisoners come to appreciate the value of routine, the protection and security that brings, but it eats at you. It's not the kind of life you should get used to. As long as there's still a voice in your head reminding you this is *not* normal, you still haven't given in. But the thought of giving in can lure you, like a drowning man succumbing to the water or the sick man to eternal sleep; it requires constant vigilance to keep it at bay.

Prison is full of ossified people, trapped inside themselves, haunting its cells. They are frozen inside someplace that no one else can get to. I started to see my role as more than protecting myself. I began to see it as a means of connection, of hope for those who hadn't turned completely petrified, not yet.

Of course, not everyone in prison deserved my help or my sympathy. These were the hard-core killers, the psychopathic, the bafflingly violent. I was familiar with survival violence, necessity violence. I didn't agree with it, but I understood it. However, Trenton's worst had been engaged in some horrific, unmotivated, mentally deranged stuff. It was literally incomprehensible to me, senselessly murdering random women or children, having no qualms and no reasons. Nothing could prepare me for the existence of these people, much less having to spend time in their company.

John List killed his wife, mother, and three children and evaded capture for nearly eighteen years. He was a tall, lanky man balding in the middle with a horseshoe of white hair accenting his head. List walked with a peculiar swagger— slow, his hips pushed forward, his arms swinging in cadence with long dragging strides. He wore black plastic-frame glasses that looked like antiques from the fifties. His eyes were round and slightly bugged out and his nose was large and protruded. He reminded me of a demented real-life version of Mr. Burns from *The Simpsons*.

List was a passive-aggressive racist and holier-than-thou sociopath. During the church service he would mock the expressive way the Blacks and Hispanics tended to worship. In the ILA office, he would refuse to even talk to any paralegals who weren't white. He would sit there for his entire legal-access period waiting for a white paralegal. If none showed up, he would lose his time, and get up and leave.

One time he was talking to Walter, a slender white paralegal at a desk across from mine. List was going on about the Black and Brown paralegals, though he used slurs to describe them. "I mean, why are these guys paralegals?" he asked Walter. I sat at my desk on the other side of the room and continued working as if I didn't hear.

"What do you mean?" Walter asked.

"I mean, c'mon. You'd think you're in a barbershop when you walk through the door."

"Well," Walter said, "you know we don't cut hair up here. I mean you're obviously not here for a haircut."

"At least I can count on quality work from you," List said.

My blood boiled but I stayed silent. Then Walter said to List, "You see that barber over there?" He pointed to me with his pencil. "He taught me everything I know. Everyone in this office attends his classes. I haven't met a better lawyer."

List didn't even look at me. "Eh, he's not a lawyer," he said, dismissively waving a hand at me.

"You know what?" Walter chuckled. "He's actually better."

List couldn't stand the idea that a Black man could be superior in anything. It seemed to go against his entire belief system. He got up and walked out of the office without saying another word.

Then there were guys like Bobby Bisaccia, a Mafia hit man and captain under John Gotti in the Gambino crime family, who was actually a pretty funny guy. In fact, Joe Pesci based his iconic *Goodfellas* character—"I'm funny how, I mean funny, like I'm a clown? I amuse you. I make you laugh?"[1]—on Bisaccia, who was a childhood friend of Pesci's back in Newark. Bobby, who had sloping shoulders, a dimpled chin, and big ears, joked from time to time, but he also had this serious edge that he could turn on in a blink. Balding in the center, with a speckle of gray hair on the sides and glasses, Bobby was a very outspoken guy, diplomatic in the way he approached people.

When he came to the balcony, he'd usually be sitting in the small office of an inmate coordinator named Gary Messina. Gary's office was a small open area on the right side of the ILA office and I'd have to walk by his office to get to my desk. Oftentimes, Bobby would be sitting there, flanked with three or four of his lieutenants, like the mayor holding court. He'd always greet me and shake my hand as I walked by, asking things like, "What case you working on today?" He had an extensive network in the prison and if I had gotten a good result for an inmate—either in prison or in court—he always knew about it. Bobby was personable to me and I think he appreciated my tenacity, especially considering my success rate.

Richard Biegenwald had a large melon head and reddish beard speckled with gray elongated at his chin. He had been on death row twice but had both sentences thrown out. Known as the "Thrill Killer," because he murdered people for fun, Biegenwald was the subject of many books and fascination. Though I was usually cordial with people, I did not hide my distaste for Biegenwald, who sought out and killed young women.

Biegenwald and a paralegal named David Russo were once in the office talking near my desk. Russo was a smaller guy with a rectangular face and speckled, duck-tailed hair. He was serving life plus twenty years for killing someone and seriously wounding two others during a gas station robbery. Russo was surprisingly personable, articulate, and well-mannered in comparison to his crime. Biegenwald was going on and on to Russo about his own case, how he was wronged by the system, how he was screwed by the lawyers, how he wanted another trial.

As I listened to all this, my frustration with my own case came to the fore and I became infuriated. Biegenwald was not only guilty as sin, but he was also a lowlife as far as I was concerned. It was people like him that made it harder for those who were really innocent. I couldn't take it anymore.

"You know what I don't understand about people who murder women," I said. "Except for the fact that they're fucking cowards, they're the first ones to beg for their fucking life. They go out and kill a bunch of innocent people, and they're the first ones who beg for their life when it's their time to die."

"Yeah, that's true," Biegenwald said with an eerie calm. "I

would beg for my life too. You know why, though? Because if I was spared, it would give me a chance to go out and kill some more people."

There was a tension and threat in his voice. I looked back at Russo, who was just laughing at the tension. The way I saw it, I had two choices: pick up one of the desk chairs and beat Biegenwald within inches of his life or walk away. I got up and left. I couldn't stand to be in the room with him and the longer I stayed, the chances grew that I would have gone for the chair.

I made a point of being able to interact with anyone and everyone, but you can't get through to someone like that. You're staring into a darkness and nothing stares back. I don't understand that void, so I didn't even try. A man who felt another's life had no meaning was beyond my comprehension. I had worked every waking hour in that prison because I believed the exact opposite.

I didn't really need a reason to go off on Biegenwald, but on that particular day I was frustrated, agitated, even a little panicked. In the mail, I had just received copies of motions from the various defense attorneys in my civil trial—lawyers for the various townships, counties, prosecutor's offices, other lawyers, cops, and public officials I was suing—informing me that they were trying to get the civil case tossed out. The reason? Unauthorized practice of law.

Let me explain: when I filed this lawsuit against the state of New Jersey and its municipalities, I was not the sole plaintiff. Sunshine was suing as well—they had lied to her, told her she'd get probation, manipulated the tapes to make it appear that we were in a drug conspiracy together. This scheme was designed to get her to take a plea—to intimidate her about her chances of winning before a jury. I insisted that she take the plea and warned her that none of them were to be trusted and to refuse the plea if anything seemed out of place. Once they got her into the courthouse for the plea, her lawyer assured her that she would get probation for the third-degree offense she would plead to as a first offender. But, in collusion with Bissell, Sunshine's lawyer drew up a plea that left the discretion for sentencing up to the judge. At the hearing, her lawyer argued for probation. Bissell stayed silent, making no argument on behalf of the state and, as planned, Imbriani slammed her, sentencing her to five years in prison.

When I heard what they did to her, I knew the hatred they had for her was grounded in their profound hatred for me. They were punishing me through her. She was owed as much recourse as I was, so we sued together. Right as I was leaving for Trenton State Prison, my standby counsel, Paul Amitrani, delivered the paperwork for our lawsuit and filed it with the court. After that, we were on our own.

However, when you are a named plaintiff in a case, the correspondence is like an avalanche. There are literally hundreds of responses, motions, and documents that you need to write, fill out, return, respond to, and deliver. Sunshine had no legal training, and no lawyer in the state would touch our civil case, so what choice did she have? What choice did I have? So I wrote all the motions for her, and signed her name, sending in anything she needed submitted to the court.

All the defense lawyers in the civil case, ten or so attorneys representing around thirty people, jumped on this. The unauthorized practice of law is a very serious breach in the court system, so they were all motioning the judge to throw out the civil case. They were claiming our lawsuit was contaminated.

I had done plenty of legal work in jail and prison but that was all within bounds. Pro se, representing myself, was protected by the Constitution. I could represent fellow inmates in courtline hearings for infractions committed in prison because those were viewed as administrative hearings, not judicial. As for inmates' criminal cases, I would always hand over my work to their lawyer or they would file it in a pro se brief. But Sunshine was a separate plaintiff in our civil case and if she didn't respond to each motion, she'd be kicked off the case.

Because I was helping her, impersonating her in the legal documents, the lawyers wanted the civil case squashed entirely. Unless I thought of something, I was in deep shit. It's not that I needed a monetary settlement—that's not why the suit mattered—it's because the civil case had been operating as my fishing net on the detectives, on the prosecutors, on everyone who put me away. Without the far-reaching discovery I was able to secure through suing these various people and offices, I would never be able to get my hands on the evidence needed to free myself.

To save the suit, I'd have to pull a rabbit out of a hat.

When I first got copies of the motions to dismiss, I read portions of them and then put them aside. The night after the Biegenwald argument, I sat on my bed and meticulously dug through them line by line. As I was doing that pains-taking analysis of the motions, something came back to me. Throughout the documents, they would refer to Sunshine by name at the top, but the rest of the documents referred to her as "Mr. Wright's wife" or "plaintiff's wife." As I read motion after motion of this, the repetitive use of the word "wife" triggered a memory—of a case holding I had once come across.

Back when I first discovered that I didn't have to read every page of the reporters, but rather the summaries and holdings in the back of those large books, the goal was to become my own legal encyclopedia. I was hoping to become a font of knowledge of every case that had gone through the court system so I would always have a precedent in mind to refer back to. I didn't have the experience that opposing counsel had, so I had to beat them through sheer volume of knowledge.

In reading through those motions to dismiss, I remem-bered coming across a New Jersey case from the early 1980s where a man was arrested for beating and sexually assaulting his wife. One of his defenses was related to something called "affinity," or the oneness of the spouses. Since the Middle Ages in England, marriage has been grounded in the bibli-cal concept of affinity, which means that when the couple is married, they become one person.* The defendant's argu-ment was that he couldn't be arrested for assaulting his wife, because they were one person.

---

* "For this cause shall a man leave father and mother and shall cleave to his wife, and the two shall be one flesh. Therefore they are no more two, but one flesh." (Matthew 19:5–6.)

Now the state Supreme Court rejected it because although affinity has been the basis for law in the Western world for centuries, there have been statutes added to it beginning in the mid-nineteenth century—the most famous of which were called the Married Women's Property Acts. These gave the wife individual rights separate from her husband. At one time, his argument would've held, but not in the late twentieth century. That part of affinity had been abridged. The court shot down his defense by going through the successive Property Acts and different statutes that had chiseled away at the husband's rights and the woman's rights for oneness purposes. Affinity was still the law, but the part that let a husband do what he wanted to his wife was gone because she was no longer a man's property. She was a separate person.

The argument got me thinking. A woman's right to own property, to not be assaulted by her husband, to vote on her own behalf—had all been instituted over the last 150 years. But a state like New Jersey was one of the United States' original thirteen colonies; its constitution came straight from English Common Law in the Middle Ages, which in itself came from the church. This means that three-hundred-to-four-hundred-year-old laws dating back to medieval England were still on the books in New Jersey. So there had to be laws that derived from the biblical concept of oneness of the spouses that were still applicable, perhaps a husband's right to represent his wife in a court of law.

So that's what I argued.

In the civil hearing, because there was no law on the books regarding this, I used persuasive law to show the judge that the common law right to affinity was still the law in New Jersey. What I was doing—representing Sunshine as though she and I were one—had not been abridged, mitigated, or nullified. I still had the right to claim Sunshine and I were one person for these legal purposes, and if the court denied me the right to represent her, they were also infringing on my constitutional right *to represent myself*.

The judge was persuaded and ruled in our favor. The lawsuit would stand, and I could continue to handle Sunshine's litigation as much as I was allowed to handle my own.

Going through all those cases, thousands and thousands of holdings, had served me well. In fact, Richard Biegenwald didn't know it, but his case was actually the very first one I came across when I first started studying the law at the Somerset County Jail. His death sentence was overturned because of the judge's instructions to the jury. When a defendant goes to trial, a jury must find that he is guilty of the charges beyond a reasonable doubt or acquit him. In order for a jury to make such a decision after hearing all of the evidence, the judge must explain what each of the charges means and what the jury must determine. This is a key point of a criminal trial, the moment where justice is handed over to the people. Before the judge releases the jury to begin deliberations, he must "instruct" them—define the elements that make up a charge. This is the crux of the judicial process, where the law travels from specific knowledge to human reasoning. If an instruction is missing something or explained incorrectly, a conviction can—and likely will—be vacated and a new trial required. In Biegenwald's case, the jury was improperly instructed during the death penalty trial. As a result, the New Jersey Supreme Court vacated his death penalty sentence. That very issue, jury instructions, would become a linchpin in my own case.

No recording, eyewitness, or DNA test was going to set me free. There was no mistaken identity or single piece of evidence that had to be exposed. There was no guilty party out there whose capture would release me. The entire case against me was a legal fiction and I needed to unravel it. I was working on my lawsuit, hoping to get a look inside the prosecutor's office and detectives' files, but I also had been working on something else. Call it a secret weapon.

Shortly after I entered prison in 1991, I created a legal theory around the kingpin law that had put me away for life. The definition of a kingpin in the criminal statute was specific, but the jury instructions on the charge were extremely broad. According to the jury instructions, a kingpin referred to anyone involved in a drug conspiracy, even a bunch of addicts conspiring to sell drugs in order to support their own habits.

I knew I couldn't use the new theory in my own case because it would be denied outright. There was too much heat on my case, too much ink spilled about how I was the first to be convicted as a kingpin. There was no way they'd overturn it, much less based on a theory that I came up with. So I waited for a carrier to test it. A host.

Enter Alexander.

In the law library, I met a dark-skinned inmate in his early thirties with tightly cropped hair framing a round face. He was tall and carrying some extra pounds, muscle turned to flab. Reserved and soft-spoken, he carried the air of someone who was beaten down, like his youth had been unceremoniously stripped away from him.

One day one of the helpers at the law library introduced us. "Isaac," he said, "this is Alexander. He has the same conviction as you. They gave him life and I'm helping him do some research."

I asked Alexander a few questions and he was just flat: "yes" and "no" and "I understand." I got to know him a little bit, learned about his case, and earned his trust. When I felt it was the right moment, I sprang.

"Listen," I said to Alexander one day in the library. "I've been reading up on your case and I think I have something that could help you."

"Yeah?" he said.

"What do you think about using it? Maybe giving it to your lawyer. There's no law surrounding it. It's new. But I think it has some meat to it. You can put it in your case in a pro se brief and see what happens."

"Sure," he said. "I got no reason to say no. At this point I'll try anything I can. I'm desperate, my family's desperate. Whatever you can do, I appreciate it."

I gave him what I'd written up about the jury instructions on the kingpin statute and scheduled a time for him to come up to the office so I could walk him through it. He sent my brief to his lawyer and to some family members. Word got back to me that Alexander's lawyer warned his client not to get any legal advice from the guys in prison. Another lawyer told the family he was not convinced that I'd even come up with it, purportedly saying, "Whoever this guy is, he's lying.

He didn't do this. A lawyer did this. Don't believe him, don't trust him, because he didn't do this."

I ended up speaking to one of the lawyers Alexander had contacted about representing him on appeal. "This is a real interesting argument," he said to me. "I don't think it's going to win, not because it's not good, but right now, this guy is down and since he's been down, a number of other people are waiting to go down."

Ultimately, unable to raise money for an appellate attorney, Alexander was represented on appeal by the public defender's office. I convinced Alexander to show the argument to his public defender, who *also* didn't believe that I wrote it. He assumed I was passing off a lawyer's work as my own and declined to put it in his legal brief. I kept pushing and Alexander eventually ended up putting it in himself, in a pro se supplemental brief for his appeal.

It landed like a guided missile. Alexander's appeal went all the way to the state Supreme Court, which reversed his life sentence, released him from prison, and as a result, created a new law around my theory. The new law mandated jury instructions that required a jury to find that a defendant not only conspired with several people to sell drugs but also that the drug conspiracy was *significant* and that the defendant occupied a *high-level leadership* position within that conspiracy as an organizer, supervisor, or manager.

Alexander's family visited me to thank me and every day until he left he was asking, "What can I do for you?" Since my trial, several other people throughout the state had already been convicted under New Jersey's "kingpin" law. Those convictions were all reversed based upon the Alexander decision.

I would later use it to get my own kingpin conviction vacated, which took away my life sentence. Unfortunately, that still left me with seventy years from my other charges. I had lifted the weight of "life" off my shoulders only to find another one still sitting there.

One of the challenges when fighting a conviction is to keep your case in the public eye. The more attention and light you can bring to a specific injustice, the more people are likely to help. There's only so much bandwidth for any individual case—in the media, in the public's consciousness, even in activist circles—and you have to find ways to shine the light on your own. My case had been in the papers, especially because of the novelty of my representing myself, but the public had moved on. I had to devise a way to get their attention again, while also simultaneously taking a shot against those who put me away.

My next move was to get the word out on what I'd collected on Bissell, as well as some things I'd learned about Judge Imbriani. Bissell was still revered and respected at this time, a big fundraiser for state politicians, and a friend of the governor. Over the years I'd been finding and holding on to illegal and embarrassing information on both men. Bissell had been dirty for some time, using drug seizure money as his own personal piggy bank, while Judge Imbriani had been engaged in embezzlement and tax fraud.

But I didn't have access to the press the way Bissell had. I couldn't just call up a reporter and feed them what I knew or send out a press release. No reporter would necessarily interview me, and even if they did, no one would believe me. I needed something dramatic, something that would get people's attention. I had to create the right moment.

There are two types of bail. There's bail when you're awaiting trial, and, after you're convicted, there's bail pending appeal. I put in a motion for bail pending appeal, knowing it would be denied. No way in hell they were going to let me out. Even if my case was *reversed*, they weren't going to let me out on bail. This was still Imbriani and Bissell. But my goal wasn't to get bail. It was just to get in front of a captive audience.

SOMERSET COUNTY COURTHOUSE
JUNE 4, 1993

Back in a Somerset courthouse for my bail hearing, everyone was there. Bissell and his underlings, Imbriani on the bench, my parents, a couple of my siblings, even my grandparents and aunts. The courtroom was also packed with media. When Imbriani gave his ruling denying bail, he started rolling out this entire narrative about my guilt, about the "overwhelming" evidence and testimony against me. Since it couldn't have been for the sake of the court, it was likely for the gallery and for the papers.

By this time my understanding of our legal system was profound. The three branches of U.S. government—executive, legislative, and judicial—are equal on paper, but inequities leave the judiciary vulnerable for one reason: the judiciary's power is dependent on the will of the executive branch.

Most orders issued by a judge have absolutely no force and effect unless given those things by the executive branch. For example, if a judge issues an order for a father to turn his child over to the child's mother and the father refuses, that order is meaningless if law enforcement is not willing to enforce it. The judiciary in this country does not have the power or authority to enforce its own orders. When you see officers in a courtroom, they do not work for the court; they are usually sheriff's officers, if it's state court,* that are assigned courtroom duty. Their job is to maintain the safety and security of the judge, the courtroom, its occupants and personnel. They *are not* under the supervision or control of the court.

I was an individual convicted of a crime, and the state guards who transported me from prison to court, and accompanied me there, worked for the Department of Corrections, which is part of the executive branch. Which meant Imbriani had no control over them. So when the judge went on and on about his ruling, I stood up and interrupted him.

"You know what," I yelled out, "these proceedings are over!"

"Mr. Wright, can you stop?" the judge said. "I'm giving my ruling, so you can appeal—"

"I'm going to appeal whether you finish or not!" I said.

Then I turned to the state guards behind me. "Get me out of here. Take me back to prison," I said, knowing Imbriani could do nothing about it. As they started cuffing me, I kept screaming over Imbriani's ruling: "You have a problem! You have a problem!"

"You are the one with the problem, Mr. Wright," Imbriani said.

As they took me away, I turned and pointed at Bissell.

---

* U.S. marshals in federal court.

"That's the man with the problem! He is a criminal. He is a thief. He is an extortionist. He doesn't pay his taxes. I know all about you. And you know that I know!" By the end of my rant I was at the door, projecting my voice as loudly as I could, rattling the courtroom. The theatrics were all part of the plan. It broke the staid and bureaucratic court atmosphere and an electric jolt filled that room.

"And I know all about you too," Bissell said.

As they took me away, I heard my mom scream at Imbriani, "You haven't heard the end of us. You both are corrupt! My son—"

"Your son's going to jail," Bissell shot back.

"Yeah," my mother responded, "and you'll be in the cell next to him!"

The door to the anteroom closed behind me and I smiled, leaving the court stunned in my wake. I had ended the hearing in a glorious, accusatory exit. I couldn't have written it more perfectly.

Sure enough, journalists printed my outburst in the paper, which had been the whole idea. Those first stories created a domino effect: Others with information on Bissell's shady business dealings started to come forward, and officials began poking around both him and Imbriani. There was a story about a superior judge whom Bissell had targeted to get pulled over and threatened with arrest because the judge had ruled against him in a previous proceeding. There were investigations into Bissell's conflicts of interests: how he earned outside income through his gas stations, was in business with his chief of detectives' brother, had filed false tax returns, was skimming from his own business, had threatened to plant cocaine on an oil company official who had filed complaints, and had not turned over cash and property seizures to the Treasury.[2]

Activists and influencers in New Jersey also began to reach out. John Paff, a Libertarian Party member and one of the most outspoken voices against corruption in Somerset County, became one of my biggest advocates. He contacted me after a full spread article appeared in the *New Jersey Law Journal* regarding the corruption in my case. Paff was instrumental in providing me with information on other victims of Bissell's and coordinating the appearance of future witnesses.

When I got back to Trenton, I heard from the warden that Bissell had called him personally, enraged, telling him to strip me of privileges, throw me in a hole, anything to punish me.

"What the hell did you do?" Morton asked, laughing. "I just got a call from the prosecutor and he was ripe mad!"

We had a brief laugh.

"Whatever you're doing out there is your business," he said, "just don't give me any problems."

Bissell's influence ended at the prison door. What did a warden in Trenton care what some county prosecutor up north was doing? Morton and I shook our heads at Bissell's efforts. The once-mighty prosecutor was raging against the dying of the light. It was only a matter of time for him and he knew it. His kingdom was about to come crashing down.

Chapter Fifteen

The knowledge of the law is like a deep well, out
of which each man draweth according to the
strength of his understanding.

—SIR EDWARD COKE

GETTING THE STATE TO SNIFF around Bissell wasn't necessarily going to get me out of prison. For that to happen, I
needed to get on the inside, to step onto his turf, explore
his territory, and see what had really happened at my arrest
and trial.

The entire case against me was dirty—a complex and
corrupt fiction—and I could prove it. I just needed to get
a look at the paper trail. Even a conspiracy can't help but
create a paper trail. I had to get my hands on prosecutors'
orders, detectives' notes, cops' communications, codefendants' deals, any and every document the prosecution had
on the *State v. Isaac Wright, Jr.*

Documents tell the truth even when they are full of lies.
Especially then.

★ ★ ★

Back when I first made the decision to represent myself, there were millions of things I didn't know about the law. But I knew one big thing: I couldn't trust anyone. I was the victim of collusion between various officials of the court, and to enlist one to get me out of prison would have been suicide. All lawyers and judges (who were at one time lawyers) are part of the same fraternity. If I hired a lawyer, I would always be on the outside looking in. I'd have to take his word for it, never knowing for real what was going on. No lawyer would ever press Bissell the way I needed him pressed. It wouldn't be worth it to them. I was just one case—and a hopeless one at that. There was too much for a defense attorney to lose by pissing off a powerful prosecutor. The courtroom is a type of theater and though attorneys are on opposite sides of an aisle and an argument, they are still working *together*. That's the nature of our justice system.

Opposing lawyers—as well as presiding judges—are, above all, colleagues. They gather behind closed doors and work out what needs to be done, with a wink and a nod, and the defendant is often left in the lurch. There was a limit to how hard defense lawyers would push for me, and none were going to push past the point of propriety. They had their own careers to think about, their own relationships to protect, their own futures to plan. But I was a young Black man with nothing more than a high school education taking on the state and I'd made it this far: I didn't give a damn about propriety.

By making it personal, Bissell had actually worked in my favor. He couldn't even bring himself to look at or talk to me. He made it clear that it was beneath him to honor any of my requests or even respond to them. But all that pride and ego backfired stupendously. Because Bissell wouldn't give me anything, I would get a crack at *everything*.

Over nearly three years, no matter how many times I put in a request for documents from the prosecutor's office in my civil trial, and motioned for the court to compel Bissell to comply, I got nothing. So the court stepped in and forced the issue. The judge in my civil trial threatened to levy sanctions against Bissell unless he produced the documents I requested. Even with the judge's threats, I knew I was still going to be engaged in a multi-year game of push-pull. So I came up with a simple fix. All the documents I needed were in one place, likely one room. I argued to the court that rather than spend even more time having the prosecutor's office go through the process of copying, cataloging, and delivering every document to me in prison, I should just go to them. I petitioned the court to transport me to Bissell's office and give me one crack at all the documents there.

The court agreed.

It was completely unprecedented, in the history of American jurisprudence, for a convicted person (especially one serving life) to be let into the prosecutor's office who put him away to scour around for exculpatory evidence. It'd be considered crazy to even make such a request. But I hadn't gotten that far by resting on precedent, so I went for it. It's not like I had anything to lose.

But getting in was the easy part; the hard part would be making it count. I could not come out empty-handed because there would be no second chance. When the day was over, and my visit concluded, Bissell could say he'd done everything required: he opened his files and given me free rein. I would have no more moves left.

BRIDGEWATER, NEW JERSEY
JULY 11, 1995

In the early summer morning hours, a prison transport van tailed by patrol cars took me the hour north to the Somerset County Administration Building, a dark gray edifice that jutted menacingly outward on both sides. My recent victory in court had been in the newspapers and some reporters were actually outside the building when I arrived. The van drove around to a back area through a guard gate. After being taken out, I was escorted through metal detectors in the rear and went up a service elevator. In my faded prison khakis, wrists and ankles cuffed, I was brought past reception into a hallway with offices on both sides. Everyone looked away as I passed or pretended they didn't see me at all. I was the invisible man.

The corrections officers escorted me inside a wood-paneled conference room. Shelved neatly along the walls were leather-bound sets of law books, and a giant oak conference table took up the center of the room. On every inch of the table, as well as in a semicircle in front, were stacks and stacks of file boxes, generic brown and white cardboard, unlabeled.

This is a common legal tactic and I expected it. If you can't prevent the opposition from seeing files, you drown them in so many that they can't find a thing. This was especially true if the opposing party only had one shot to look through them. While still abiding by the judge's ruling, Bissell would try to plunge me into the deepest water possible, hoping I'd drown.

The officers uncuffed my arms and legs, closed the stately door, and took their post outside. It was just me in there, alone with the long sordid history of what the state had done to me. The court order stated that if the prosecutor's office believed a document was privileged and that I shouldn't have it, they could hold it and go to court to argue that.

I opened the first box and got to work. I didn't know exactly what I was looking for, but I knew I was not going to find anything obvious. Those kinds of revealing documents, if they existed at all, would have been hidden or destroyed long ago. Even if they somehow remained six years after my arrest, someone in the prosecution office would have had it removed before I showed up that morning. What I needed was a diamond in the rough, a document that proved the case against me was fraudulent without it sticking out so much that Bissell would've gotten rid of it.

But how? How was I going to find in the remaining documents that which no one else, not even Bissell himself, could see? I realized that in order to see something they didn't, I needed to approach things differently. I wouldn't just read the documents in the files. I would *listen* to them. Allow the documents to speak to me. I would not only read the words but would heed the secrets behind the words—a buried meaning, motive, or revelation that the documents would show only me. If there was something that I could use, something with the capacity to change the course of my case and, by extension, my life—the documents would tell me. So I began to read. And to listen.

I didn't eat or drink a thing all day—no one offered anything, as I'm sure Bissell instructed—though I found a gracious young assistant who agreed to photocopy what I needed.

As I sat on the beige carpet, reading in the low light, hours passed quickly. I felt the pressure of time clamping down on me. Ringing phones, footsteps, and elevator dings bled through the walls, but mostly I just heard the quiet thump of my own heart. It took superhuman focus to ignore the jitters, the vacant stomach, the strained neck, as I made my way through the boxes, through file after file after file.

For the most part, I was poring through papers with which I was already very familiar. Most of it had been provided in discovery before my trial took place: police reports, search warrant and wiretap applications, motions and legal arguments, evidence logs, trial and motion hearing transcripts, lab reports, codefendant plea agreements, and witness statements. Hour upon hour I went through it all—from morning to the height of day to dusk—taking meticulous notes on a legal pad I'd brought.

Then sometime in the early evening, with the summer light slanting through the blinds, it appeared. Almost as a whisper. At the bottom of a folder filled with interoffice correspondence, I came across a memo signed by Bissell and each of the five detectives in my case. My heart sped up rapidly as my brain processed what I was holding. I read and reread it to be sure it was what I thought it was. It sparkled like a divine revelation and my hands shook. I had gone in there with this quiet faith that if I kept digging, kept listening, I would find it. And I did.

I exhaled slowly, trying to hide my excitement, and got up off the ground to find the helpful assistant. "Listen," I told her, as nonchalantly as I could, "I need a copy of this."

"One second," she said. "I just need to check." She took the memo to Bissell and came back. "OK, that's fine," she said and took it to the copier. It didn't even register to him what it was.

The memo, dated a week before the trial began in spring 1991, was from Bissell to the five lead detectives in my case. It instructed them, in preparation for my trial, to read over all the case files and reports ahead of their testimony.

At the top it read: *Somerset Co. Prosecutor's Office*, with the seal on it, *Nicholas L. Bissell, Administrator*.

To all the detectives listed below, please read all the case files in the case of State v. Isaac Wright, indictment #_____. Once you have finished reading them, please sign, date and hand it over to the officer below your name.

Nicholas L. Bissell
Head Prosecutor, Somerset Co.

Beside each detective's name was their signature and a date.

The document seemed monotonous, not even worth a second look. But it was exactly what I was searching for. While it read as an inconsequential bureaucratic directive, if used correctly, its impact would be colossal. It would give me the opening I needed to attack the detectives' veracity and credibility in the hopes that one of them would cave, admit they'd been lying all this time. It would require meticulous and unconventional planning, but I could use this document to push a detective to the point where telling the truth—in essence, confessing to misconduct—was in his best interest.

Let me explain: Before they testify, cops are well-prepared and trained to say exactly the right thing. They look over each other's files, statements, and testimony so their stories all line up. In order to help the case and to protect each other, they have to maintain the fiction that they're all just telling the truth. The memo from Bissell's office proved that all the detectives had read each other's files in my case even though they claimed, during the trial, that they hadn't. They had only admitted to reviewing their own.

Cops must deny reading another officer's report even when they have. When police officer A reads police officer B's report, a defense attorney is allowed to question police officer A about the contents and contradictions of police officer B's report. In other words, if police officer A admits to reading police officer B's report, an experienced and skilled defense attorney can impeach the credibility of police officer B through police officer A, without calling police officer B to the stand. Because of this danger, cops make sure that their testimonies remain consistent with each other. Further, they are also trained to deny this on the witness stand. Quite simply, they are taught to lie.

At my trial, every cop I questioned claimed they hadn't read the other officers' reports. Over and over again they told this lie, clung to it because this lie undergirded all their other lies. I needed to get the detectives back on the stand and ask them if they read any other reports in my case, so they could again deny it. Those same detectives would have no idea that I possessed a memo proving they had read all the reports in my case, had even signed a document attesting to that fact. The memo would cut through all the lies like a clean, sharp blade.

In order to keep the element of surprise, I was only going to have one chance to use that memo. So I had to pick the specific detective who I thought would be the weakest link, the one most likely to break. The plan was to lay it all on a single officer who couldn't hold the burden.

I took a scientific approach to selecting the right detective. I did my own psychological analysis of these men, went through reports on my case and others', talked to anyone in prison who knew any of these cops, and constructed profiles of each detective. I spent my days reviewing, studying, and scrutinizing their investigative reports, affidavits, and notes, examined the way they articulated the facts, measured the discrepancies between different versions of incidents, and measured the level of ease with which they lied. It was crude but I worked with what I had in order to make a calculated guess as to who'd be the most likely to crack.

When I was done, one cop stood out: Detective James Dugan. From his reports I could sense a softness in him, a humanity that made it harder for him to deceive, a touch of an independent streak. In Dugan's writing, I saw an inner struggle triggered by his own honor and integrity. At times, he didn't even bother to rewrite a report that needed a correction; he just scratched words out and drew lines through paragraphs, changing it right there on the document itself. The other cops made sure their lies looked unblemished—practiced and pristine. But Dugan was different. I could see him wrestling with his conscience. I had to get him on the stand and pin him so far back against the wall that he would see it was in his best interest to confess. It was unorthodox, and any legal expert will tell you that cops just don't break like that, but I literally had no other choice.

Those years behind bars taught me so much, about where my strength came from, about the spirit inside other people, about what keeps some going while others give in. I learned about power, how it is gained, abused, and manipulated. Working as my own lawyer showed me that the state—government leaders, prosecutors, judges, and police—cannot be blindly trusted to protect and defend us. Those institutions are built on a desire for power and an impulse to protect and defend *themselves and each other.* I knew that as well as anyone alive, had gone to sleep every night among cold stone and thick steel understanding that fact down in my bones.

My goal was to get one of them to admit it.

When I talked to people inside and outside prison about what my strategy was—getting a cop to confess—they literally thought I was crazy. Most of them didn't say it, but I could tell they thought something was wrong with me, that prison had eaten away at my good sense, that it was time for medication. That's how ridiculous it seemed. The one bet

I was making on my freedom and the rest of my life made people think I needed serious help.

That year at Trenton, there was an uptick in violence and two consecutive riots. One spilled out after a fight on the basketball court, while the other was part of the war between the Nation of Islam and the Five Percenters, a gang that had spun off from them. The two gangs had gotten along for years after the split, but there was underlying tension. Rumors floated around about a problem simmering between them. Then in the yard one day, it ignited. Two rival leaders were talking, in an intense conversation, hands waving. Then the Nation of Islam leader just screamed out, "Jihaaaaaad!"

After that, all hell broke loose, echoes of "Jihad" and "Allahu Akbar" ringing through the yard as inmates came running from all ends. It was complete chaos, and inside the scuffle were multiple stabbings. Then a gunshot from the tower. A warning. The next one would be directed at the yard. At the sound of the gunshot I hit the ground, as did everyone else, lying on my belly with my hands behind my head. The guards lined up at the gate, twenty or thirty deep, to come in and extract everyone. After that, the violence just migrated inside. They had to shut down the prison and keep everyone on lockdown, impacting my work at a time when every hour was precious.

I was more annoyed than afraid by that point. I had found a quiet space inside my mind where I knew fear was pointless. Whatever was going to happen was going to happen. Fear doesn't change anything. Thinking is what changes it. If it's going to change, it's only going to change based on how you deal with it. The only thing fear does is weaken you when you can least afford it. I refused to let it.

During my seventh year behind bars, 1996, with all my appeals exhausted, I reached the end of the line. My last shot would be a single post-conviction relief (PCR) hearing, scheduled for early September. The law recognizes the vulnerability of human error and the overzealousness of obtaining convictions, so it provides the option for a PCR hearing, which is essentially a hearing to vacate a conviction. It is the final bite at the apple, giving the defense one last chance to raise new issues, whether legal or factual errors that occurred during a plea or trial, or an actual claim of innocence. The PCR hearing is like a strainer for any remaining imperfections left inside a conviction. I had the interoffice memo from Bissell's office, reams of compromising information on him and Imbriani, and the files of the five detectives on my case. I was gambling on Detective James Dugan in the hopes that with the right approach I could get him to give up the game.

The night before I was to be transferred back up to Somerset for my hearing, the warden shuffled by my cell for a chat. We had come a long way and I could feel a grudging respect in the way he sent me off.

Warden Morton came to my cell with a captain and a lieutenant. "Listen, Wright," he said. "Come to the bars. I want you to do me a favor." He was talking loudly and a bunch of other inmates on the tier could hear him, so I laughed.

"What?" I asked. "Do you a *favor*?"

Favor was the wrong word coming from a warden to an inmate surrounded by the paranoid and angry. So I pushed back, not having a clue what he was talking about.

"No, no, no," he said. "I'm sorry. Not a favor. I know we're transferring you back to the county tomorrow. I want you to promise me something."

"What?"

He came closer to the bars. "When you leave," he said, "you don't come back."

I laughed and even heard a few other inmates laughing. "Well, I'm not trying to come back, but it's surprising to hear that."

"Don't get me wrong," he said. "I'm glad you'll be out of my hair, but custody and the administration have a betting pool. They believe you'll be back and we believe you won't. If I don't see you again, we win. So promise me you're not coming back."

I came to the bars and shook his hand. "I promise you that I won't come back on this side," I said. "But, you know, I may be coming back from the outside to come to your office to get some of that money you won."

It was couched in a joke and a bet, but underlying it I could tell: he had faith in me. He knew I didn't belong in prison any more than he did.

The next morning, as I rode back up north Route 206 to Somerset, I allowed myself to dream that it would be for the last time. It was a powerful feeling. But it was mixed with something else. Something unexpected. A sadness for those left behind.

There was an inmate with me at Trenton who went to

prison for something he didn't do. I knew his people and everyone in the street knew who really did it. They always do—especially a violent crime. He didn't ask for my help because his family had money; he was their only child, and they had brought in some high-priced lawyers. By the time I left Trenton, his family had lost all their money. His father had died and his mother was in a shelter. His case had drained away every dime they had. And he was still in there.

There was also Alfred, an inmate serving a life sentence for murder whom I was helping up until the day I left. The evidence was clear: Alfred was not at the scene of the crime and had neither participated in the murder nor even *knew* that it had occurred. His friend, Sam, the sole perpetrator, received less time because he took a deal and received a thirty-year sentence. In Sam's statement, he confessed that he had borrowed Alfred's gun for the murder, which was how Alfred got a life sentence. The backwardness of it made me ill. And every day that Alfred stayed in prison was an injustice.

Alfred was an anxious guy, jittery and irrational. In desperation, he had someone unqualified do the paperwork for him who screwed up his whole case. At the time I was sent back up to Somerset for the hearing, I was doing what I could to fix it. But I could only do so much. In my mind he stood in for all the other guys I left behind. He reminded me that even if I passed through this crucible, there was still so much unfinished business.

Chapter Sixteen

SOMERSET COUNTY JAIL, SOMERVILLE, NJ
AUGUST 1996

I WAS A DIFFERENT MAN when I was transported back to Somerset County Jail in the summer of 1996. But it was also a different jail, part of the wave of modernized facilities that were built in the wake of the War on Drugs and the epidemic of mass incarceration. The new jail could hold ten times as many prisoners as the old one. It had also been automated and updated, with buzzed doors instead of metal bars, swiped cards replacing heavy keys. The horror was depersonalized, giving visitors and staff some distance from what really went on in there. The cold technology just drove home that we were objects being stored, not flesh-and-blood men carrying on with our lives any way we knew how.

Many of the administrators and COs hadn't changed, though. They knew me, and the damage I could do, so they went out of their way to isolate me from the population, even locking the jail down on the day I arrived. I was a convict with vast legal knowledge, a chip on his shoulder, and a desire to educate fellow prisoners. In their minds, the less I associated with other inmates, the better. I was separated from virtually the entire general population and

I only saw one or two other people in my pod. During gym time, I was alone, shooting hoops by myself. At mealtime, I was close to alone at the empty tables. I spent my days in the small law library, the place where I first discovered the law, which brought my whole journey back in a full cosmic circle.

Legally, the custodial staff had to let me prepare for my hearing. I stored my case files in a special adjoining cell, and was allowed to interview and prep witnesses in a private visiting room in the jail's high-security pod. But the last thing they needed was my stirring up shit. I was being separated not because of the danger I posed to inmates, but because of the danger I posed to the system itself.

In the post-conviction relief hearing, I was requesting a Dismissal of the Indictment based upon police and prosecutorial misconduct. If I won, the most likely scenario was that I'd get a new trial. The prosecution must've seen that momentum was in my favor. The legal situations I'd stirred up in both jail and prison, my constant transport back and forth to court, the news coverage on Bissell and Judge Imbriani—it was all spiraling out of control for them. Bissell was already going under, having been convicted in federal court a few months prior on "all charges in a 33-count tax fraud and corruption indictments,"[1] which included charges related to professional misconduct and violations of the public trust. Imbriani had been removed from the bench and would face jail time the following year.

In addition, witnesses from my trial had been coming forward to recant. My friend Rhoda had given a statement that Bissell had pressured her to perjure herself, as did my acquaintance John (who came out of nowhere to testify against me at trial). Both were willing to take the stand to say so at the hearing. Even Gator said in a deposition that he was promised a lighter sentence in exchange for testimony against me.

Recantations seem like they should be enough on their own, but it's not like the movies when people change their story and they let you out. Courts are suspicious of recantations from defendants, though that goes against common sense. Clearly there's an incentive to lie the first time and a *disincentive* to lie the second time, but recanting defendants are generally treated as liars who can't be trusted.

Still, the recantations were yet another thing on the pile in my favor. Given all this—plus the fact that they now knew I was never going to give up—the prosecution came to me with what they thought of as a generous offer: plead guilty and be eligible for parole after three more years, completing a ten-year sentence.

I wasn't even tempted.

Judge Leonard Arnold wore glasses and had thinning dark brown hair that was bald on top. Even-handed and fair, Arnold had actually written the first criminal procedure book I studied when I got to the jail's law library. He replaced the disgraced Imbriani in my case and his presence was another sign to me that things might be coming around, like the universe was swinging back in my favor. The jurist who first taught me the law was going to rule on whether or not I would have another shot at justice.

After hearing from the prosecution that I'd turned down the deal, Judge Arnold looked at me, perplexed. "Mr. Wright, do you know what you're getting into?"

His confusion was understandable. I was already awaiting a retrial on the lifetime-carrying kingpin charge that had been vacated on appeal. I was currently burdened by a sentence totaling over seventy years on the remaining convictions that the appellate division refused to vacate. If I lost my PCR hearing, I'd be retried on the kingpin charge. In essence, I was risking the chance of getting a life sentence reimposed, along with the time I was currently serving.

"I do understand what I'm getting myself into, Your Honor," I said. "They stole seven years of my life. If I have to spend the rest of my life proving my innocence, then that's what I'll do."

I wanted to take this thing to its natural conclusion, to clear my name and punish those who put me away. They took my identity, my career, my family, and my freedom. They robbed me of things I will never be able to get back. I could have done three more years standing on my head; it wasn't the time that mattered. Taking the deal was against the very core of who I was, who I'd become. I understood the collateral damage a loss would wreak upon my parents, my siblings, my daughter—the people I loved more than myself. But pleading guilty would be stabbing myself in the heart. I would spend the rest of my life dead on the inside, no good to myself or anyone else. If I came home, I refused to come home as Isaac Wright Jr., the convicted felon, the loser who served ten years on a drug charge, the coward who gave up his integrity because avoiding prison was more important than fighting for justice. It was a huge gamble, but at that point my innocence mattered more than anything.

So I rolled the dice.

The assistant prosecutor assigned to my case, James Mc-Connell, successfully delayed the PCR hearing for another month, so by the time the guard came to get me that first morning for court, I was primed for battle. From the jail's holding cell, I was chained and duckwalked across the polished cement floor, passing men on the stainless steel bench bolt-welded along the wall. A few knew where I was headed and gave me a nod, a brief gesture of solidarity. The chains on my ankles clanged against each other and the floor, bouncing a familiar jangle. I was escorted to the courthouse, now located across the street, and then to the familiar holding cell, where I changed into a modest outfit of a button-down shirt and blue denim slacks with a pair of dress shoes.

Though Rhoda and John were going to be recanting on the stand, I didn't expect their testimony to move the needle. Having them there, and padding my brief with their recantations, was something of a diversionary tactic, a misdirect. I didn't want anyone—Bissell, former Chief of Detectives Thornburg, Dugan—to expect anything about the memo I'd found in Bissell's office. Through discovery rules, court procedure requires that both sides reveal to the other party the evidence they possess. The genius of using the Bissell memo was that I didn't have to tell the prosecution what I was holding because *it was their document.*

In her leopard-print blouse, sunglasses resting on top of her head, Rhoda was fearless and confident on the stand. She seemed eager to undo the testimony she'd been forced into seven years prior. I think her own guilt about helping to put me away had something to do with it as well. Prompted by my questions, she said everything she'd testified about me at my trial was untrue, orchestrated by Bissell and police.

"Mr. Bissell told me he was going to be pushing for life for you," she said, "and if I didn't testify I would get the same."

"And Prosecutor Bissell told you what to say?" I asked.

"Word for word," she replied.

When the prosecutor, McConnell, pushed Rhoda on why she had perjured herself, she pushed back right at him. "I wanted to see my son again," she said. "I mean, anyone in that predicament would have done the same thing—including you."

McConnell went at her credibility, at her motivation, at her history, but she was defiant. She reached a point where she got fed up with the prosecutor's line of questioning and refused to answer.

"You need to answer or I'll hold you in contempt," Judge Arnold said.

"Another threat," Rhoda said. "Threats, I'm sick of them."

At the sight of Nicholas Bissell entering the courtroom, the entire gallery went silent. Bissell was still under house arrest after his thirty convictions the previous May, wearing an ankle monitoring device, and awaiting sentencing. The fact that with that many counts, that many lives ruined, that much public trust squandered, this man still got to be with his wife and sleep in his home—while the innocent until proven guilty rotted away in jail—made me seethe. It drove home to me how the problem was so much larger than this already disgraced prosecutor.

The courtroom was eerily quiet, recognizing the inherent drama of the situation: a man sentenced to life in prison was getting the chance to grill the man who put him there. The reporters, former prosecutor's office employees, and onlookers in the gallery focused on him tentatively, studying his every move. Journalists moved around on the hard wooden benches, anxious to record the next step in Bissell's tumble down the ladder.

Though the standoff might have seemed ripe for drama, the reality was less so. Bissell wasn't going to give up anything and I didn't expect him to. After all, the captain has to go down with the ship. I put Bissell up there with a clear purpose: to get his lies on the record. I wanted to lay a foundation that I could systematically ax with each successive witness. During my questioning, I asked Bissell about countless issues in my case and his lies flowed freely. At one point, Judge Arnold intervened. "Where is this all going, Mr. Wright?"

"Bissell's credibility is an issue," I argued. "That's the reason why I called him." It was *the* issue and he walked right into it.

Bissell was calm bordering on cocky, the condescending laughter in his voice, that familiar superiority like he couldn't believe he had to answer questions from me, of all people. Of course, he was well-versed in his version of the "facts," and moved from lie to lie with the fluid ease of a public speaker, peppering in various legal terms throughout.

"Is it not true that your office had an arrangement to make secret deals with defense attorneys?" I asked.

"That is not true," he said.

"You didn't secretly promise one sentence while putting a different one in the plea agreement?"

"Not to my knowledge. No."

"Not to your knowledge?" I asked, my voice slightly raised. "This was your office, how could you not know?"

"No," he said. "No—we didn't do that."

"Never?"

"No."

Then I grabbed a document from my table and methodically went through a list of cases where defendants pleaded to time but in reality were given much less, sometimes probation or time served. I went through sentencing transcript after sentencing transcript that didn't match up with the accepted plea.

"Can you explain that?" I asked. Again and again, one after another, I asked, "Can you explain that?" I hit him with case after case of deals that were meant to circumvent the process, until he got frustrated and began to feign ignorance.

"Can you explain the case of Victor Travino," I asked, "who was arrested with hundreds of kilos of cocaine yet after he turned over nearly a million dollars he was not charged as a kingpin and given a flat ten-year sentence, which would allow him out in three?"

"I'm not familiar with that," he said, coolly.

"You're not familiar with Victor Travino?"

"With the case, yes. With that agreement, I—I can't remember."

I took a beat. "Would you agree that a prosecutor's primary role is not to convict but to see that justice is done?"

"Objection!" the prosecutor interjected.

"I believe I did," Bissell said.

If it wasn't sad, it would've been comical. This man had been removed from office, convicted on thirty counts, put under house arrest, forced to wear an ankle monitor, and was awaiting sentencing. Yet he continually claimed that he was honest, that he had integrity, that he never acted improperly in his job. I didn't even bother to drive the absurdity home; I didn't need to. He hung himself out there to dry.

As we progressed through Bissell's four hours on the stand, I noticed a fatalism creep into his testimony. It was like he didn't even care whether his words matched up with the facts, like a kamikaze pilot barreling with abandon toward his final end. This was not the same Nicholas Bissell who came to taunt me in my cell seven years ago. It was a resigned, pathetic man who knew it was over, his testimony his requiem. He seemed far older than his fifty years, a husk of his former self.

SOMERSET COUNTY COURTHOUSE
SEPTEMBER 4, 1996

James Dugan carried himself sturdy and upright, like a Marine, as he made his way into court that morning. After spending so much time inside this man's mind, I spotted a wariness there. I sensed in him an effort to keep wearing a mask. My strategy in court was to carefully, almost imperceptibly, get him to take it off.

I began with his biography, his entire career from the moment he started in law enforcement to the day of that hearing. I highlighted all the awards he had won, his promotions and commendations, his role as chief of the police academy—the uniform he was wearing that day—and emphasized how he was the molder of impressionable minds. The text of my questioning was his accomplishments, but the subtext was his honor and integrity. Then I hammered on that theme.

"You've testified many times during your career, correct?"

"Yes, I have," Dugan said.

"Some of those testimonies would include criminal trials?"

"Yes."

"And how many times, if you can remember, did the trials you testified in result in a conviction?"

"I don't remember exactly . . . Many."

"During any of those times you testified," I asked, "were you ever untruthful?"

"Absolutely not."

"You'd never lie under oath, would you?"

"Never," he said.

"Not only is lying under oath a crime, but it would cast doubt on your integrity and credibility as a law enforcement officer, correct?"

"I would think so."

"That goes for your testimony today. You intend to be truthful with this court?"

"I'm always truthful, Mr. Wright."

"Yes, as you testified earlier, dishonesty, especially under oath, is something you've never engaged in, right?"

"That is correct."

"OK, let's turn to your reports," I said. "You did prepare reports during your investigation in this case, didn't you?"

"I did."

"In fact, several officers prepared reports, correct?"

Dugan nodded. "I would think so."

"Let me ask you about Detective Racz's report. Isn't it true that Detective Racz's report regarding the events of my arrest contains glaring inconsistencies in the timeline?"

"I'm not sure what you're asking," he said, "but I wouldn't know. I didn't read Racz's report."

"What about Detective Buckman, did you read his report?"

"No."

"Detective Smith?"

"Mr. Wright," Dugan said, a bit exasperated, "I read no other report but my own."

"Out of all the reports prepared by other officers in this case, you didn't read any of them?"

"I only read my report."

I wanted it to be clear what I was asking and what he was answering. "Please remember, Officer Dugan, you're under oath. You've testified that you'd never lie under any circumstances. So I'm going to ask you again. Did you read any reports other than your own?"

"I did not."

"Objection, Your Honor." The prosecutor stood. "The question has been asked and answered numerous times."

"Objection sustained," Judge Arnold responded. "Mr. Wright, it is clear from Officer Dugan's testimony that he's read no other report but his own."

I'd gotten what I wanted on the record: an objection from the prosecutor and a ruling from the judge specifically finding that Dugan read no one else's report.

I walked over to my files and removed the memo from Bissell's office. That thin page I'd found at the bottom of an unmarked box had a sense of destiny about it, like it had traveled years and miles from briefcases to boxes to file cabinets to folders, in order to be in my hands at that moment.

That's the thing about truth. Long after people think it's dead and buried, it keeps breathing.

I stepped in front of Assistant Prosecutor McConnell's table and put the document behind my back, holding it by the corners so he could read it. This wasn't just a taunt. I wanted the prosecutor, in desperation, to project panic. I wanted Dugan to feel it and I wanted Judge Arnold to see it. If I had any chance of breaking a police officer on the stand, it would have to come from the pressure pushing in from all sides.

As I continued to ask Dugan questions, I saw him trying to meet McConnell's eyes. When I turned around, I could see the blood rushing up the prosecutor's neck and turning his entire face red. He was rattled and, more importantly, Dugan noticed.

"I'm sorry, Officer Dugan," I said, "you're looking at the prosecutor. Is there something wrong?"

"No, I'm fine, Mr. Wright."

"Would you like to call a recess so you can talk to the prosecutor about your testimony today?"

"No," Dugan said. "I'm fine."

"Can I see that document?" McConnell interrupted.

"No," I quickly answered, moving back to my side of the court. The rules of evidence required me to show him the document only if I was going to show the witness. But I had not yet decided to show it to Dugan. What I had wanted was McConnell's reaction. I was going to taunt him, frustrate him, beat him down in order to trigger his protest.

"Objection, Your Honor," McConnell said. "May we approach the bench?" McConnell stood to his feet.

He played right into my hands. Discrediting the detective was not going to be enough. I needed Dugan to see there was trouble, so I could bring him to a confession. Causing anxiety and confusion before I ultimately approached him with the document was part of the strategy.

Both McConnell and I walked up to Judge Arnold at the bench, Dugan eyeing us warily from the stand.

"Your Honor," McConnell said, his voice low and furtive, "this is a prosecutor's office memo. An interoffice memo that is privileged and confidential that he should not have. He should not be allowed to examine the witness . . ."

"I haven't examined the witness yet," I said. "I haven't even marked the document for identification."

"Are you planning to?" the judge asked.

"Yes," I said, "and once I do, I'll give it to the prosecutor."

"He can't even use it," the prosecutor said. "It's privileged and confidential."

"Can I see the document?" the judge asked. I handed it to Judge Arnold. As he read the memo, he looked up at McConnell. "Are you asking me to prevent Mr. Wright from using this document?"

"Yes, Your Honor, it's privileged."

At that, Judge Arnold's patience dropped off a cliff. "Mr. McConnell, this officer just testified unequivocally that he didn't read any of the files. In fact, Mr. Wright pressed him so hard on it that you placed an objection on the record. An objection *I* sustained. Are you now telling me that you want me to prevent Mr. Wright from cross-examining the officer about this document that clearly shows he has read other reports in the case and has been untruthful in my court?"

"Your Honor," McConnell said, "we wouldn't normally be making this objection but this document is privileged. It's an interoffice document, it belongs to the prosecutor's office."

"I see that it is," the judge said. "Mr. Wright, how did you obtain this document?"

"Your Honor, the prosecutor himself copied and gave it to me in the civil case."

McConnell went white. "Your Honor, that document is a—"

"Then it's not privileged," Judge Arnold said, cutting him off. "You gave it to him! Mr. McConnell, go sit down! Mr. Wright, please proceed."

I marked the document for identification and brought it over to McConnell to see, though he waved me off—he knew what it said. I approached Dugan on the witness stand and handed the document to him.

"Officer Dugan," I said with theatrical confidence, "do you recognize this memo?"

He took it and then hesitated, his eyes shifting to the prosecutor. "Yes," he said, the word catching in his throat. "Yes."

"Based on your testimony today—which had the air of integrity and appeared to be cloaked with honor—I now would like you to read this document to yourself, please."

Dugan readjusted in his seat. That single sheet shook in his hands, its flapping cutting through the room's stillness. He took a long time reading it, his eyes shifting back and forth across the text. I could see his Adam's apple moving up and down, like a tremor.

I had him.

All of my uncertainty and caution slowly drained out of me, traversed the ten feet between us, and then pooled around him as fear. Did he know it was over? Did the sound of it all collapsing echo in his mind?

"Have you read it?" I asked.

"Yeah," he said, a quaver in his voice, then a cough. "Yes, I read it."

"I'd like for you to now read it aloud, please, for the record," I said. I could feel the eyes of everyone in the gallery boring through my back. The silence of the room was tight and pinched, just the whir of an air-conditioner high in the back corner.

Dugan's eyes were darting away from mine, trying to meet McConnell's. With no objection from the prosecution and no choice, Dugan began to read aloud.

"To all the detectives listed below, please read all the case files in the case of *State v. Isaac Wright, Jr.* Once you have finished reading them, please sign, date, and hand it over to the officer below your name. Nicholas L. Bissell, Head Prosecutor."

"Is your name on that document?" I asked.

"Yes."

"Did you sign it?"

"Yes."

"Did you date it?"

"Yes."

"And you passed it to the detective under your name?"

"Apparently," he said, exhaling heavily, "I did."

I took the memo from Dugan and proceeded to walk toward my table. "So you lied in this courtroom today," I said, turning halfway.

"No!" Dugan yelled out, almost panicked. "I didn't lie."

"Yes. You not only lied, you lied repeatedly, didn't you?"

Under his breath he mumbled, "I didn't lie."

"What's that?" I asked.

"I didn't lie."

"You lied here today or you lied to the prosecutors," I said, my voice raising. I proceeded to the defense table and grabbed Dugan's reports from a folder. "Either way, how can the court believe that you're not lying right now?"

"Mr. Wright, I didn't lie," Dugan repeated. He seemed stuck on this protest, as though he could will it to be true.

"You lied under oath!" I exploded. "What happened to that honor? Where's that integrity?" I approached the witness stand and slammed Dugan's own report in front of him. "You lied about the Carlos search. You lied at my trial!"

"I didn't—"

"Just tell the truth! Redeem yourself," I said.

A quiet passed over the courtroom.

Dugan's eyes were darting over to the memo, to the prosecutor, his mind circling, searching for a way out. But there was none. I could feel the entire gallery holding their breath.

"I think what troubles me about saying this in this courtroom today, Mr. Wright, is that I am fighting with myself to tell the truth." Dugan then said something that made it harder for me to empathize at all with him, about how he regretted telling the truth if it meant helping me out. But I ignored that, holding my breath. I almost had him—just a little push.

"All you stand for rests on your words," I said. "You know what you have to do."

"I've been . . ." Dugan's voice caught and he began to tear up. "I've been holding this in for . . . for seven years."

"You don't have to hold it in any longer," I said, a touch of sympathy in my voice. "Tell the court what really happened."

"We obtained the warrant after the drugs had already been discovered in Carlos's house."

A collective gasp. Then whispers, which rose up into full-on noise. Judge Arnold pounded his gavel. "Order!"

"What is not in my report," he said, the words seeming to pool out of him, "and what I have done some soul-searching with is that at one point during the investigation I had learned that, upon securing the home, there were people who saw narcotics in the basement. But this was after I had been going under the premise that we got a search warrant the first time. Not taking responsibility for what I heard, and quite frankly, being scared to think that if I brought this into the situation at that point it would make it look like I am hiding something. I did not include that in my report."

I had appealed to the better angels of his nature, the man underneath who would reach for the truth. I knew his honor mattered to him—and that it would be my own saving grace.

The significance of Dugan's testimony was far-reaching. He confessed to a lie that was reiterated in just about every detective's report in the case. Those lies were repeated by many of those detectives under oath in affidavits to the judge issuing the search warrant, to the grand jury that indicted me, and to the trial jury that convicted me. Now, every single one of those detectives was tainted by misconduct. Dugan had exposed the poisonous tree.

Dugan even confessed to something I didn't know. After I was arrested, the detectives all got together and talked about how to write their reports in a way to make the search look good. The search was in fact so illegal that they conspired with each other on how to falsify the reports, to make sure the drug evidence wouldn't be suppressed.

"Was Prosecutor Bissell at that meeting?" I asked.

"Yes," he said.

"Wait," the judge said. "Wait, you're telling me that the head prosecutor was *there*?"

"Yes, Your Honor," Dugan said.

"I don't need to hear anymore," the judge said. "I've heard enough."

"Wait," McConnell said and jumped up. "We haven't put on our case yet. We have a right to call witnesses—"

"Are you listening here?" Judge Arnold asked. "Are we in the same courtroom? Did you hear what the witness just said?" The judge was livid because Bissell, the head prosecutor, the man who tried my case, was personally involved in the cover-up. He had wanted to bury me so badly that he headed a conspiracy in order to do so.

Dugan, who was full-on crying by now, turned to the judge. "I'm really sorry about what I did." The judge passed over a box of tissues, and Dugan took one to wipe his face.

Arnold called a recess. With the sound of that gavel, I felt like I'd snapped out of my body. I saw myself, the other Isaac, the one whom I didn't bring to court, the one who had done over seven years, standing there—watching me, seeing my father, my mom. She was crying and screaming at them, "Why? Why did you do this to my son? Why did you do this?" It was a question without an answer, but her voice rose up inside that crowd and pierced into my brain. It was like all her pain left her body and traveled, transferred over to me. I was burning up inside as I thought of all she had endured these years. As tears came to my eyes, I finally released it all.

I knew it was over. No matter what the state tried to pull after that, it would all be futile. I would be going home.

I could almost see the walls tumbling down around me and a shaft of light darting through the rubble. I could hear my daughter in her high-pitched voice: *Daddy Duna.* Though she no longer had that child's voice and was well past the age where she mispronounced words, was a full teenager, in fact, I still heard her as a little girl. It was the sound that had helped me get through thousands of days fearing I'd never get to see her again. *Daddy Duna.*
Daddy Duna.

Chapter Seventeen

Possession is a figment of the imagination.
Control is the ultimate level of ownership. It is the
only thing a man can take with him to the grave.

—ISAAC WRIGHT JR.

WHEN THE TIDE GOES OUT, they say, you get to see everyone who has been swimming naked.

After Dugan's admission, and his incrimination of Bissell and his colleagues, I called former chief of detectives, Richard Thornburg, to the stand. Thornburg had been the one trying to get me to give up the combination to my safe on the day of my arrest, the man I faced down after seeing my wife in shackles. Thornburg had already been disgraced—he was a cooperating witness against Bissell—but his arrogance did not allow him to accept it until it was too late.

A cardinal rule for attorneys is never to ask a question you don't know the answer to. An unknown answer can devastate a case. But I realized the opposite could also be true, especially when using the question "Why?" "Why" can be one of the most explosive pieces of a defense attorney's arsenal because the question itself can be a statement. It can highlight what the court is *already feeling.* "Why" underlines the stupidity or ridiculousness or maliciousness of a subject's actions. It is a question an attorney can ask only after setting the stage for there to be no acceptable answer.

I methodically carried Thornburg through his impressive career and followed its evolution period into corruption under Bissell's tenure. Thornburg revealed that Bissell was indeed present during meetings regarding the covering up of police misconduct in my case, and that secret deals were a customary practice of the prosecutor's office.* I moved from one corrupt act to another until I got Thornburg to admit that winning, even if it took breaking the law, was what mattered in that office. They were willing to forgo or subvert justice just to do so. Then, when he was so stuck that there was no way out, I put forth that simple question. "Why?"

I waited for an answer, but none came. While Judge Arnold glared at him, Thornburg remained silent, unable to speak.

Judge Arnold was shocked, enraged even, that both Bissell and Thornburg were at the meeting to discuss the cover-up of the bad search. We were clearly far beyond any bad-apple

---

* Rhoda's attorney from the time of my trial would even later admit on the stand that the deal he struck for his client in exchange for testimony against me was secret and that they both knew she wouldn't do any jail time, even though the plea agreement signed by Bissell, Rhoda, and her attorney revealed that the second-degree drug crime she pled guilty to required mandatory jail time. A year later, in front of an ethics committee, this attorney denied the existence of a secret deal, even though he had admitted it under oath in front of a superior court judge and witnesses and in the court transcript. He was cleared of any ethics violation. In my opinion, it was yet another example of the system protecting their own at the expense of justice and the lives of the people victimized by it—a continuation of the conspiratorial culture that had wronged me.

scenario. A corrupt head prosecutor and chief of detectives meant that the entire office—both the administrative and the investigative branches—was dirty. All of their cases could be thrown into doubt. The wide-reaching conspiracy was now exposed, front and center for the public to see. Who knows where that could lead?

I had forced Arnold's hand to the point where he had to act. The judge went for Thornburg's head, taking over the questioning. He clarified that Thornburg knew the drugs were seized illegally, that they should be suppressed because of it, and that the officers had falsified their reports. It was like a grand unraveling.

"I take offense at this right now," Thornburg said, "because you are saying that I should have known this, that, and the other thing."

"I'm trying to find out what you did know!" Arnold said. "Are you telling me that when you received this information you didn't recognize the significance that as a result of a search for narcotics, the evidence might have to be suppressed."

"Yes," Thornburg said, "I am well aware of that."

"But you directed none of the officers who reported to you to make that fact known in their reports?"

"Your Honor, I didn't tell anyone to do anything in their reports."

Thornburg lost it up there, frustrated that he was being left to sink. At one point, he jumped up and screamed at the prosecutor, "Stand up and talk!"

But McConnell knew it was no use. No objections were going to save him.

When Thornburg came down off the stand, any lingering

doubt had been removed. I had successfully proven that the whole case against me was fraudulent. Then I brought in esteemed defense attorney Francis Hartman as a closer. It was merely insurance for myself, making it easier for the court and the system to do what it knew it had to do.

In his forty-five-minute ruling, Judge Arnold was direct. "I don't see how, in light of these facts, cold facts, this conviction can stand." He found a "pervasive pattern of disinformation" in the Somerset County prosecutor's office. "The deceptions of the judge and jurors by the state offend the rudimentary demands of justice," he told the court. "The totality of these errors requires a new trial."

The court vacated all of my remaining convictions, finding that police and prosecutorial misconduct had occurred under Bissell. Judge Arnold imposed a half-million-dollar bail, which friends, supporters, and activists immediately began to raise for me.

I was in the hole when I found out about Bissell's suicide. An officer wandered by, told me what had happened, and kept walking.

Less than three weeks after I was granted a new trial, and on the eve of his own sentencing, Bissell fled from house arrest. A week later, U.S. marshals tracked him down to a casino motel outside Las Vegas. He shot himself rather than face the jail time he had coming, time that he so cavalierly dropped on me and so many others. Before he pulled the trigger, his final words were: "I can't do ten years."

It is not within me to celebrate a man's death, not even that of a man who did me so much harm.

I was placed in disciplinary detention after a couple of new Somerset guards decided they weren't going to allow me access to my court-ordered phone time. In response, I refused to lock in my cell during the count and the riot squad was called in. As they got ready to take me down in my pod, a lieutenant who knew me played peacemaker. I was charged with an infraction and was escorted to the dark, dank box.

In the hole, they had a policy that in order to be fed, the inmate had to turn his back to the door, get on his knees, and put his hands behind his head. Only then would the guard open the door, put the tray on the floor, and close the door. It was a psychological tactic meant to dominate and humiliate. They didn't need to do it that way; there was a slot in the wall made for the tray to slide through. The guards just wanted to put the prisoner in his place, intimidate, dehumanize, humiliate. So they didn't feed me for the five days I was in there.

I wasn't getting on my knees for anyone.

On a cold December day, seven and a half years after I went in, I walked out the front door of the jail, pushing a laundry cart filled with my computer and boxes of documents from my case. My bail had been cut in half by Judge Arnold after prosecutors delayed my retrial. It would be postponed until after the completion of a state investigation into the prosecutors and police. I made bail that afternoon.

There was never going to be a new trial. They had lost the credibility of all of the detectives in my case, including the chief, not to mention that of the disgraced prosecutor. They had lost Rhoda's, John's, and Gator's testimony, and, most significantly, they had lost the cocaine found at Carlos's house. There was no case against me. Its hollowness—which had always been there—was finally exposed in court and to the world.

The prosecutor's office put on a façade in the press like they were absolutely going to try me again, but that was just them trying to save face. They had no case and if they did try me again, they knew it could only bite them. "I can't wait for this new trial," I said to one reporter, "because not only will I get acquitted but the prosecutorial misconduct that comes out in this new trial will be ten times what came out before. I can't wait for a new trial."

A year later, my indictment was thrown out. Six months after that, the prosecutor said they wouldn't retry me. As for my civil case, in 2001, the New Jersey Supreme Court ruled, for the first time, that the state was liable for the actions of prosecutors. In 2005, my civil case was settled, successfully ending a conflict that had spanned over sixteen years.

They say you only do two days in prison: the day you come in and the day you go out. But that's just bravado, a way to absorb the hell that you've been through. The reality is that each day is a lifetime and it burrows itself deep into your bones.

I left prison a changed man. Once I got my freedom, I realized it was no longer the only thing that mattered. There was a magnetic pull for me to return—for all the Maurices and O.D.s and Alfreds I left back there. Getting out was a turning point in my story, but it was not the end. There are thousands suffering behind bars who don't need to be there, families and communities destroyed in that wake, injustices that need to be corrected as mostly men of color, and mostly poor, are left to rot in our country's prisons.

As I began to rebuild my life, I made the only decision that made sense at the time: I began law school. I would enter with more life and trial experience than likely any incoming student in the world. And I was just getting started.

As I write this in the spring of 2022, there is a hope in the air; the country has finally woken up to the fallibility of the police, the cruelty of our institutions, the repair that needs to happen. There are justice warriors in every corner and pocket of this nation. With their fierce spirit, I know we can take down the Goliaths all around us. I stand with them, knowing our cause is righteous and that the future is not yet written.

There is a reckoning to be had with the criminal justice system in this country. We're living in an era when people are tearing off the covers of institutions that they once blindly trusted and are now looking inside. What we're seeing is the systemic oppression that has long run through these places like veins, like blood. The truth that we're finally seeing we cannot unsee.

"Marked for life" was once a curse on me, a branding of me as a lost soul. But I now see it as a badge of honor, a crucible that fortified me for the work I was meant to do.

It took years to fight the state for my law license, but today I am a lawyer, "slaying giants for a price," as I like to say. I bring something to the table that virtually no other lawyer on the planet can bring. My intimacy with the law is unassailable because it saved my life. My trust in it is total because it was forged in fire.

But I'm just a drop in the ocean.

There are so many men and women out there who feel alone, who are sure their cases are hopeless. I am here to tell them they are not. We all must band together to do our part. The injustices of this world are not accidental; they are committed by *people*. And it is people who must work to bring the reckoning that is long overdue.

It is my job to keep making the noise, shaking the bars loud enough for everyone to hear me. I hope my story will inspire others to take up the fight—to meet life's challenges head-on and to never give up. There are more of us than them, and with right on our side, we can win this thing. The war is still raging and I haven't been unscathed in battle. But I'm still out here, on the front lines, with mud on my boots and blood on my knife.

As my enemies and adversaries fall at my feet, I know that I am far from done. The moment one falls, another rises to take his place. Perhaps one day the natural order of things will bring my mission to an end. But that day is not today. So I can use all the help I can get.

I hope to see you out here.

Ooh ra.

Notes

CHAPTER THREE

1. Paul Butler, *Chokehold: Policing Black Men* (New York: New Press, 2017).

CHAPTER FIVE

1. Eric Bentley Jr., "Alleged Dealer Flaunted Perks," *The Central Jersey Home News*, July 28, 1989.
2. Mary Romano, "Drug Ring Leader Claims Unfairness," *The Courier-News*, June 7, 1990.

CHAPTER SEVEN

1. William Glaberson, "In Prosecutor's Rise and Fall, a Story of Ambition, Deceit and Shame," *New York Times*, December 1, 1996.

CHAPTER NINE

1. Upton Sinclair, *I, Candidate for Governor: And How I Got Licked* (Berkeley: University of California Press, 1994).

CHAPTER TEN

1. Joseph T. Hallinan, *Going Up the River: Travels in a Prison Nation* (New York: Random House, 2001), xvi.

PART TWO: OUT

1. Michael Morton, *Getting Life: An Innocent Man's 25-Year Journey from Prison to Peace: A Memoir* (New York: Simon & Schuster, 2015), 118.
2. Jerry Metcalf, "The Everyday Chaos of Incarceration," *The Marshall Project*, March 1, 2018.

CHAPTER ELEVEN

1. Elizabeth Greenberg, Eric Dunleavy, and Mark Kutner, *Literacy Behind Bars: Results from the 2003 National Assessment of Adult Literacy Prison Survey*, Report NCES 2007–473 (Washington, D.C.: National Center for Education Statistics, U.S. Department of Education, 2007).
2. Hallinan, *Going Up the River*, 17.
3. Hallinan, *Going Up the River*, 104.
4. Timothy Hughes and Doris James Wilson, *Reentry Trends in the United States* (U.S. Bureau of Justice Statistics, U.S. Department of Justice, 2002), http://www.bjs.gov/content/pub/pdf/re entry.pdf.
5. "Mental Health," *Prison Policy Initiative*, https://www.prisonpolicy.org/research/mental_health/.
6. "Incarceration Nation," *Monitor on Psychology* 45, no. 9 October 2014, www.apa.org/monitor/2014/10/incarceration.
7. "Incarceration Nation."
8. Hallinan, *Going Up the River*, 5.
9. Christine Montross, *Waiting for an Echo: The Madness of American Incarceration* (New York: Penguin Press, 2020), 7.
10. Montross, *Waiting for an Echo*, 186.

CHAPTER TWELVE

1. Bryan Stevenson, *Just Mercy: A Story of Justice and Redemption* (New York: Spiegel & Grau, 2014), 18.
2. Hallinan, *Going Up the River*, 25.
3. Heather Ann Thompson, *Blood in the Water: The Attica Prison Uprising of 1971 and Its Legacy* (New York: Pantheon, 2016), 8.
4. Thompson, *Blood in the Water*, 142.

CHAPTER THIRTEEN

1. Nancy S. Kim, "The Cultural Defense and the Problem of Cultural Preemption: A Framework for Analysis," *New Mexico Law Review* 27, L. Rev 101 19 (Winter 1997).
2. Taryn F. Goldstein, "Cultural Conflicts in Court: Should the American Criminal Justice System Formally Recognize a 'Cultural Defense'?" *Dickinson Law Review* 99, no. 1 (1994–95): 141–148.
3. Michelle Maiese, "Dehumanization," *Beyond Intractability*, posted July 2003, last modified June 2020, https://www.beyondintracta bility.org/essay/dehumanization.

4. Mark Godsey, *Blind Injustice: A Former Prosecutor Exposes the Psychology and Politics of Wrongful Convictions* (Berkeley: University of California Press, 2017), 39.
5. Thompson, *Blood in the Water.*

CHAPTER FOURTEEN

1. Martin Scorsese, dir., *Goodfellas*, (1990; Burbank, CA: Warner Bros.).
2. William Glaberson, "In Prosecutor's Rise and Fall, a Story of Ambition, Deceit and Shame," *The New York Times*, December 1, 1996; William Glaberson, "Missing Felon Obsessed with Spotlight," *The New York Times*, November 25, 1996; Dale Russakoff, "Fraud, Flight, and a Fatal Finale," *The Washington Post*, November 27, 1996.

CHAPTER SIXTEEN

1. Michael Drewniak, "Resentencing Rejected, Inmate Wants New Trial," *The Star-Ledger*, July 2, 1996.

Index

music producing, 8
Muslims, 233

Nation of Islam, 269
near death experience, 181–88
new identity, 78, 85
New Jersey, 4, 5, 9, 14
   Franklin Township, 17
   kingpin statute, 60–61
   Passaic County, 17
   Somerset County, 72, 90
"new kid," 24–25
new suit, 137
"New York" (inmate), 188–89, 193
New York City, 8–10, 53, 111
   childhood in, 165–66
New York Stock Exchange, 114
newly arrested, 14
newspapers, 84–85, 194
nickname, B.I.G., 217
Nolan, Veronica, 32, 108–9, 138,
   145–46
nonviolent offenders, 191–92
not guilty plea, 34
Notice of Claim, 230–31
nullification, jury, 159–60

obstacles, 80–81
O.D. (inmate), 223–26, 230–32
office, of Bissell, 262–63
opening arguments, 139–42
"orchard parties," 86
Orlando, Florida, 130
ownership lesson, 132
oyako shinju (parent-child suicide),
   227

package delivery, 112–13
Paff, John, 258
pager, Carlos's, 145–46
paralegal assistance, 197–98
paralegals, at Trenton, 191–92,
   194–95, 233–34, 242–43
paralysis, 182–83
paranoia, 70, 120, 204

parent-child suicide *(oyako shinju),*
   227
parents, 28
   visitation from, 234–36
parole, 97
Passaic, New Jersey, 4
Passaic County, 17
passion, 77
Patrick, 112–17
pawns, inmates as, 100
PCR. *See* post-conviction relief
   hearing
penal reform, 209–10
penalty, trial, 71
penitence, 176
penitentiary, 176
People v. Kimura, 1985, 227
Peter DeMarco (alias). *See* Thornburg,
   Richard
phone call, 94
   with daughter, 74–75
photos, of family, 76–77
plaintiff, 246
plea
   guilty, 71, 127, 158
   not guilty, 34
plea deal, 59–60, 61, 108, 125, 153,
   158–59
   Raquel, 128–29
   Sunshine, 245–46
Plymouth Duster, 43
police, 5–6, 7, 11–12, 298
   Black people and, 54–55
   Franklin Township, 14
   at house, 42–43
   lying and, 143–44
   prosecutors and, 69
   systemic abuse, 85
police brutality, 12
police confession, 268–69
police reports, 266–67, 268, 283–84
police testimonies, 146, 266–67
policy, custodial, 216
political motives, 141
possession, 132